LANGUAGE AND

Dorothy S. Strick
Celia Genishi and Donna
ADVISORY BOARD: *Richard Allington, K*
Anne Haas Dyson, Carole Edelsky, Mary Juzwik, Susan Lytle, Django

MW01073874

Remixing Multiliteracies: Theory and Practice from
New London to New Times
FRANK SERAFINI & ELISABETH GEE, EDS.

Culturally Sustaining Pedagogies:
Teaching and Learning for Justice in a Changing World
DJANGO PARIS & H. SAMY ALIM, EDS.

Choice and Agency in the Writing Workshop:
Developing Engaged Writers, Grades 4–6
FRED L. HAMEL

Assessing Writing, Teaching Writers: Putting the
Analytic Writing Continuum to Work in Your Classroom
MARY ANN SMITH & SHERRY SEALE SWAIN

The Teacher-Writer: Creating Writing Groups
for Personal and Professional Growth
CHRISTINE M. DAWSON

Every Young Child a Reader: Using Marie Clay's
Key Concepts for Classroom Instruction
SHARAN A. GIBSON & BARBARA MOSS

"You Gotta BE the Book": Teaching Engaged and
Reflective Reading with Adolescents, Third Edition
JEFFREY D. WILHELM

Personal Narrative, Revised:
Writing Love and Agency in the High School Classroom
BRONWYN CLARE LAMAY

Inclusive Literacy Teaching: Differentiating Approaches in
Multilingual Elementary Classrooms
LORI HELMAN, CARRIE ROGERS, AMY FREDERICK, & MAGGIE STRUCK

The Vocabulary Book:
Learning and Instruction, Second Edition
MICHAEL F. GRAVES

Reading, Writing, and Talk: Inclusive Teaching Strategies
for Diverse Learners, K–2
MARIANA SOUTO-MANNING & JESSICA MARTELL

Go Be a Writer!: Expanding the Curricular Boundaries of
Literacy Learning with Children
CANDACE R. KUBY & TARA GUTSHALL RUCKER

Partnering with Immigrant Communities:
Action Through Literacy
GERALD CAMPANO, MARÍA PAULA GHISO, & BETHANY J. WELCH

Teaching Outside the Box but Inside the Standards:
Making Room for Dialogue
BOB FECHO, MICHELLE FALTER, & XIAOLI HONG, EDS.

Literacy Leadership in Changing Schools:
10 Keys to Successful Professional Development
SHELLEY B. WEPNER, DIANE W. GÓMEZ, KATIE EGAN CUNNINGHAM,
KRISTIN N. RAINVILLE, & COURTNEY KELLY

Literacy Theory as Practice:
Connecting Theory and Instruction in K–12 Classrooms
LARA J. HANDSFIELD

Literacy and History in Action: Immersive Approaches to
Disciplinary Thinking, Grades 5–12
THOMAS M. MCCANN, REBECCA D'ANGELO, NANCY GALAS,
& MARY GRESKA

Pose, Wobble, Flow:
A Culturally Proactive Approach to Literacy Instruction
ANTERO GARCIA & CINDY O'DONNELL-ALLEN

Newsworthy—Cultivating Critical Thinkers, Readers, and
Writers in Language Arts Classrooms
ED MADISON

Engaging Writers with Multigenre Research Projects:
A Teacher's Guide
NANCY MACK

Teaching Transnational Youth—
Literacy and Education in a Changing World
ALLISON SKERRETT

Uncommonly Good Ideas—
Teaching Writing in the Common Core Era
SANDRA MURPHY & MARY ANN SMITH

The One-on-One Reading and Writing Conference:
Working with Students on Complex Texts
JENNIFER BERNE & SOPHIE C. DEGENER

Critical Encounters in Secondary English:
Teaching Literary Theory to Adolescents, Third Edition
DEBORAH APPLEMAN

Transforming Talk into Text—Argument Writing, Inquiry,
and Discussion, Grades 6–12
THOMAS M. MCCANN

Reading and Representing Across the Content Areas:
A Classroom Guide
AMY ALEXANDRA WILSON & KATHRYN J. CHAVEZ

Writing and Teaching to Change the World:
Connecting with Our Most Vulnerable Students
STEPHANIE JONES, ED.

Educating Literacy Teachers Online:
Tools, Techniques, and Transformations
LANE W. CLARKE & SUSAN WATTS-TAFFEE

Other People's English: Code-Meshing,
Code-Switching, and African American Literacy
VERSHAWN ASHANTI YOUNG, RUSTY BARRETT,
Y'SHANDA YOUNG-RIVERA, & KIM BRIAN LOVEJOY

WHAM! Teaching with Graphic Novels Across
the Curriculum
WILLIAM G. BROZO, GARY MOORMAN, & CARLA K. MEYER

The Administration and Supervision of Reading Programs,
5th Edition
SHELLEY B. WEPNER, DOROTHY S. STRICKLAND,
& DIANA J. QUATROCHE, EDS.

Critical Literacy in the Early Childhood Classroom:
Unpacking Histories, Unlearning Privilege
CANDACE R. KUBY

Inspiring Dialogue:
Talking to Learn in the English Classroom
MARY M. JUZWIK, CARLIN BORSHEIM-BLACK,
SAMANTHA CAUGHLAN, & ANNE HEINTZ

Reading the Visual:
An Introduction to Teaching Multimodal Literacy
FRANK SERAFINI

continued

For volumes in the NCRLL Collection (edited by JoBeth Allen and Donna E. Alvermann) and the Practitioners Bookshelf Series
(edited by Celia Genishi and Donna E. Alvermann), as well as other titles in this series, please visit www.tcpress.com.

REMIXING
MultiLITERacies

Theory and Practice from
New London to New Times

Edited by

Frank Serafini
Elisabeth Gee

TEACHERS COLLEGE PRESS

TEACHERS COLLEGE | COLUMBIA UNIVERSITY

NEW YORK AND LONDON

Published by Teachers College Press, 1234 Amsterdam Avenue, New York, NY 10027

Library of Congress Cataloging-in-Publication Data is available at loc.gov

Names: Serafini, Frank, editor. | Gee, Elisabeth, editor.
Title: Remixing multiliteracies : theory and practice from New London to New
    Times / [edited by] Frank Serafini and Elisabeth Gee, EDS.
Description: New York : Teachers College Press, [2017] | Series: Language and
    literacy series | Includes bibliographical references and index.
Identifiers: LCCN 2017012062 (print) | LCCN 2017023693 (ebook) | ISBN
    9780807776148 (ebook) | ISBN 9780807758649 (pbk. : acid-free paper)
Subjects: LCSH: Literacy--Social aspects. | Sociolinguistics. |
    Semiotics--Social aspects. | New London Group.
Classification: LCC LC149 (ebook) | LCC LC149 .R47 2017 (print) | DDC
    302.2/244--dc23
LC record available at https://lccn.loc.gov/2017012062

ISBN 978-0-8077-5864-9 (paper)
ISBN 978-0-8077-7614-8 (ebook)

Printed on acid-free paper
Manufactured in the United States of America

24 23 22 21 20 19 18 17   8 7 6 5 4 3 2 1

This book is dedicated to the original members of the New London Group for their wisdom to see the future, and their determination to work to improve the lives of teachers and students everywhere.

Contents

Acknowledgments

We would like to thank Stephanie Reid for her help in the preparation of the manuscript. In addition, we would like to thank all of the fabulous doctoral students in the Learning, Literacies, and Technology doctoral program at Arizona State University. Thanks for keeping us on our toes and forcing us to become better faculty members.

Acknowledgments

Introduction

Frank Serafini and Elisabeth Gee

We are finishing this introduction in January 2017, in the midst of considerable social and political upheaval. As academics in the United States, we were particularly affected by the 2016 presidential election, which drew attention to stark political, social, and economic divides in our nation. The wider global situation reflects similar divides and trends, in particular the ascent of conservative, ethnic nationalism in response to the growing economic uncertainties, political instability, and environmental devastation. The challenges facing scholars and educators are significant, complicated by a strong current of popular distrust in science, the proliferation of false or misleading information on the Internet, and at least in the United States, heightened struggles over private versus public control of schools and curricula.

In this introduction, our goal is to briefly review the original contexts and purposes of the New London Group (NLG) manifesto and examine the continued relevance of the manifesto, including its political and social aims, as well as its theoretical and pedagogical contributions, in today's social and cultural landscape (New London Group, 1996).

THE BEGINNINGS OF THE NEW LONDON GROUP

In 1994, a group of literacy educators, linguists, and educational researchers convened in New London, NH, to discuss the state and future of literacy education in America and around the world. Two years later, they published the manifesto "A Pedagogy of Multiliteracies: Designing Social Futures" in the *Harvard Educational Review* (New London Group, 1996), and coined the term "multiliteracies," which brought new perspectives to bear on literacy education, pedagogy, and research. This landmark publication has been cited thousands of times and has been used as a foundation for literacy educators working to abandon autonomous models of literacy in favor of situated, ideological models (Barton, Hamilton, & Ivanic, 1999; Heath, 1983; Street, 1984).

In 1994, members of the original NLG included Mary Kalantzis, Bill Cope, Allan Luke, James Paul Gee, Norman Fairclough, Gunther Kress, Courtney Cazden, Martin Nakata, Sarah Michaels, and Carmen Luke. At the time of publication, these distinguished scholars worked across Australia, England, and the United States in various faculty and administrative positions in colleges of education and centers of educational research.

In their manifesto, members of the NLG posed two main arguments, one focusing on "the increasing multiplicity and integration of significant modes of meaning-making, where the textual is also related to the visual, the audio, the spatial, the behavioral, and so on," and the second focusing on "the realities of increasing local diversity and global connectedness" (p. 64). In addition, they suggested that the term "multiliteracies" designate a conception of literacy that "creates a different kind of pedagogy, one in which language and other modes are dynamic representational resources, constantly being remade by their users as they work to achieve their various cultural purposes" (New London Group, 1996, p. 64).

The first argument acknowledged the expanding complexity of the multimodal nature of contemporary communication. In other words, the texts used in and out of school were becoming more complex, both visually and textually. The second argument focused on the new array of literate practices and the situated and political nature of these practices and abilities.

In the manifesto, they presented the following four components of a multiliteracies pedagogy:

1. Situated Practice—drawing on the experience of meaning-making in lifeworlds
2. Overt Instruction—developing an explicit *metalanguage* of vocabulary for discussing elements of design
3. Critical Framing—interpreting the social contexts and purposes of designs of meaning
4. Transformed Practice—students, as meaning-makers, become designers of their social futures.

The NLG worked to understand the dynamic changes occurring across the landscape of literacy teaching and learning by rethinking the resources, both analog and digital, that supported the representation and communication of meanings through an ever-expanding set of semiotic resources used for representing and communicating ideas. The NLG manifesto was a response to social and cultural conditions that shaped the goals and perspectives of the academics involved in creating it. The manifesto is often viewed primarily as a declaration of theoretical assumptions about literacies and language and a corresponding pedagogical approach. However, as the original manifesto makes clear, the authors were also motivated by goals of activism and social change; they hoped to intervene politically in debates about the changing nature of capitalism, growing worldwide inequality, and education at a time when neoliberalism was becoming hegemonic across the developed world. Their manifesto was at once a pedagogical framework and a political treatise about literacy instruction in changing times.

In this introduction we begin by addressing the "what" and "how" of multiliteracies pedagogy. In addition, we will address the "why" of multiliteracies in both the original context and contemporary times. We will include a brief discussion of the impetus for the book and conclude the introduction with brief descriptions of each of the chapters.

THE "WHAT" OF MULTILITERACIES

The concept of multiliteracies was intended to challenge views of literacy as involving primarily written language and as the mastery of a relatively stable and unitary set of rules and conventions for the use of this language. The more complex view of meaning-making reflected in the NLG's definition of multiliteracies recognized the importance of multiple modalities in meaning-making as well as the value and necessity of diversity in representations and meaning-making, whether that be specialist forms of language used by scientists or the mixture of text, visual images, or video on a pop-culture fan website.

A multiliteracies perspective, however, raises questions about the focus of contemporary literacy pedagogy. Students could not possibly master all forms of meaning-making in school, while text forms and their use are constantly evolving. For the NLG, the answer was that literacy pedagogy should introduce students to "a metalanguage of multiliteracies based on concept of design" (p. 73). The NLG felt that this metalanguage, a new means of understanding and talking about meaning-making across varied modalities, was crucial to transforming literacy pedagogy. They reframed the process of meaning-making around the concept of designer, as opposed to the traditional use of reader/writer, to emphasize the active and creative aspects of meaning-making and the use of multiple modalities, as well as the role of conventions (such as existing genres, styles, grammars) in representing and communicating meanings.

Perhaps the greatest attention among multiliteracies scholars currently is devoted to multimodality, both as a feature of more "traditional" texts that increasingly are digital, and as a way of understanding the representation of meaning in forms as diverse as video games, social media, and children's imaginative play. The concept of multimodality has been presented as a theory, as an analytical framework, and as a way of describing a particular form of social phenomenon or complex text. As a theory, multimodality "approaches representation, communication, and interaction as something more than language" (Jewitt, 2009, p. 1). Theories of multimodality investigate how various semiotic resources represent and communicate ideas across varied channels of dissemination or media. Scholars have developed multimodal analytical frameworks utilizing a variety of approaches and research methodologies, including systemic functional linguistics (Machin, 2007; O'Halloran, 2004), social semiotics (Kress & van Leeuwen, 1996), and multimodal interactional analysis (Norris, 2004; Scollon & Scollon, 2003). Others have drawn upon linguistic, semiotic, literary, and artistic perspectives to analyze multimodal phenomenon, such as picture books (Serafini & Reid, in press). Finally, scholars have simply used the concept of multimodality to describe or define an object of study. Scholars talk about multimodal texts as if they are a special type of text that incorporates images, design features, sound, gestures, and video clips, in addition to written language for representational and communicative purposes.

However, these approaches to multimodality also have their critics. Stockl (2007) suggested that the recent focus on multimodality is the "late discovery of the obvious," while other theorists question whether there are any truly monomodal texts (Mitchell, 2005). Dressman (2015) called into question the use of Saussure's (1910) theories as a foundation for multimodal analysis. His compelling argument for drawing upon Charles Sanders Peirce's (1960) triadic conception of the sign (object, representamen, interpretant) rather than Saussure's dyadic (signifier, signified) challenges the use of linguistic frameworks for analyzing nonlinguistic phenomenon. Regardless of these theoretical debates, the presence of multimodal phenomenon will only increase in the future, and understanding how these complex entities affect students' literate lives should remain a focus of current literacy scholarship.

Lastly, the NLG's focus on design as central to meaning-making deserves more attention. The NLG argued that the design of meaning occurred in the act of interpreting texts as well as creating them, a point often overlooked. *Reader as designer* extends the constructivist metaphor or role of reader as text-participant, to assert that readers of multimodal texts not only construct meaning from what is depicted or represented, but also design the way the text is read, its reading path, what is attended to, and in the process construct a unique experience during their transaction with a text (Serafini, 2012, p. 157).

THE "HOW" OF MULTILITERACIES

The NLG did not want to simply propose a new theory; they were deeply concerned with spelling out the implications of this theory for literacy pedagogy. How might teachers best facilitate students' fluency with meaning-making in the context of multiliteracies? They took as their starting point a view of the human mind as "embodied, situated, and social" and laid out an approach to pedagogy that integrated immersion in literacy practices, direct instruction in the metalanguage of multiliteracies, critical analysis of the relationship among particular representations and their social and cultural context, and engagement in new practices informed by what was learned. The NLG argued that this integration was crucial to overcoming the limitations of any one component, and they also hoped to transcend the often polarizing advocacy of one practice versus another, such as the critique of direct instruction often associated with more progressive pedagogies.

No single element of the NLG approach to pedagogy is likely to seem new or surprising to literacy educators today. The rise of "balanced" approaches to literacy instruction, at least at the elementary levels, have made the integration of literacy practices (i.e., storybook reading, independent reading) and direct instruction (i.e., word study, phonics) more common. However, as Cope and Kalantzis (2009) note, the transformative goals of the NLG pedagogy do not fit well within an educational system that increasingly emphasizes some version of a Common Core curriculum, high-stakes standardized testing, and the steady erosion of teacher autonomy and expertise.

At the same time, this pedagogy of multiliteracies does align well with more recent pedagogical innovations, including the broad framework known as Connected Learning and the various educational methods associated with the Maker Movement. The Connected Learning framework (Ito et al., 2013) focuses on providing more young people with opportunities to engage in sustained, interest-driven learning experiences that cross-cut in-school and out-of-school spaces, supported by peers as well as teachers, and enhanced by the capacities of new technologies. The Maker Movement refers to people's engagement in a wide range of creative activities aimed at producing physical devices and objects, as well as to a particular set of values and commitments (often called maker culture) that stress informal knowledge sharing, learning by doing, and a DIY ethos. Makerspaces often incorporate the use of new technologies for making (such as 3D printing) and for sharing designs and information with broader communities of makers. Educators have adopted making primarily as a way to interest children in science and develop their technology skills (Halverson & Sheridan, 2014).

Notably, neither Connected Learning nor Making educational initiatives tends to address the importance of literacy learning in how participants acquire specialist knowledge related to their interests, how they become fluent in multiple discourses as they move across different school and out-of-school spaces, or how becoming skilled in Making is caught up with the making of meaning, not simply with the making of physical objects. We see tremendous opportunity for the integration of a multiliteracies pedagogy with such initiatives.

Even in the context of these more expansive initiatives, a multiliteracies pedagogy poses numerous challenges to educators. How to move among pedagogical practices is a particular issue, since the intent was not to present them as a recipe or series of steps. The "weaving" (Cope & Kalantzis, 2009) of practices requires considerable skill and expertise of teachers, as well as a deep knowledge of literacy not cultivated by most teacher education programs. A second issue is how situated practice might be defined and integrated within the constraints of typical classroom spaces and schedules. Too often, literacy practices are stripped of their original context and transformed into "doing school" by well-meaning educators, losing much of their potential as rich resources for a multiliteracies approach. Thirdly, instruction in the metalanguage of multiliteracies often seems to be overlooked, despite the importance of these conceptual tools for students' mastery of diverse representational forms. As we noted above, this may be due partly to the primacy still given to the written word in mainstream literacy education, which works against the adoption of the broader perspective associated with the NLG's design terminology.

THE "WHY" OF MULTILITERACIES

The NLG manifesto argued that a new theory of literacy pedagogy was necessary because the "languages needed to make meaning" (New London Group, 1996, p. 59) were changing due to dramatic shifts in the nature of work, citizenship, and people's private lives. Literacy pedagogy needed to account also for the great diversity in the nature of texts and communication resulting from societies that were becoming increasingly culturally and linguistically diverse and globalized. Literacy pedagogy has to address the great variety of new forms of representation supported by digital technologies—in particular, at that time, the growing importance of visual images. The group's concern was not simply to keep literacy education up-to-date, but rather to promote a form of pedagogy that would work against widening economic disparities resulting from changing organizational and technological structures of work.

Business and management practices such as distributed leadership, emphasis on communication and teamwork across specializations, and the rise of knowledge workers as a key segment of the workforce would, they argued, disadvantage students who were not fluent in dominant discourses. The NLG also hoped to address a weakening in the social fabric of communities and nations, reflected in and reinforced by the ascent of neoliberalism, tensions over local cultural diversity (immigration in the United States hit an all-time high by 2000), and a corresponding growth in identity politics. The NLG hoped that schools could support "civic pluralism" in which differences among people in language, culture, and identity were viewed as a resource for a more robust and inclusive society. They also noted the growing opportunities, made possible in part by new technologies, for people to engage with a multiplicity of lifeworlds in their private lives. These lifeworlds—virtual or material spaces for community life characterized by distinctive subcultures and languages—could allow for varied forms of self-expression, social connections, and participation.

However, just as boundaries between lifeworlds were becoming more permeable, so were traditional boundaries between public and private, again fueled by the reach of new digital media into all aspects of people's lives. The NLG stressed that to navigate this multiplicity of lifeworlds required all people to become proficient in recognizing and negotiating differences in discourses, as well as able to adopt a critical stance towards the potential co-option and exploitation of these worlds by corporate or other nefarious interests.

Ultimately, the NLG argued that "dealing with cultural differences and linguistic diversity has now become central to the pragmatics of our working, civic, and private lives" (New London Group, 1996, p. 64). The role of schools, and literacy pedagogy in particular, should be to support "an epistemology of pluralism" (p. 72) that gives more people access to forms of language and culture necessary for economic gain and social power, while at the same time supporting their continued engagement in diverse lifeworlds. Curriculum was to be viewed as "a design for social futures" (p. 73) and school as a space to instantiate the kinds of social relationships and identities that might comprise these visions of the future.

Since the mid-1990s, some of these trends have accelerated, while others have shifted in unanticipated directions, with significant implications for the continued relevance of the NLG's ideas. New digital technologies have contributed to each, but we believe that societal culture and values are the primary forces behind these trends. We start with changes in the workforce and nature of work, and then move to changes in our civic and private lives.

THE POLITICS OF MULTILITERACIES

The Great Recession of the late 2000s through early 2010s heightened public awareness of inequitable economic trends. While multiple influences contributed to the economic downturn, a significant factor was the removal of government regulation from banking, and a proliferation in risky new means of financial speculation. Financial capitalism has become a predominant force in the global economy, emphasizing the generation of wealth through speculation rather than through the manufacture of tangible goods, the provision of services, or even the creation of new knowledge (Peet, 2011). Financial capitalism has been linked to neoliberal policies that allowed the over-accumulation of wealth among a small elite, giving them enormous amounts of surplus income with which to speculate. The knowledge economy, in which corporations have little need for investment capital, also created a need among banks and investment firms for new sources of income, as traditional commercial lending dwindled in volume and profitability.

Taken to an extreme, speculation displaces the reinvestment of profit in productive activities (i.e., job creation, business expansion, research, and so forth). Notably, over the last five years the vast majority (up to 90%) of the largest American companies' profits have been allocated to stock buybacks and dividends (Lazonick, 2014). One feature of this allocation of profits is that worker productivity has lost its historical relationship with increased wages, further exacerbating income inequality. Since the late 1970s, in fact, worker compensation grew at a very small rate (9%) while productivity soared (74% increase) in part due to new technologies and globalization, which has allowed corporations to outsource work to the most inexpensive labor market (White, 2015). Since work is increasingly distributed geographically, corporations are also less inclined to invest in community resources such as education or infrastructure that benefits workers as well.

Increasing value for shareholders (who often include corporate leaders) has become a priority of many organizations, rather than retaining and rewarding employees or even meeting the needs of consumers. The ideal of the "flexible" worker has been translated into the growth of contingency employment. Almost 40% of U.S. workers are now contingent, and even those who hold more traditional positions change jobs more frequently than ever (Pofeldt, 2015).

Amidst these workforce trends are reports of widespread alienation and dissatisfaction with work. Even many so-called knowledge workers are engaged in routine, predictable tasks, or what has been described as "shallow" as opposed to "deep" work (Newport, 2016). Contrary to the notion that knowledge work would be the most secure in the 21st century, such positions are ripe for automatization. For example, routine legal tasks can now be computerized, replacing legal secretaries and paralegals, as well as novice lawyers.

What does this mean for literacy educators? Fluency with multiple discourses seems just as important, or even more important than, at the time of the NLG, as workers move from job to job, workplace to workplace, and workers leverage new media and companies to find work as well as hire others. Identifying and mastering the kinds of discourses that are important to achieving status and power may be even more difficult in this fluid economic context, in which "selling yourself" again and again is crucial. Lastly, acquiring the specialist discourses associated with highly skilled and highly compensated positions can be particularly challenging since traditional career ladders have been truncated and increasingly unavailable.

The Nature of Citizenship

Problems associated with weakening civic ties and tensions over cultural and ethnic diversity identified by the NLG have heightened dramatically over the past 20 years. In the United States, the 2016 election drew attention to widespread public dissatisfaction with mainstream political parties; increasing polarization around key civic issues; and the impact of "fake news" disseminated largely online, particularly through social media. Neo-nationalism arose as a powerful rhetoric in the United States and Western Europe, associated with anti-globalization and protectionist trade policies, opposition to immigration, ethnocentrism, and anti-elitism (Fotopoulos, 2016). The core appeal of neo-nationalism is the promise of bringing back jobs to lower- and middle-class workers and a return to traditional values perceived as threatened by liberal social policies.

Long before the 2016 election, the growth in formerly minority populations, particularly Hispanics, was predicted to have an effect on U.S. politics. The election of the country's first Black president was a symbol of the success of liberal social policies and at the same time unleashed a torrent of racist reactions. Commentators have rushed to blame "identity politics" and in particular the marginalization of the White lower and working class as a key factor in the divisiveness that arose in 2016. The aftermath of the Great Recession was undoubtedly a factor, combined with the continued strength of neoliberalism as a rhetorical as well as an economic force. Neoliberalism not only gives the wealthy increasing influence on the political process and the aims of economic policy, but also promotes the equation of self-worth and knowledge with financial success. People forced into long-term unemployment or lower paying jobs experience a diminished sense of self-worth and alienation, and often lose important social ties, since so many of Americans' social connections outside of family result from their jobs.

While factionalism due in part to race and income was readily identified by the NLG, another concern emerged more recently with additional relevance for literacy educators: the rise of so-called fake news and the broader notion of post-truth politics, a political culture in which appeals to emotion and ideology outweigh factual evidence, and where even general notions of truth are rejected (Roberts, 2010). Fake news is not a new phenomenon, and its role in the 2016 election can be linked to broader trends in current media, including the conflation of reality and fiction in entertainment media (e.g., "reality" television), a focus on attracting viewers ("clickbaiting"), and the reinforcement of misinformation and cultural tribalism in the "echo chambers" of polarized social media networks (Samuel, 2016). Along with many calls for traditional news outlets and social media platforms to reform their approaches and tools for reporting news, there have been heightened demands to make media and information literacy an educational priority.

The NLG's proposal that schools should promote civic pluralism, rather than assimilation into a dominant value system, still seems like a promising and even imperative ideal. Their vision was, however, based on the assumption that we could develop a sense of common purpose—that is, after all, the basis of human societies, however flawed. While the NLG did not state this explicitly, we assume they also believed that students should learn to form and assess opinions or perspectives based on evidence (not emotion alone), and in the possibility of consensus on at least some facts or "truths." While many calls for critical media literacy education assume that readers or viewers lack the ability to judge the quality of sources, there is a deeper problem, and that is whether people really care about the quality of information they receive. Plenty of evidence suggests that even well-educated people tend to ignore information that disconfirms their existing beliefs. Do people even want to know the "truth," and why should they, if the truth is that they are increasingly at risk and seemingly powerless to improve their life situations?

What does this have to do with multiliteracies? We know that people's affiliations with particular social groups are integral to the kinds of literacy practices they engage with, as well as their beliefs about the world and the trust they place in particular sources of information and authority. We also know that traditional forms of school-based literacy education can be alienating to students whose background and affiliations do not make school literacies relevant. As literacy educators, we need to keep in mind that a goal of multiliteracies pedagogy was not simply to celebrate diversity in meaning-making, but to forge common bonds among people whose lives are enhanced by access to powerful forms of language and culture.

Our Not-So-Private Lives

The NLG noted the role of new media in providing us with access to multiple and divergent communities and potential identities, while acknowledging the dangers of a global commodity culture and consumerism. In 2017, these communities and opportunities are being increasingly co-opted by the very commodity culture that the NLG warned against. Not anticipated even less than a decade ago is how social media platforms, online advertising, and Internet search engines narrow rather than broaden our exposure to different perspectives and social groups. Our personal lives are increasingly commodified as our online behavior is observed, quantified, and sold as data to advertisers and corporations. Certainly new digital tools and the Internet give people unprecedented abilities to create and share their creations, whether that be a YouTube video, a game mod, or even a particularly witty tweet. However, a relatively small percentage of people are creators in any kind of community and those who do create are encouraged to monetize their creations with ads on platforms such as YouTube.

The NLG argued that education should promote "a vision of meaningful success for all" that is not defined in purely economic terms (p. 67). This goal is more crucial than ever, and at the same time, education should provide people with tools to resist exploitation in all aspects of their lives. This is no simple task.

IMPETUS FOR THIS BOOK

In the spring of 2015, Frank created a seminar for doctoral students in the Learning, Literacies, and Technology PhD program in the Mary Lou Fulton Teachers College at Arizona State University. The seminar centered around the work of the New London Group and the concept of *multiliteracies*, and students would read the NLG manifesto as their first assignment. Throughout the seminar, students would be introduced to a range of perspectives, including those of the original members of the NLG and other contemporary scholars working to expand the concepts laid down in the manifesto.

In addition to selecting an array of readings, Frank had contacted noted scholars, including several members of the original NLG, to share their ideas with my students via videoconference technology and face-to-face meetings. The first scholar to share with the class was James Paul Gee. He attended the class in person and offered his perspectives on the contexts and circumstances that led to his involvement in the NLG. This discussion became the basis for his chapter in this volume.

Allan Luke was the first scholar to video chat with the class. Through our Skype connection, Allan welcomed us to his beach house in Australia and students watched the sunrise over the South Pacific Ocean through his computer camera as Allan's coffee finished brewing. Throughout the course of two semesters, other noted literacy educators shared their expertise with students. Students were required to read selections of each scholar's work and developed questions for each of these guests as part of our videoconferences.

During the course of the semester, Len Unsworth conferenced in from Australia to discuss types of multimodal discourse analysis, and Colin Lankshear shared his ideas on new literacies. In addition, Donald Leu talked about new literacies and technology, and as a final surprise guest, Gunther Kress conferenced in from his offices in London and shared his current thinking on multimodality. Overall, it was an experience that the students and I will never forget. In fact, it was such an amazing experience that Frank approached Betty with the idea of using the seminar as a framework for a possible publication. Noting that 2016 would be the 20-year anniversary of the original NLG manifesto, it seemed like the perfect opportunity to revisit this groundbreaking work and spend some time considering how the manifesto affected the field of literacy education since its publication. And that is how the book you are reading came to be.

To expand on the ideas shared and discussed in the doctoral seminar, Betty and I started talking about which original members of the NLG might be interested in writing a piece for the book. Several agreed to write a piece, while the rest wished us luck with our project and were interested in reading what we eventually published.

In addition, we started talking about which contemporary scholars were working to expand the concept of multiliteracies and multimodality into new areas and fields of inquiry. We made a "wish list" of all the people we would love to have as part of the book and sent out invitations. To our surprise, and happiness, many of the scholars we contacted agreed to contribute to the project and are included in the second section of this book.

THE CHAPTERS IN THIS BOOK

In the opening chapter of the Original Voices on Multiliteracies section, James Paul Gee offers a retrospective on the formation of the NLG and his initial involvement with the group. His chapter describes the educational and political context in which the original manifesto was published. At the end of this chapter, Jim's doctoral student Kewman Lee offers a brief response to Jim's work and describes how the work has featured in his own scholarship.

Bill Cope, Mary Kalantzis, and Sandra Abrams review 2 decades of work on multiliteracies in Chapter 2. Their purpose is to explore emerging directions in the digital era, and to discuss the relevance of multiliteracies in contemporary times. They consider what can be done to leverage the social affordances of new technologies in the service of improving learning opportunities for all students.

In Chapter 3, Kate Cowan and Gunther Kress consider the multimodal aspects of the original manifesto and consider how moving meaning across modalities, through the processes of transcription and transduction, affects the meaning potential and affordances and limitations of various modes and systems of meaning.

In the final chapter of this Original Voices on Multiliteracies section, Jie Y. Park, Elvis Arancibia, Saint Cyr Dimanche, Deborah Diaz Lembert, and Kevin Sanchez join original member Sarah Michaels to provide a description of multiliteracies in action in an intergenerational poetry project. The chapter documents and theorizes the nature of poetry-based, multiliteracies-aligned practice and programs.

The second part of the book, Contemporary Voices on Multiliteracies, begins with Jennifer Rowsell and Julianne Burgess discussing four different "turns" or paradigm shifts associated with contemporary work on multiliteracies. They explore the following strands of change in multiliteracies pedagogy: (a) design, (b) temporal, (c) spatial, and (d) posthuman.

In the next chapter, Rebecca Rogers and Lina Trigos-Carrillo consider the connections and associations between critical discourse analysis and multiliteracies. They offer an overview of critical discourse analysis, then consider aspects of literacy, design, critique, and learning that are associated with these two concepts.

Carey Jewitt connects multiliteracies with research on touch and haptic modes of communication. She views touch as an emerging communicational form that is becoming more prevalent with new technologies, for example digital tablets, and tries to explain the new roles and potentials for touch in communicational and pedagogical contexts.

The chapter by Julie Coiro, Carita Kiili, and Jill Castek focuses on pedagogies associated with personal digital inquiry. Their framework blends new literacies, new technologies, and inquiry-based pedagogy with concepts from multiliteracies to offer a new vision of literacy education in the new millennium.

Jeffrey Holmes pushes our thinking forward into digital culture as he situates a multiliteracies pedagogy in spaces beyond traditional classrooms. He offers a vision of "multipedagogies" by presenting ways that teaching occurs in video games and other digital spaces.

In the next chapter, Mary McVee, James Gavelek, and Lynn Shanahan explore theories of how the body plays a role in cognition and its connection with theories of multimodality and multiliteracies. They contend that researchers must attend to the foundational theoretical perspectives of multimodality and embodiment to fully excavate semiotic signs related to literacy learning and teaching.

Karen Wohlwend connects multiliteracies with her work in early childhood classrooms based on the concepts of play and multiliteracies. She uses mediated discourse theory as a foundation for considering how children navigate digital and analog technologies in their play, and how this connects to the NLG's concepts of design and redesign.

Dawnene Hassett and Christiane Wood draw upon multiliteracies, multimodality, and semiotics to reconsider the connections among imagination, modes, and classroom pedagogy. In this chapter, they argue that imagination is both serious and playful, guided and spontaneous, and, overall, an integral part of the design process within a pedagogy of multiliteracies.

The epilogue is written by the doctoral students who participated in the seminar on multiliteracies. These emerging scholars talk about their experiences in the seminar and connect their future work to the concepts presented therein. The students discuss the various guests to the seminar and connect their work with these giants of literacy education.

The epilogue was written by the doctoral students in the LLT program in which Betty and I teach. These students were part of the doctoral seminar mentioned above and drew upon these experiences to share their understandings with the readers of this book.

CONCLUDING REMARKS

Critical analysis relies on a deep understanding of social, political, and economic influences on how meanings are represented and interpreted across situations and people. This kind of analysis requires interdisciplinary perspectives that are not commonly cultivated among teachers or students. Furthermore, critical analysis without transformed practice can simply be debilitating, yet all too often opportunities for students to participate in meaningful change are limited.

The NLG assumed that learning about the increasingly complex forms and varieties of languages, texts, and modalities involved in meaning making, as well as opportunities to participate in the redesign of these texts and practices, would help people improve their lives. They also suggested that educators needed to play a role in resisting the encroaching view that success and self-worth should be measured in material wealth and economic gain. At the same time, we need schools and education that enable all students and teachers to take an active role in designing social futures that do not disenfranchise growing numbers of people. In the current debates over a "post-truth" society, we can see very clearly how powerful both new and traditional languages and media can be in shaping our collective, or disparate, views of the world and each other. While as scholars and educators, we should debate some of the specific concepts and practices associated with the NLG's view of multiliteracies, we remain inspired by their efforts to reimagine a better future.

REFERENCES

Barton, D., Hamilton, M., & Ivanic, R. (Eds.). (1999). *Situated literacies: Reading and writing in context.* London, UK: Routledge.

Cope, B., & Kalantzis, M. (2009). Multiliteracies: New literacies, new learning. *Pedagogies: An International Journal, 4*(3), 164–195.

Dressman, M. (2015). Reading as the interpretation of signs. *Reading Research Quarterly, 51*(1), 111–136.

Fotopoulos, T. (2016). Globalization, rise of neo-nationalism and the bankruptcy of the Left. *Global Research.* Retrieved from http://www.globalresearch.ca/globalization-the-massive-rise-of-neo-nationalism-and-the-bankruptcy-of-the-left/5527157

Halverson, E. R., & Sheridan, K. (2014). The maker movement in education. *Harvard Educational Review, 84*(4), 495–504.

Heath, S. B. (1983). *Ways with words: Language, life, and work in communities and classrooms.* New York, NY: Cambridge University Press.

Ito, M., Gutiérrez, K., Livingstone, S., Penuel, B., Rhodes, J., Salen, K., . . . Watkins, S. C. (2013). *Connected learning: An agenda for research and design.* Irvine, CA: Digital Media and Learning Research Hub.

Jewitt, C. (Ed.). (2009). *The Routledge handbook of multimodal analysis.* London, UK: Routledge.

Kress, G., & van Leeuwen, T. (1996). *Reading images: The grammar of visual design.* London, UK: Routledge.

Lazonick, W. (2014). Profits without prosperity. *Harvard Business Review, 92*(9), 46–55.

Machin, D. (2007). *Introduction to multimodal analysis.* London, UK: Hodder Arnold.

Mitchell, W. J. T. (2005). There are no visual media. *Journal of Visual Culture, 4*(2), 257–266.

New London Group. (1996). A pedagogy of multiliteracies: Designing social futures. *Harvard Educational Review, 66*(1), 60–92.

Newport, C. (2016). *Deep work: Rules for focused success in a distracted world.* New York, NY: Grand Central Publishing.

Norris, S. (2004). *Analyzing multimodal interaction: A methodological framework.* New York, NY, and London, UK: Routledge.

O'Halloran, K. (Ed.). (2004). *Multimodal discourse analysis: Systemic functional perspectives*. London, UK: Continuum.

Peet, R. (2011). The contradictions of finance capitalism. *Monthly Review, 63*(7). Retrieved from http://monthlyreview.org/2011/12/01/contradictions-of-finance-capitalism/

Peirce, C. S. (1960). *Collected papers* (Vols. I–II). Cambridge, MA: Harvard University Press.

Pofeldt, E. (2015). Shocker: 40% of workers now have "contingent" jobs, says U.S. government. *Forbes*. Retrieved from http://www.forbes.com/sites/elainepofeldt/2015/05/25/shocker-40-of-workers-now-have-contingent-jobs-says-u-s-government/#2d5827922532

Roberts, D. (2010). Post-truth politics. *Grist*. Retrieved from http://grist.org/article/2010-03-30-post-truth-politics/

Samuel, A. (2016). To fix fake news, look to yellow journalism. *JSTOR Daily*. Retrieved from http://daily.jstor.org/to-fix-fake-news-look-to-yellow-journalism/

de Saussure, F. (1910). *Course in general linguistics*. New York, NY: McGraw Hill.

Scollon, R., & Scollon, S. W. (2003). *Discourses in place: Language in the material world*. London, UK: Routledge.

Serafini, F. (2012). Expanding the four resources model: Reading visual and multimodal texts. *Pedagogies: An International Journal, 7*(2), 150–164.

Serafini, F., & Reid, S. (in press). Linguistic, semiotic, literary, and artistic perspectives for analyzing picturebooks. In K. Coats & D. Stevenson (Eds.), *The Blackwell Companion to Children's Literature*. London, UK: Wiley-Blackwell.

Stockl, H. (2007). In between modes: Language and image in printed media. In E. Ventola, C. Charles, & M. Kaltenbacher (Eds.), *Perspectives on multimodality* (pp. 9–30). Amsterdam, The Netherlands: John Benjamins.

Street, B. (1984). *Literacy in theory and practice*. Cambridge, UK: Cambridge University Press.

White, G. B. (2015). Why the gap between worker pay and productivity is so problematic. *The Atlantic*. Retrieved from http://www.theatlantic.com/business/archive/2015/02/why-the-gap-between-worker-pay-and-productivity-is-so-problematic/38593

PART I

ORIGINAL VOICES ON MULTILITERACIES

CHAPTER 1

A Personal Retrospective on the New London Group and Its Formation

James Paul Gee

This chapter is a retrospective and personal look back at the New London Group (NLG) and its origins. The social, political, and academic context that provided an impetus for the NLG's formation, goals, and ideas may seem like ancient history to current readers. However, an appreciation of this context, as well as the role of individual participants in the NLG's work, is crucial for understanding its significance. In addition, by telling the story of the NLG, I hope to illuminate more broadly how academic theories are influenced by the worldviews and social positioning of the people involved. I tell some anecdotes and share some personal information about the participants (including myself) to convey some of the interpersonal dynamics and relationships that were important to our work together. Along the way, I also will discuss some foundational ideas from linguistics about grammar and meaning that were at the heart of the NLG's efforts to reimagine literacy pedagogy. Of course, the views I express are only my opinions and others might well disagree.

A STARTING POINT: AUSTRALIA AND THE GENRE WARS

The origins of the NLG lie in Australia, in a debate over literacy education called the "genre wars." Very simply put, the genre wars concerned the most appropriate focus for literacy education. On one side were scholars and educators who argued that children (particularly poor children) should receive direct instruction in the "rules" of particular genres of written communication, such as writing reports or persuasive essays. On the other side were scholars and educators who believed that (a) teaching universal rules for genres left children without the awareness of how genres are modified to meet the expectations of particular contexts, and (b) more emphasis should be placed on the development of critical literacy, an understanding of how language forms such as genres serve social and political ends.

I will return to the genre wars shortly, but I would like to start the story with how I first travelled to Australia, because this helps explain my perspective on the NLG. I started my career as a generative, "Chomsk-yan" theoretical linguist working on syntactic theory or "grammar." In the 1980s, I transitioned from syntax to sociolinguistics and discourse analysis. Such a transition was rare. Chomskyan linguists were, by and large, hostile to social and cultural approaches to studying language. Chomsky has long argued that humans cannot achieve scientific rigor in studying social issues (Chomsky, 1959, 2015).

My work in these areas first came together in a special issue of the *Journal of Education* (1989) devoted to my papers and in my first book, *Social Linguistics and Literacies: Ideology in Discourses* (1990). Not long after the book was published, I received, on the same day, two letters in the mail inviting me to give talks in Australia, a place I had never visited before and knew nothing about.

I went to Australia in 1992 and gave talks to two different groups. They both told me they liked my book and agreed with me. However, I discovered that they deeply disagreed with each other. In fact, unbe-knownst to me, they were on opposite sides of the genre wars. Each group had interpreted my book to agree with their views and disagree with their opponents'. Such is ever the pain and glory of reading and writing.

The genre wars began in Australia, but later spilled over to Cana-da and the United States (Freedman & Medway, 1994; Swales, 1990). Nonetheless, the genre wars were, in their original formation, uniquely Australian. Since at the time more Australians read my work than did Americans, over the next few years I spent a good deal of time giving talks all over Australia and trying to better understand the arguments on both sides.

CONFLICTING VIEWS OF GRAMMAR

The Australian genre wars were tied to linguistics as a field in a way that could not have happened in the United States. In the United States "ap-plied linguists," and linguists who studied the social and cultural aspects of language, did not have the status they did in Australia or England. Furthermore, in Australia, academics can have a more direct link to, and effect on, both state and national level educational policy and practices than they can in the United States. And, too, in Australia, educators and educational policymakers pay more attention to linguists than they do in the U.S., where psychology has long been the "go-to" discipline for education.

As another factor, mainstream Australian linguistics at the time was quite different from mainstream American linguistics. Noam Chomsky's approach to linguistics dominated the United States and most of the rest of the world, while M. A. K. Halliday was the leading linguist in Australia. Halliday's theory had many more potential implications for education. I will briefly describe both perspectives below.

For Chomsky, grammar was an inborn or innate property of the human mind/brain (1975). Much like the ability to build nests in some species of birds, grammar develops in a child's mind/brain without instruction, provided the child engages in normal social interaction to set the process off. He believed that all children can effortlessly learn any language as their first language, because the basic template for grammar in the brain is the same everywhere, a property of human nature.

For Chomsky, *universal grammar* is the basic template for the grammar of any and every human language. This template, instantiated in the brain, specified the limits or parameters within which the grammars of different languages could vary, and the basic or core properties of human language everywhere. Chomsky saw the grammatical differences across languages as relatively superficial variations on a basic plan. This core grammar is not aligned in any straightforward way with meaning or communicative functions. It is a product of evolution (see Pinker & Bloom, 1990) or an accidental by-product of the evolution of some other cognitive capacity (see Chomsky, 1996, p. 30). The communicative functions of language, what we do with language to communicate and engage in social interaction, are simply social and cultural conventions that vary across cultures and are variable products of history. These conventions can be described, but not studied in any scientifically rigorous way.

Halliday's views of language and grammar differ significantly from Chomsky's. For Halliday, grammar is not hardwired, but has evolved as a set of resources to serve particular functions in specific social contexts. In Halliday's theory, Systemic Functional Grammar (Halliday, 1985), grammatical structures at every level of writing or speaking—for example words, phrases, sentences, discourse and texts—carry out specific communicative functions and are mastered through experience in social settings with other people. Halliday (1978) looked at grammar as what he called "social semiosis," as opposed to originating in an innate, universal template. By this he meant that grammar was composed of symbols or representations that existed to do the social work of communication and interaction. Again in contrast to Chomsky, Halliday and his fellow linguists believed that grammatical rules and properties could be studied systematically in terms of the functions they carried out in communication.

GENRE AND LITERACY PEDAGOGY

So, what were the genre wars? They originated in Halliday's view of language, as elaborated by the brilliant, but controversial, linguist Jim Martin (James R. Martin). Martin is a Canadian transplanted to Australia. He was trained by Halliday and worked side by side with him at the University of Sydney. He was, in many ways, the heir apparent to Halliday.

Martin (1992; Martin, Christie, & Rothery, 1991; Martin & Rose, 2007, 2008; Rose & Martin, 2012) argued that grammatical structures at every level of grammar (from words to texts) were the entrée to mastering communicative functions. Some of these functions were necessary for success in school and society. As in the U.S., in Australia, disadvantaged children fare less well in school, in part because more advantaged children often have educated parents who have mastered and facilitated their children's development of socially powerful forms of oral and written communication. So, Martin argued, let's teach grammar explicitly and overtly as a set of tools for powerful forms of communication (ways of meaning and doing things with language), especially those forms that lead to success and power in society.

Martin argued that schools did not usually teach grammar directly in terms of functions, and when they did, teachers shared no common way to talk about grammar with each other or with their children. Thus, they could not talk with their students in consistent and coherent ways about grammar and communication. They often did not teach grammar directly or taught traditional forms of it unrelated to communicative functions.

Teachers, especially progressive teachers, often left children's learning of communication and writing, and their connections to grammar and function, to immersion in curricular activities with little or no direct instruction. In turn, this often meant that advantaged children looked smart because they had learned "the (communicational) rules of the game" at home and knew already what their immersion in activities at school was supposed to teach them. Disadvantaged children needed to be told the "rules of the game." And the "game" that led to power in society was grammar, because mastery of grammar as functional meaning-making led one to be able to function in society at the highest levels of communication, interaction, and social activism.

The level of grammar that was most important for school success and later success in society was, Martin argued, "genre." Of course, genre was a relatively high level of grammar and so one had to master all the levels beneath it (word, phrase, sentence, aspects of discourse) to master it. It is important to note that, for Chomskyans, grammar stops at the level of the sentence, the "highest" level of grammar for them (morpheme, word, phrase, sentence). For Hallidayans, grammar goes on past the level of the sentence to include elements of discourse, text types, registers, and genres.

As you can very well imagine, lots of ink was spilled over exactly what "genre" meant or should mean, even within Halliday's theory of grammar. Some of these definitional issues came down to how many angels could sit (or dance) on the head of a pin. We will (sadly or not, depending on your view of these sorts of things) skip the technicalities here. It is important to remember, though, that for a Hallidayan functional linguist, describing the grammatical steps that lead up to composing a genre is actually a description of functionally meaningful steps, not just "structures" unencumbered by socially significant meanings (which is what syntax is for Chomskyan linguists). Genres for Hallidayan linguists are recurrent configurations of meanings (functions) that let people enact social practices. For example, a recipe is written in a way intended to enable you to gather ingredients, estimate preparation time, and so forth, as part of a larger social practice of preparing a meal.

A genre is a conventional way of carrying out a communicational activity. People in various cultures, groups, and institutions develop ways of doing things that carry out social practices. People who "follow the rules" tend to gain more status, power, and success. The language genres that seemed to Martin to matter most in school and society were activities like giving reports, constructing narratives, offering clear descriptions, developing explanations, writing essays, engaging in arguments, and other such conventional "ways with words" meant to accomplish larger social (and sometimes political) deeds.

Martin argued that (Hallidayan) linguists knew the "rules" for these genres (both in terms of their lower-level grammatical properties and the special properties at their own level). They knew, as well, a consistent and coherent way to talk about grammar and genre. So, why not teach teachers this way of talking about grammar and then have them teach their children "the rules" of important genres through overt and explicit instruction, leaving nothing to be inferred from mere unguided immersion in practice.

Martin's pedagogy involved teachers writing the rules for each genre on the board and explicitly analyzing them in Hallidayan terms; showing and explicating models of the genre; writing a whole-class teacher-guided version of the genre; and then letting the students practice writing in the genre on their own or in groups, with copious and explicit feedback from the teacher again couched in the language of functional grammar. Martin and his associates (like Frances Christie, Claire Painter, Joan Rothery, David Rose, and Robert Veel), all top scholars in their own right, brought this pedagogy to what Australians called "disadvantaged schools" (see Martin's and Christie's retrospectives on their work in schools in de Silva Joyce & Feez, 2016). The (functional) linguist had "well and truly" (this is an Australianism) gone to school. Martin and his associates gained some impressive and widely touted results, even in mainstream media in Australia.

Martin's project was a political one. He is a leftist, as are Halliday and many Hallidayan linguists (and, for that matter, almost all Chomskyan linguists). He believed that if you taught the poor and disadvantaged the "rules of power" (the grammatical rules that underlie the "discourses of power"), they would master these rules, gain power, and then radically change the structure of society to be more equitable and humane (because they had experienced, when at the bottom, how unfair and inequitable society was). This was, by the way, a theory that had long been popular with Irish nuns teaching working-class kids in Australian Catholic schools (and Martin was influenced by this, at least indirectly via his wife at the time, the Australian feminist scholar Anne Cranny-Francis, who went to such a school).

Martin's argument that immersion in activities at school without direct instruction often hid the rules of the game from the more disadvantaged kids, and that we needed to tell them overtly the rules via direct instruction, got a global boost when Lisa Delpit (1986, 1988) published two papers in the prestigious *Harvard Educational Review* making much the same argument as Martin (though without knowing about his work at the time) in regard to African American children.

What made this approach significant was that in the United States direct instruction was always considered traditional and "right wing," and immersion in rich practices without direct instruction was always considered progressive and "liberal" ("left wing"). Hence, for example, the ever enduring phonics (direct instruction) versus Whole Language (immersion) debates in the United States.

Here was an African American author—a liberal as evident in her work—in Delpit's work, who critiqued immersion from the left, not from the right. Martin had already reversed this polarity, since he was a left-winger (like Halliday and Chomsky, more left, in fact, than most liberals in America) critiquing progressivism and immersion. Delpit's voice licensed a global left wing/liberal critique of progressivism in a way that Martin's never could have. In turn, she made Martin's work more exportable to the United States. Today, it is not uncommon to see certain progressive ideas critiqued from the left (indeed, in my view, this has been more important in the "death" of Whole Language than the long-running right-wing critiques of Whole Language). (I should note that Delpit is not anti-progressive, but critical of some progressivist practices and claims.)

Opposing Perspectives

Who were Martin's opponents in the genre wars? They were a motley crew from different academic areas. Unlike Martin and his associates, these opponents were not from one "camp," though they all shared a belief in the social and situated nature of language use. Two of them were both brilliant and highly charismatic scholars, Allan Luke (1997, 2000; Muspratt, Luke, & Freebody, 1997) and Gunther Kress (1989, 1997, 2003, 2010; Kress & Threadgold, 1988).

Allan Luke is a second-generation Asian American born and raised in Los Angeles who earned his doctorate in Canada before moving to various Australian universities for his distinguished career. He works in the area of critical literacy and the sociology of literacy. Luke was known in particular for developing, with Peter Freebody, the Four Resources model of literacy, which attempted to bring together ideas from competing approaches to literacy education (Freebody & Luke, 1990).

Gunther Kress is a German transplanted to Australia, where he worked at various universities before moving to the University of London. Kress works in the area of social semiotics, an area he helped create in its modern form. Kress is an advocate of Hallidayan grammar, though he does not usually couch his work in terms of grammatical details in the way Martin and Halliday do.

Two other opponents were the married pair of academics Bill Cope and Mary Kalantzis (1993, 2000), the founders of the NLG, about whom we will hear more later. It is perhaps worth noting that Bill Cope is the first native-born Australian I have mentioned in this recap (aside from Martin's associates) while Mary Kalantzis was born in Greece.

While Martin's opponents differed on many things (though Martin tended to refer to them all as "critical literacy" people), they shared the belief that genres were important but not defined by or teachable by rules. If there were strict rules for genres, we did not know what most of them are, they argued. And there are probably not strict and teachable rules for genres anyway.

Genres (like reports, explanations, arguments, narratives, and so forth) always come in versions that fit the contexts or situations in which they are used. Any model of a genre, including Martin's list of rules, that was not adapted to a specific context was at best a generic "type" that always, in application, had to become a more nuanced, adapted, and context-specific token. Martin's opponents argued that when children were trained to write genres by direct instruction and rules, they produced at best routinized versions unfit for any specific purposes or social contexts. Far from gaining power with such products, they would come across as "wannabes" mimicking forms they could not put into fluent concrete practice in the real world.

Martin's opponents argued for teaching genres, which they, too, believed were a source of power in society, in their social, cultural, historical, and political contexts as part and parcel of "critical literacy." Critical literacy names an approach to studying and teaching literacy that stresses not just mastering literacy, but also learning how to think about literacy practices and genres in terms of their full range of purposes and uses, some that have, in the past, led to political quiescence and others that have been more liberatory. Kress added to this mix a stress on children and adults as active sign-makers, not mere passive followers of conventions or rules.

The problem Martin's opponents faced was this: They had general and theoretical ideas about pedagogy, but no specific pedagogy to offer, unlike Martin. Martin's approach had spread to many teachers and schools, and this was hard to compete with minus your own pedagogy and loyal team of dedicated associates. Furthermore, the opponents faced the dilemma that in the absence of specific ideas about pedagogies, they might be seen as progressive immersionists. We have already seen that Martin and Delpit let loose a worldwide critique of progressivism from the left, not the right. The fact that here the left and right came to some agreement and could join forces made for hard competition, indeed.

THE NEW LONDON GROUP

This is where Cope and Kalantzis come into the picture. They wanted to settle the genre wars once and for all. Mary Kalantzis is a Greek Australian. In Australia, Greeks count as a minority in much the way Latinos and African Americans do in the United States. Mary was a national figure in Australia as an activist and spokesperson for multiculturalism.

Bill Cope is a combination of erudite European intellectual and working-class bricoleur. The phrase "marching to your own drummer" was invented for him. There is one and only one Bill Cope. He was the note-taker at the NLG meeting and the draftsman for the paper that came out of the meeting.

Cope and Kalantzis as a team are movers and shakers. They called the NLG together, surely with their own private agenda (i.e., win the genre wars back home by using outside validation), but with a public agenda that seemed to me to include the following elements:

1. Get an "international" group of scholars (sadly, in the first meeting, only Australia, England, and the United States were represented) to rethink the importance of genre and the issues in the genre wars and then come to a consensus view that could spread internationally.
2. Find a way to talk about grammar, language, and literacy across the many competing views on these subjects, determine how to study them, and how to incorporate them into education.
3. Find a wider and more accessible language that transcended words like "genre" and "grammar," and the other terms of art in

the genre wars, so that conversations about language, literacy, and education could broaden and include more people, including teachers and people struggling for liberation across the world.

4. Develop a pedagogy or, at least, a take on the sorts of pedagogies that could compete with the Martin-inspired genre pedagogy. The pedagogy to be developed must be relevant to classrooms, adult education, and community activism in struggles for liberation.

5. Intervene politically in debates about the changing nature of capitalism, growing worldwide inequality, and education at a time when neoliberalism was becoming hegemonic across the developed world.

6. Gain a consensus view about literacies as multiple, social, and cultural, and the implications of this viewpoint, for pedagogy and social change. (The so-called New Literacy Studies [Gee, 1990] was just coming into its own in those days.)

7. Stress that learning to "play by the rules" is a way station on the route to people being pro-social agents able to innovate and transform language, literacy, and genres for their own purposes and for the creation of a better world.

The first meeting of the NLG was held in the small town of New London, NH. Like so many of these sorts of meetings, in my experience, the first meeting was the best and energy dissipated in each subsequent meeting (in London and in Alice Springs, Australia).

The group was put together entirely by Cope and Kalantzis from people they knew or people who knew people they knew. The group shared a view of language and literacy as social, cultural, and political, but did not share a lot more. The people in the group came from different academic and intellectual backgrounds and used different registers (styles) of academic language. When they used the same words, words like "grammar," "sign," "language," and "genre," they did not always mean the same things. These differences had to be worked out in order to produce the white paper–style document that was the intended product of the meeting (and became the famous NLG paper that first appeared in the 1996 *Harvard Educational Review*).

Sadly, I do not have the space here to detail the original NLG members' biographies or (better yet) personalities. So let me just offer something that is little more than a word-association game:

Courtney Cazden: Former student of Roger Brown, the founder of the field of child language development. Courtney was a leading figure on literacy, child language development, and teaching practices.

Bill Cope: From 1995 to 1996, he was the First Assistant
Secretary and Director of the Office of Multicultural Affairs in the
Department of the Prime Minister and Cabinet for the Australian
Government. Unfortunately, the Labor Government fell soon after
Bill was appointed to this post; otherwise I suspect he may well
have left academics for politics. He is a polymath.

Norman Fairclough: Founder of his own widely used approach
to critical discourse analysis (CDA). He has been influenced by
Halliday, European critical theorists, and varieties of neo-Marxism.

James Paul Gee: Generative linguist, discourse analyst, one of the
founders of the New Literacy Studies and, later, of the modern
field of digital games and learning.

Mary Kalantzis: A national figure in Australia and a leading
academic worldwide on multicultural issues. She was a Dean at
RMIT University in Melbourne and was the dean of the school of
education at the University of Illinois at Urbana-Champaign.

Gunther Kress: Founder of a highly influential approach to social
semiotics and multimodality. He has applied his work in important
ways to learning and classrooms.

Allan Luke: A major force in critical literacy studies and educational
policy in Australia and across the world. He worked on the history
and sociology of literacy and issues of race and equity.

Carmen Luke: A leading figure in Australia and worldwide on
feminism, media literacy, and sociology. She did important work
on "critical pedagogy" as well.

Sarah Michaels: Trained by the anthropological linguist John
Gumperz at Berkeley and influenced by Irving Goffman and Dell
Hymes, as well. Interested in talk and texts as forms of social
interaction.

Martin Nakata: A leading indigenous scholar in Australia. He
is a Torres Strait Islander, a lesser-known group of indigenous
Australians than the aboriginal peoples.

I am not going to comment on what the NLG paper "means" (see the Introduction for a brief overview of key ideas in the paper). It was a document
written by a committee and it reads like it. It has taken on different meanings
and led to different practices in different parts of the world, as it was meant
to. I will, however, comment on two key words that allowed us to get past
our individually favored terms and adopt a shared language.

First is the word "multiliteracies," which was invented by the NLG
and has spread widely. Literacy is multiple in many different ways, and
different people in the group focused on some ways rather than others.
The term "multiliteracies" allowed us to include all forms of literacy's
multiplicity in one term.

Literacy is multiple in that there are different sorts of literacy events and literacy practices even within one culture or society. It is multiple in that there are differences in literacy practices and different literacy practices across different cultures, institutions, social groups, and cultures. It is multiple in that print combines with other modalities (images and sounds) to create a plethora of multiple multimodal literacy events and practices. It is multiple in that there are many different semiotic systems that can be looked at as "literacies," such as digital literacy, emotional literacy, gamer literacy, scientific literacy, and so on.

The NLG recommended that teachers combine, connect, integrate, compare, and contrast all the multiples in literacy in their pedagogies as a way for students to achieve mastery, critical insight, and the power to innovate and creatively oppose oppression. Many people have read a good deal about digital media into the NLG paper, but the paper was written before digital and social media were highly prevalent.

Second is the word "design." This is the word we finally chose to replace "grammar" and to background our academic differences as linguists and language and literacy scholars. We wanted to foreground the idea that grammar is a set of tools that people actively use to design communication and interaction in order to carry out activities and accomplish purposes. Using these tools is a type of art, much in the way a painter understands and uses paint, color, light, and composition to achieve meaning and impact.

Students need to think critically about how oral and written language and multimodal forms of communication are designed to function, mean, and accomplish things—and sometimes to manipulate people. They need to be able to design in socially and culturally conventional ways to achieve success in school, society, and life. But they also need to know how to redesign, transform conventions, and create new designs in the name of human development as agentive people, global citizens, activists, and proactive creators.

I should note that the NLG sought to avoid the binary of overt instruction and immersion in activities. We espoused a strong role for teachers engaged in a variety of practices, including overt instruction. And we espoused a need for students to be producers (not just consumers), participants (not just spectators), and transformers and innovators (not just followers).

REFRAMING THE PROBLEM: SYSTEM AND SITUATION

To end my discussion, I want to couch the dilemma at the heart of the genre wars and the NLG's work in terms not used at the time. This dilemma is central not just in the study of language and literacy, but also in many other areas of academics. This is the problem of what I will call "system and situation" (Gee, 2015).

A great many things in life are adaptive systems. For example, the U. S. Constitution is a set of rules and principles (a system), but these rules and principles have to be adapted to specific situations, some that did not exist at the time the Constitution was written. A dilemma often arises as to how far and how much a system should be adapted to particular situations. Some members of the Supreme Court have argued that adaptations should be small and that we should stick very closely to the original meanings of the 18th-century document. Other members of the court have argued that adaptations need to be much more extensive given the massive changes in the United States since its founding.

We face the system/situation dilemma in the case of language, as well. The lexicon (the mental dictionary in speakers' heads) and grammar of any language set the rules or conventions for using that language, but the rules or conventions vary somewhat in different specific situations of use. For example, the word "coffee" has a general meaning in the lexicon of English. However, the word takes on different nuances of meaning, and more specific meanings, in different situations of use. Compare: The coffee spilled, go get a mop. The coffee spilled, go get a broom. The coffee spilled, stack it again. Big Coffee is as bad as Big Oil. Here too, issues can arise as to how much one can adapt the meaning of a word to new situations. For example, some people object to using the word "literacy" in a phrase like "computer literacy" and others do not.

As another example, the United States clearly fits the general system-level definition of a "democracy" (representation and voting), but some people do not consider it a "real democracy" because of the power money has in elections. Others do not see this as a reason not to extend the word "democracy" to the political system in the United States.

Genres are systems of conventions. But they are adapted to (varied in) different specific situations of use. A person who does not adapt a genre system to different situations but rather uses an unvarying form in every situation looks inept, and will not get the social power the genre can bring. But, too, a person who varies it too much or in the wrong ways will look inept and won't get power either. However, even granted these tensions, genres change over time and new ones arise. We need to ask who has the power to bring about this creativity, when, and where.

Liberals (progressives) in education have often overplayed situation (variation, adaptation, creativity) and underplayed system (convention, sharing, mutual "ways with words"). Conservatives have often overplayed system (sticking close to models and traditions) and underplayed situation (variation for and adaptation to changed or new situations and new times). However, without a system there is no way to know what to do in a situation and no way for people to share meanings and communicate. But without variation across different situations, the system becomes moribund, since it cannot speak to changed or new situations.

There needs to be a balance between system and situation, and this is often hard and a matter of contestation and negotiation. Purists and ideologues don't help us much here. Polarized, binary debates in education achieve little but grief. Neither left nor right is correct, and there are a myriad of positions between and beyond them. The NLG made some small steps in dealing with the hard issue of system versus situation in the case of language, literacy, and genres. But there is room still for a great deal more progress; there is lots more work to do.

Rejoinder: The New London Group, A Short Look Forward

Kewman M. Lee

Society has changed greatly since the New London Group (NLG) met. We live in a much more digital world now and the forces of globalization have changed considerably. Furthermore, the nature of diversity has changed, something that even much current scholarship has not yet caught up with.

Digital media enables people from all over the world to join interest-driven sites (what Gee calls affinity spaces; see Gee and Hayes, 2011) to assume identities that are often transnational and translingual. These identities are based on such shared endeavors as media production, gaming, citizen science, fan fiction, activism, anime, and a great many more things. Sites devoted to, say, Korean popular culture are inhabited by Koreans, Korean Americans, non-Koreans, people who speak Korean, people who don't, and people who want to learn Korean or English. Such sites are not "Korean" in any traditional sense. Korean popular culture is an "attractor" that spreads globally, much as anime spread Japanese culture as an "attractor." Such sites are simultaneously culturally specific and universal, much like what T. S. Eliot called a "concrete universal" (based on the Hegelian idea that the universal is constituted by its particulars; see Habib, 1999).

Even when English is used as a lingua franca it is used in a variety of different ways, each of which counts as "native" if it reflects the shared interest, passion, and identity of the site. For example, on a site devoted to the Japanese manga series and trading cards called *Yu-Gi-Oh*, you have to speak "*Yu-Gi-Oh* language," whether you use English or not.

Furthermore, your English has to be *Yu-Gi-Oh* correct, not grammatically correct. The whole notion of "native speaker" changes. Here, for example, is some *Yu-Gi-Oh* language:

> Equip Spell Cards are Spell Cards that usually change the ATK and/or DER of a Monster Card on the field, and/or grant that Monster Card special abilitie(s). They are universally referred to as Equip Cards, since Equip Cards can either be Equip Spell Cards, or Trap Cards that are treated as Equip Cards after activation. When you activate an Equip Spell Card, you choose a face-up monster on the field to equip the card to, and that Equip Spell Card's effect applies to that monster until the card is destroyed or otherwise removed from the field. (Gee, 2014, p. 4)

This is no one's first language. It is only acquired by participation in shared activities and identities, and those identities are both rooted in Asia in this case (the game is based on the fictional manga series, *Yu-Gi-Oh! Duel Monsters* created by Kazuki Takahashi) and global and universal, as well. A paradox, yes, but a common one now.

When the NLG met, diversity tended to mean big things like "Black people," "people of color," "White people," "Latinos," or "Asians." These labels hide all the interesting diversity they seek to name. Real diversity exists at the next level down, in different types, different ways of being African American, White, Asian, Korean, or what have you. These different types are rooted in the different lived experiences different sorts of people in these groups have thanks to all their other identities and their uniqueness. As we have seen, digital media have made things yet more complex. There are ways to affiliate with Korean as an identity that do not require you to be Korean.

Once we see the diversity of different ways that different people live an identity like being African American or Asian, then we quickly realize that people today live out all sorts of identities based on a passion for shared activities, like Korean pop music, Japanese anime, real-time-strategy gaming, astronomy citizen science, *Yu-Gi-Oh*, or graphic fan fiction based on *The Sims* (the best-selling videogame). Big labels like "African American" or "Asian" efface these seemingly small and concrete identities, but, in reality, all identities are concrete.

Labels like "African American" or "Korean American" are lived in different concrete ways, connected to different shared interests, passions, and activities, by different types of African Americans and Korean Americans. Furthermore, there are times where one's identity as a teen fan-fiction author writing for other teens across the world trumps big-label identities. Denying or ignoring such identities becomes a particularly modern and pervasive form of discrimination.

REFERENCES

Chomsky, N. (1959). A review of B. F. Skinner's *Verbal Behavior. Language, 35*(1), 26–58.

Chomsky, N. (1975). *Reflections on language.* New York, NY: Pantheon Books.

Chomsky, N, (1996). *Powers and prospects: Reflections on human nature and the social order.* London, UK: Pluto Press.

Chomsky, N. (2015). *What kind of creatures are we?* New York, NY: Columbia University Press.

Cope, B., & Kalantzis, M. (Eds.). (1993). *The powers of literacy: A genre approach to teaching writing.* London, UK: Falmer.

Cope, B., & Kalantzis, M. (Eds.). (2000). *Multiliteracies: Literacy learning and the design of social futures.* London, UK: Routledge.

Delpit, L. D. (1986). Skills and other dilemmas of a progressive educator. *Harvard Educational Review, 56*(4), 379–385.

Delpit, L. D. (1988). The silenced dialogue: Power and pedagogy in educating other people's children. *Harvard Educational Review 58*(3), 280–298.

Freebody, P., & Luke, A. (1990). Literacies programs: Debates and demands in cultural context. *Prospect: Australian Journal of TESOL, 5*(7), 7–16.

Freedman, A., & Medway, P. (Eds.). (1994). *Learning and teaching genre.* Portsmouth, NH: Heinemann.

Gee, J. P. (1989). Literacy, discourse, and linguistics: Essays by James Paul Gee (Edited by Candace Mitchell). Special issue of the *Journal of Education, 171*(1), 5–17.

Gee, J. P. (1990). *Social linguistics and literacies: Ideology in Discourses* (5th ed., 2015). London, UK: Falmer Press.

Gee, J. P. (2014). *An introduction to discourse analysis: Theory and method* (4th ed.). London, UK: Routledge.

Gee, J. P. (2015). *Literacy and education.* New York, NY: Routledge.

Gee, J. P., & Hayes, E. R. (2011). *Language and learning in the digital age.* London, UK: Routledge.

Habib, R. (1999). *The early T. S. Eliot and Western philosophy.* Cambridge, UK: Cambridge University Press.

Halliday, M. A. K. (1978). *Language as social semiotic: The social interpretation of language and meaning.* London, UK: Edward Arnold.

Halliday, M. A. K. (1985). *An introduction to functional grammar* (2nd ed.). London, UK: Edward Arnold.

Kress, G. (1989). *Linguistic processes in sociocultural practice.* Oxford, UK: Oxford University Press.

Kress, G. (1997). *Before writing: Rethinking paths to literacy.* London, UK: Routledge.

Kress, G. (2003). *Literacy in the new media age*. London, UK: Routledge.

Kress, G. (2010). *Multimodality: A social semiotic approach to contemporary communication*. London, UK: Routledge.

Kress, G., & Threadgold, T. (1988). Toward a social theory of genre. *Southern Review, 21*(3), 215–243.

Luke, A. (1997). Genres of power: Literacy education and the production of capital. In R. Hasan & G. Williams (Eds.), *Literacy in society* (pp. 308–338). London, UK: Longman.

Luke, A. (2000). Critical literacy in Australia: A matter of context and standpoint. *Journal of Adolescent & Adult Literacy, 43*(5), 448–461.

Martin, J. R. (1992). *English text: System and structure*. Philadelphia, PA: John Benjamins.

Martin, J. R., Christie, F., & Rothery, J. (1991). Teaching functional grammar. In: *Teaching Critical Social Literacy: A project of national significance on the preservice preparation of teachers for teaching English literacy* (Vol. 2: Papers, pp. 88–125. Canberra, Australia: Department of Employment, Education, and Training.

Martin, J. R., & Rose, D. (2007). *Working with discourse: Meaning beyond the clause* (1st ed., 2003). London, UK: Continuum.

Martin, J. R., & Rose, D. (2008). *Genre relations: Mapping culture*. London, UK: Equinox.

Muspratt, S., Luke, A., & Freebody, P. (1997). *Constructing critical literacies*. Sydney, Australia: Allen & Unwin; and Cresskills, NJ: Hampton.

New London Group (1996). A pedagogy of multiliteracies: Designing social futures. *Harvard Educational Review, 66*(1), 60–92.

Pinker, S., & Bloom, P. (1990). Natural language and natural selection. *Behavioral and Brain Sciences, 13*(4), 707–784.

Rose, D., & Martin, J. R. (2012). *Learning to write, reading to learn: Genre, knowledge and pedagogy in the Sydney School*. Sheffield, UK: Equinox Publishing.

de Silva Joyce, H., & Feez, S. (2016). *Exploring literacies: Theory, research and practice*. New York, NY: Palgrave.

Swales, J. (1990). *Genre analysis: English in academic and research settings*. Cambridge, UK: Cambridge University Press.

CHAPTER 2

Multiliteracies
Meaning-Making and Learning in the Era of Digital Text

Bill Cope, Mary Kalantzis, and Sandra Schamroth Abrams

Since the publication of the original New London Group (NLG) manifesto, we have been actively involved in further developing the concept of multiliteracies and its pedagogical applications. At the core of this current work is the question, "What will an education look like that is appropriate to the rapidly evolving knowledge economy and that uses the new media?" In this chapter, we share our thoughts about the contemporary relevance of multiliteracies and our current efforts to leverage the social affordances of new technologies in the service of improving learning opportunities for all students.

THE DEVELOPMENT OF MULTILITERACIES AS A CONCEPT

When they first met in 1994, the NLG developed a proposal for a pedagogy of multiliteracies that addressed three fundamental concerns: the changing "why" of literacy's importance in the emerging social conditions of work, citizenship, and social life; the "what" of literacy in terms of new communications media and social diversity that challenged the traditional orientation of literacy; and the "how" of literacy in terms of a series of complementary pedagogical orientations that combined immersion in authentic practices, overt instruction, and critical understanding as a basis for acquiring new meanings and practices. Addressing each of these points, the group concluded that the term "literacy" needed to be used in its plural form, "literacies," to attend to the diversity of social settings in response to "why"; the wide range of multimodal and socially varied forms of meaning in response to "what"; and the large, more balanced scope of pedagogical traditions in the case of "how" (New London Group, 1996).

With the digital revolution over the past several decades, our means for the production of meaning have changed fundamentally, first with email and the World Wide Web, later social media and the smartphone, and then with algorithmically driven apps. We sensed in 1994 that big changes were afoot. Although the specifics of these changes were barely imaginable, the concepts we developed then have proved surprisingly durable. We have refined and extended them, and now we are trying to make sense of the transformations still underway in the creation and communication of meanings mediated by digital resources.

Despite efforts to integrate "21st-century learning" in schools, big change has not yet come to many schools. Diversity and equity were a major focus in the pedagogical agenda we developed in 1994. However, there has not been the equity revolution that we may have hoped for back then, though our senses of realism or pessimism may have predicted the perennial failure to alleviate social inequalities. Yet we wanted to present a case that was grounded in strategic optimism, addressing what could possibly be achieved, even if realistically it was not going to be achieved without a more fundamental regime change that goes beyond the institutions of schooling.

These beginnings of the notion of multiliteracies back in the mid-1990s had deeply rooted antecedents in the field of literacy pedagogy: Cazden's work on classroom discourse and "whole language plus" (Cazden, 2001; Cazden, Cordeiro, Giacobbe, Clay, & Hymes, 1992); Cope and Kalantzis's work on genre approaches to literacy (Cope & Kalantzis, 1993); Fairclough's critical discourse analysis (Fairclough, 1992, 1995); Gee's social linguistics (Gee, 1992/2013, 1996); Kress's work on semiotics and images (Hodge & Kress, 1988; Kress, 1976; Kress & van Leeuwen, 1996); Allan Luke's new literacy studies (Luke, 1988, 1993); Carmen Luke's research into gender and technologies (Luke, 1994, 1995); Michaels's work on classroom talk (Michaels, 1986; Michaels, O'Connor, & Richards, 1993); and Nakata's insights into learning at and from the margins (Nakata, 1993, 1997). If there was something new in the first NLG manifesto, it was bringing these strands of thinking into one room (literally, in New London, New Hampshire, for a week in September 1994), and thrashing out a new synthesis as a basis for a new approach to literacy pedagogy.

EVOLVING IDEAS ABOUT MULTILITERACIES

Since the publication of the NLG manifesto in 1996, Kalantzis and Cope have elaborated and extended the theory of multiliteracies and applied a multiliteracies pedagogy to practice in a number of iterations (Cope & Kalantzis, 2000, 2009a, 2015a; Kalantzis & Cope, 2012a, 2012b, 2016;

Kalantzis, Cope, Chan, & Dalley-Trim, 2016). Other members of the group have gone on to do pathbreaking work, consistently in the spirit of the multiliteracies agenda: Gee on video games and situated learning (Gee, 2003/2007, 2004); Kress on multimodality (Kress, 2009); Allan Luke on literacy pedagogy (Luke, 2008; Luke & Dooley, 2009); Michaels on accountable talk (Michaels, O'Connor, & Resnick, 2002); Nakata on Indigenous education (Nakata, 2007).

In our own work on multiliteracies, our focus is not only "communication" (making meanings for others, and the interpretation of those meanings according to the experience and interests of the interpreter), but also "representation" (making meanings for oneself, or literacies as tools for thinking). Representations are always created prior to communication, and interpretation entails another representation. We represent and communicate via a range of modes and textual, visual, spatial, object-oriented, embodied, aural, and oral meanings. Though each mode works as a distinct system, the full panoply of human meanings can be represented comprehensively in each mode, for instance, in gesture by signing for the hearing-impaired, via touch for the sight-impaired. However, in the representational and communicative practice of "multimodality," modes inseparably overlay and/or cohere with each other.

Across all modes, meaning is simultaneously expressed at five levels, which we call *meaning functions*: reference, agency, structure, context, and interest. Level 1, *Reference*, points to specific and general things, persons, time, space, and qualities. Level 2, *Agency,* speaks to patterns and relationships of human action and the movements and forces of nature. Level 3, *Structure*, accounts for devices that organize meaning. Level 4, *Context,* consists of the meanings created by surroundings, close and distant. Level 5, *Interest,* accounts for the purposes that underlie meaning. Acts of meaning in every mode work at all five levels. The parallelism of functions across different forms of meaning supports "synesthesia," or mode shifting, for example when a sound is seen as a color, or a word has a texture. Since any particular mode has intrinsic affordances as well as limitations for meaning-making, we often combine modes in our meaning-making practices (Cope & Kalantzis, 2009b; Kalantzis & Cope, in press).

The question of pedagogy also has been high on the multiliteracies agenda since the 1996 manifesto. Initially, the NLG formulated four pedagogical orientations: *situated practice*, in the tradition of progressivist and experiential approaches to literacy learning; *overt instruction*, in the conceptual spirit of traditional academic disciplines; *critical framing*, aligning with critical pedagogy; and *transformed practice*, consistent with functional approaches to literacy. We advocated a repertoire of such practices, rather than a single orientation, where the strength of the pedagogy is its movement among the different orientations. More recently, we have conceptualized these as epistemological frames, or different types of learning-action: experiencing (the known and the new); conceptualizing (by naming and with theory); analyzing (functionally and critically); and applying (appropriately and creatively) (Cope & Kalantzis, 2015b). These four frames become especially helpful as we consider shifts in epistemological and social norms. For instance, there are expectations today that, beyond the conceptual and empirical orientations of didactic pedagogy, students will also be creative and critical thinkers, intellectual risk-takers and innovators. This is why an expanded range of pedagogical moves or knowledge processes has become necessary.

NEW MEDIA AND NEW NORMS FOR MULTILITERACIES

With the rise of modern mass institutionalized education in the 19th century, literacy in schools existed in a range of distinctive artifactual forms, including the printed word (textbooks and reading books for reading) and the practice of writing. In the 21st century, readable matter also is found on phones and tablets and in e-books, as reading has come to be about meaning-making, not only about decoding alphabetic and image-based text. For instance, we "read" in video games, apps, searchable web sources, and data mashups created on the fly. Written text is integrally juxtaposed with image, video, data visualization, and sound. Though traditional print may remain privileged in some schools, there is a growing understanding that meaning-making extends beyond the page, and that learners are layering literacies (Abrams, 2015) to contextualize, individualize, and characterize information and meaning.

Practices and participation transform according to contemporary resources and norms, and new media continue to influence communication structures, contributing to the evolution of workplace cultures and skills. As such, pedagogy and practice need to adapt to and address how the media we use in our working, public, and community lives are changing, and in some quite fundamental ways.

The behavior of the next generation, the millennials, has become a topic in the news, with the *New York Times* featuring an article about norms in millennial-run workspaces (Widdicombe, 2016). In addition to portraying fraternity-like banter in the workplace punctuated by the use of hoverboards to move about the office or the presence of dart guns and megaphones as part of daily interaction, the article focused on unabashed boundary pushing, with media communication as central to the change. The article centered on the issue created when one employee, Joel Pavelski, fabricated a family death in order to get time off from work and then tweeted the following about his deception: "I said that I was leaving town for a funeral, but I lied." Whereas face-to-face insubordination, such as an entry-level employee scolding the CEO, was not tolerated, the Twitter-based cyber confession was excused because Pavelski, "who had been working grueling hours," was perceived as needing the respite.

Though the 28-year-old CEO told Pavelski that such behavior would not be tolerated in the future, this example suggests that there is a new communicational norm in this particular workplace culture: There seems to be an accepted tolerance of social-media-as-confessional or as a space for free expression. This new genre of meaning-making transcends public and private boundaries and potentially supports the human side that historically has been exploited or ignored in the face of capitalist production, which was a concern identified in the original NLG manifesto.

The example also calls into question necessary workforce skills amidst a changing business culture. In her introduction to the second edition of *Classroom Discourse: The Language of Teaching and Learning*, Courtney Cazden (2001) noted that "two of the abilities necessary to get good jobs in the changing economy are also necessary for participation in a changing society: effective oral and written communication and the ability to work in groups with persons from various backgrounds" (p. 5). These abilities remain essential, especially as the literacies necessary for the workforce include participatory agility, or the flexibility necessary for engaging in "critical thinking, problem-solving, and collaborating with and influencing others," skills contemporary employers value (Kalantzis & Cope, 2012a, p. 43). When we examine these skills, however, in relation to the example above, we question what it means to effectively communicate and work with others. For Pavelski's millennial-owned business, the expectations for effective communication seemed to differ according to the context, and much of that may have been due to the conditions associated with specific social media.

Twitter's 140-character maximum requires short bursts of condensed information, and though print text remains integral to tweets, hyperlinks and images are equally important. In fact, the ubiquity of phones and cameras has supported a pictorial turn; many social media sites have features to modify images, privileging creativity and agency. This shift suggests that effective communication also means critically understanding potential interpretations and forms of multimodal representations.

Multiliteracies, as it was defined in 1996, called for a literacy pedagogy that not only was culturally responsive, but also "account[ed] for the burgeoning variety of text forms associated with information and multimedia technologies" (New London Group, p. 61). But what about the nuances and finesse related to using these text forms, the knowledge of when and how to use the media? Even though Joel Pavelski's boss warned him against future lying, he was remarkably forgiving of the Twitter confessional. In this case, we see the possibility of a new culture that may value critical thinking, but is tolerant of the blending of personal and public beliefs and practices.

REMIX AND MULTIMODALITY

Variation in text and divergence in cultural norms have become more pervasive as digital enhancements and remix are easy to accomplish. Given that "remix means to take cultural artifacts and combine and manipulate them into new kinds of creative blends" (Knobel & Lankshear, 2008, p. 22), there are possibilities to deconstruct, reconstruct, extend, and create texts and ideas. There are possibilities to create divergent identities. For the greater integration of personal experiences via new media, there is the capacity to express varied identities, to highlight and revel in our differences, as much as to bring them into convergence.

Among millennials and those younger, remix has become quite commonplace, as "today's young adolescents have never known a world in which remix, even in its mildest form, was uncommon" (Shelby-Caffey, Caffey, R., Caffey, A, & Caffey, K., 2014, p. 48). Creativity and imagination seem to be promoted in place of prescriptive roles and expectations. This translates into a cultural shift that veers away from a singular, traditional practice and toward multifarious options that hinge on the remixing of modes and meaning.

Remix, indeed, seems to be an inherent component of ideating and sharing. Evans-Tokaryk (2014) called attention to how this culture of remix is coupled with a general and blanket understanding that authorship is fluid:

> So-called millennial students express originality or creativity through pastiche and collaboration, and they understand "authorship" as the process of mixing two or more existing (i.e., Internet) sources together—some obvious examples are uncited quotations or images on Facebook pages, mash-ups that combine a song with unrelated video footage, and cut-ups of literature (para. 9).

Just as the boundaries between private and public seem to blur, so, too, do the well-established traditions of citing sources and acknowledging the origin of an idea. Though Evans-Tokaryk (2014) explained that rules can be context bound, he also acknowledged how the shift that is occurring is not solely led by those under 40 years old: "Architectural design, a variety of web applications, and many research/writing projects undertaken in the Creative Commons embrace the same kind of uncited intertextuality that millennials use in their everyday lives, and these domains are by no means populated entirely by millennials" (para. 10). In other words, new media bring with them new norms that stem from new affordances, and, likewise, human needs and social and cultural values and practices spur the need for new or different resources and pedagogies.

After the Digital Incunabula

We are living in a time that Jean Claude Guédon calls the "digital incunabula" (Guédon, 2001, 2013). The first incunabula ("cradle" in Latin), were works printed in the half century after Johannes Gutenberg printed the first book using movable type and the printing press, around 1450. By 1500, 8 million books had been published. Print created a remarkable, new mode of telepresence, supporting for the first time the mass production of meanings-at-a-distance. However, it was not until about 1500 when a recognizably modern textual regime was established. Supported by simple and revolutionary textual inventions—continuously numbered pages, for example—there were intratextual features, such as graduated types, spatial page design, section breaks, chapter headings, tables of contents, title pages, and intertextual aspects, such as author, title, and publisher identification to facilitate citation, quotation, footnoting, bibliography, and the cataloguing practices of librarianship.

Both these intratextual and intertextual orders sat within the context of a new extratextual regime, dimensions of which included the veracity of assertions through authorial voice distinguished from externally verifiable sources (Grafton, 1997), the demarcation of private ownership rights to textual meaning through copyright (Rose, 1993), a new premium placed on accuracy through editing and proofreading, and the linguistic standardization of vernacular languages in the form of the literature and literacy practices of modern nation-states (Eisenstein, 1979; Febvre & Martin, 1976). This was the basis of the regime of modern literacy, brought to school as an instrument of mass socialization in the 19th century with its textbooks, readers, grammars, spelling, and learning a single, "standard" form of the language (Kalantzis & Cope, 2011).

We live in a time of an equally transformative change in our means of production of meaning, in the forms of our telepresence. In the 1980s, the first generation of mass digital composition, made possible with word processing, revolutionized 16th-century typographic practices. It was no longer only practitioners of the arcane trade of typesetting who used concepts such as "font" and "point size"; everyone learned these terms as they adopted the visual design logics of print to mark textual architectures. This was a back-to-the future move from which digital textual practice has only slowly recovered.

In a crucial and now mostly forgotten moment in 1969, an IBM lab scientist, Charles Goldfarb, led a team that invented Standard Generalized Markup Language (SGML), a radical departure from typographic markup because texts became marked structurally and semantically. A <p> tag marked the beginning of a paragraph, a structural concept in text, and a semantic concept that indicates the beginning of a new idea. Something about the structure of a text immediately and unambiguously became scrutable. These and other markups made aspects of meaning readily machine-readable. A convoluted story follows, in which Tim Berners-Lee misunderstood the logic of SGML in his simplification into HTML by introducing typographic tags. Five torturous reiterations later, and HTML became closer to original, semantic, and structural principles. Meanwhile, the latest generation of digital composition and communication spaces has largely or completely removed typography. Facebook and Twitter need to be semantically aware because they need to know about the users in order to customize their feeds and sell them things. Following typography, we are now in an emerging regime of semantic publishing (Cope, Kalantzis, & Magee, 2011), including markup methods of XML and tagging, domain-specific structured vocabularies and ontologies, informal taxonomies, and word clouds.

It has taken half a century so far to shake off 16th-century textual practices. We are just beginning to see the effects. Unlike Web 1.0, in Web 2.0 (O'Reilly, 2005) machines create text on the basis of algorithmic formulations. Almost every Facebook wall and every Twitter feed is unique and created algorithmically and mostly on-the-fly. Every rendering of information through an app includes combinations of user, location, time and other germane data. Natural language processing algorithms are able to read meanings when markup does not tell enough. Machine learning processes draw inferences between textual and data inputs about human-defined activities or outcomes. Largely gone in these dynamic spaces, and necessarily so, are the first-generation digital artifacts of typography, documents, folders, and books. These are all legacy notions from the universe of print that get in the way of today's digital textuality.

Perhaps the biggest changes are social. The traditional demarcations of writing and reading are blurred as we become simultaneously writers and readers. "Users" and "producers" are better words. And the world of "mass" is replaced by a world of difference, where nobody's social media activity stream is quite the same as anyone else's, depending on their friendships, interests, purchases, proclivities, and fetishes. The more we come together by participating in this universal web of meaning, the more different we style ourselves to be. Mass production of meaning is replaced by algorithmic mass customization.

There is something paradoxical at work here. The mass usership of social network sites is far greater than that of the mass media of newspapers, radio stations, and television channels. However, instead of reading/hearing/viewing the identically replicated texts of mass culture, today's digitally-mediated news, information, and culture feeds are customized according to data collected about users' purchasing patterns, interests, demographics and identities. Massification and divergence are dialectically and paradoxically interconnected in these algorithmically manufactured media. Despite these forces shaping media production and consumption, users have more opportunities now than ever before to (re)create, present, and distribute remixed images, ideas, and identities.

PROSPECTS FOR PEDAGOGICAL CHANGE

So what to do in schools? What does it mean to develop "literacies" in the plural, distinct from the literacy in the singular of the earlier modernity? And how will workforce culture drive a new approach to expression and learning? In the most general of theoretical terms, we would answer with the multiliteracies precepts of multimodality, active learning, and diversity of meanings according to interest and context.

However, we have wanted to be practical, too. None of the digital tools available to learners realizes to our satisfaction the scope of potentials for multimodality, semantically aware text, and actively engaged meaning-makers. So, we have since 2009 been building a website-based social space for meaning-expression, *Scholar*.[1]

Just as the first generation of digital writing tools replicated 16th-century typographical design processes, the first generation of e-learning tools replicated the didactic pedagogy of the 19th-century classroom. The e-textbook simply repeats the epistemic logics of content transmission and knowledge consumption of the print textbook. The "flipped classroom" often replicates the teacher-lecturer, where the student quiescently listens. Learning management systems lay out the content to be covered. Intelligent tutors and educational games march students through domains via a sequence of procedures where each decision point is a right or wrong answer. Computer adaptive tests replicate the deeply flawed tradition of item-based testing now well over a century old (Cope & Kalantzis, in press).

Scholar aims to take on each of these textual and pedagogical conventions. In textual terms, it is centered around a semantic editor, where a quote is marked by selecting a block quote button. The effect is an indent, but the machine knows this stretch of text is not the author's (for the purposes of grade-level analysis of writing, for instance, or detection of plagiarism), because the action is unambiguous. With no typography, the editor is simpler and also much more sophisticated as image, sound, math, dataset, and external media can be embedded inline, allowing fully multimodal knowledge representation.

In pedagogical terms, with *Scholar's* Learning Module the educator curates the digital world of authentic sources in all their polyphony and shares these resources with others. Instead of consuming transmitted content (reading the chapter, viewing the lecturer), the student works on projects that structure peer collaboration as an integral part of the work; they become a knowledge (re)producer rather than a knowledge consumer. In classroom discussion in *Scholar,* everyone talks and all at once, in contrast to the turn-taking routines of classical classroom discourse.

Finally, instead of summative assessments, *Scholar* offers a wide range of formative assessment mechanisms that exist throughout the production process: measures of contribution to classroom discussion; peer-, self- and teacher-reviews against guiding rubrics; coded annotations; machine assessments using natural language processing and machine learning tools; and surveys of knowledge and information. There are hundreds and thousands of small feedback loops: a machine writing suggestion; a coded peer annotation; an answer to a knowledge question. Every piece of feedback is semantically legible to the student and immediately actionable (unlike the grade at the end of a unit of work). *Scholar* also features a rich view of learner progress via retrospective visualizations. In fact, there is so much data about the learning process (the phenomenon of "big data"), that summative assessments have become obsolete, awkward, and limited inferential artifacts (Cope & Kalantzis, 2016).

Designs for Schools of the Future

We contend that, just as textual architectures are undergoing fundamental transformation, so a fundamental transformation of pedagogical architectures is possible. If the trend in the realm of text is towards remix, then the trend in education may be towards a regime we call "reflexive pedagogy" (Cope & Kalantzis, 2015b).

Applying this idea of reflexivity experimentally, our research in *Scholar* trials thus far shows some modest impact on teaching and learning (Abrams, 2013; Ahn & Greene, 2013; Carlin-Menter, 2013; Cope, Kalantzis, Abd-El-Khalick, & Bagley, 2013; Kline, Letofsky, & Woodard, 2013; Lammers, Magnifico, & Curwood, 2014; McCarthey, Magnifico, Woodard, & Kline, 2014; Olmanson & Abrams, 2013; Woodard, Magnifico, & McCarthey, 2013). What more might be possible?

We have involved ourselves in this hands-on platform building and experimental intervention as an act of strategic optimism, or what Antonio Gramsci called optimism of the will, notwithstanding a certain pessimism of the intellect.

Is it possible to move beyond e-learning routines that merely replicate the 19th-century classroom, especially if social norms beyond school walls demand epistemological shifts? Might it be possible to use the affordances of digital networks to create a paradigm shift in the processes of learning, a transformation as great as were the artifacts of textbooks, lectures, classroom discussions, and tests in their time? Can education respond to the demands of and changes in new media? Schooling, we contend, could change dramatically, indeed should change dramatically. A pedagogical revolution is possible, is necessary. As ambitious as this may be, we need to hold onto the hope that such a pedagogical revolution could play a part in a social revolution that recognizes diversity, redistributes social resources more equitably, and engages learner-citizens as collaborative and reflexive meaning-makers.

NOTE

The development and testing of *Scholar* was supported by a series of research grants from the Institute of Educational Sciences in the United States Department of Education, the Bill and Melinda Gates Foundation, and the National Science Foundation. US Department of Education, Institute of Education Sciences: "The Assess-as-You-Go Writing Assistant: A Student Work Environment that Brings Together Formative and Summative Assessment" (R305A090394); "Assessing Complex Performance: A Postdoctoral Training Program Researching Students' Writing and Assessment in Digital Workspaces" (R305B110008); "u-Learn.net: An Anywhere/Anytime Formative Assessment and Learning Feedback Environment" (ED-IES-10-C-0018); "The Learning Element: A Lesson Planning and Curriculum Documentation Tool for Teachers" (ED-IES-lO-C-0021); "InfoWriter: A Student Feedback and Formative Assessment Environment for Writing Information and Explanatory Texts" (ED-IES-13-C-0039). Bill and Melinda Gates Foundation: "Scholar Literacy Courseware." National Science Foundation: "Assessing Complex Epistemic Performance in Online Learning Environments." *Scholar* is located at http://CGScholar.com

REFERENCES

Abrams, S. S. (2013). Peer review and nuanced power structures: Writing and learning within the age of connectivism. *e-Learning and Digital Media, 10*(4), 396–406.

Abrams, S. S. (2015). *Integrating virtual and traditional learning in 6–12 classrooms: A layered literacies approach to multimodal meaning making*. New York, NY: Routledge.

Ahn, J., & Greene, J. C. (2013). Evaluating the developmental stages of digital educational programs: Challenges and opportunities. *e-Learning and Digital Media, 10*(4), 471–483.

Carlin-Menter, S. (2013). Exploring the effectiveness of an online writing workspace to support literacy in a social studies classroom. *e-Learning and Digital Media, 10*(4), 407–419.

Cazden, C. B. (2001). *Classroom discourse: The language of teaching and learning*. Portsmouth, NH: Heinemann.

Cazden, C. B., Cordeiro, P., Giacobbe, M. E., Clay, M. M., & Hymes, D. (1992). *Whole Language Plus: Essays on literacy in the United States and New Zealand*. New York, NY: Teachers College Press.

Cope, B., & Kalantzis, M. (1993). *The powers of literacy: Genre approaches to teaching writing*. London, UK: Falmer Press.

Cope, B., & Kalantzis, M. (2000). *Multiliteracies: Literacy learning and the design of social futures*. London, UK: Routledge.

Cope, B., & Kalantzis, M. (2009a). "Multiliteracies": New literacies, new learning. *Pedagogies: An International Journal, 4*(3), 164–195.

Cope, B., & Kalantzis, M. (2009b). A grammar of multimodality. *International Journal of Learning, 16*(2), 361–425.

Cope, B., & Kalantzis, M. (2015a). *A pedagogy of multiliteracies: Learning by design*. London, UK: Palgrave.

Cope, B., & Kalantzis, M. (2015b). Assessment and pedagogy in the era of machine-mediated learning. In T. Dragonas, K. J. Gergen, S. McNamee, and E. Tseliou (Eds.), *Education as social construction: Contributions to theory, research, and practice*. Chagrin Falls, OH: Worldshare Books.

Cope, B., & Kalantzis, M. (2016). Big data comes to school: Implications for learning, assessment and research. *AERA Open, 2*(2), 1–19.

Cope, B., & Kalantzis, M. (in press). Conceptualizing e-Learning. In B. Cope & M. Kalantzis (Eds.), *e-Learning Ecologies*. New York, NY: Routledge.

Cope, B., Kalantzis, M., Abd-El-Khalick, F., & Bagley, E. (2013). Science in writing: Learning scientific argument in principle and practice. *e-Learning and Digital Media, 10*(4), 420–441.

Cope, B., Kalantzis, M., & Magee, L. (2011). *Towards a semantic web: Connecting knowledge in academic research*. Cambridge, UK: Elsevier.

Eisenstein, E. L. (1979). *The printing press as an agent of change: Communications and cultural transformation in early-modern Europe*. Cambridge, UK: Cambridge University Press.

Evans-Tokaryk, T. (2014, November 24). Academic integrity, remix culture, globalization: A Canadian case study of student and faculty perceptions of plagiarism. *Across the Disciplines, 11*(2). Retrieved from http://wac. colostate.edu/atd/articles/evans-tokaryk2014.cfm

Fairclough, N. (1992). *Discourse and social change.* Cambridge, UK: Polity Press.

Fairclough, N. (1995). *Media discourse.* London, UK: Edward Arnold.

Febvre, L., & Martin, H. J. (1976). *The coming of the book.* London, UK: Verso.

Gee, J. P. (1992/2013). *The social mind: Language, ideology, and social practice.* Champaign, IL: Common Ground.

Gee, J. P. (1996). *Social linguistics and literacies: Ideology in discourses.* London, UK: Taylor and Francis.

Gee, J. P. (2003/2007). *What video games have to teach us about learning and literacy.* New York, NY: Palgrave Macmillan.

Gee, J. P. (2004). *Situated language and learning: A critique of traditional schooling.* London, UK: Routledge.

Grafton, A. (1997). *The footnote: A curious history.* London, UK: Faber and Faber.

Guédon, J. C. (2001, May). *In Oldenburg's long shadow: Librarians, research scientists, publishers, and the control of scientific publishing.* Paper presented at the meeting of Association of Research Libraries, Toronto, Canada.

Guédon, J. C. (2013). Sustaining the "Great Conversation": The future of scholarly and scientific journals. In B. Cope and A. Phillips (Eds.), *The future of the academic journal* (pp. 85–109). Cambridge, UK: Woodhead.

Hodge, B., & Kress, G. (1988). *Social semiotics.* London, UK: Polity Press.

Kalantzis, M., & Cope, B. (2011). The work of writing in the age of its digital reproducibility. *Yearbook of the National Society for the Study of Education, 110*(1), 40–87.

Kalantzis, M., & Cope, B. (2012a). *Literacies.* Cambridge, UK: Cambridge University Press.

Kalantzis, M., & Cope, B. (2012b). Multiliteracies in education. In *The Encyclopedia of Applied Linguistics.* doi:10.1002/9781405198431.wbeal0809

Kalantzis, M., & Cope, B. (2016). Multiliteracies. In M. Peters (Ed.), *Encyclopedia of Educational Philosophy and Theory* (pp. 1–8). Singapore: Springer.

Kalantzis, M., & Cope, B. (2017 [in press]). *Making sense: A grammar of multimodality.* Cambridge, UK: Cambridge University Press.

Kalantzis, M., Cope, B., Chan, E., & Dalley-Trim, L. (2016). *Literacies* (2nd Ed.). Cambridge, UK: Cambridge University Press.

Kline, S., Letofsky, K., & Woodard, B. (2013). Democratizing classroom discourse: The challenge for online writing environments. *e-Learning and Digital Media, 10*(4), 379–395.

Knobel, M., & Lankshear, C. (2008). Remix: The art and craft of endless hybridization. *Journal of Adolescent & Adult Literacy, 52*(1), 22–33.

Kress, G. (1976). *Halliday: System and function in language*. Oxford, UK: Oxford University Press.

Kress, G. (2009). *Multimodality: A social semiotic approach to contemporary communication*. London, UK: Routledge.

Kress, G., & van Leeuwen, T. (1996). *Reading images: The grammar of visual design*. London, UK: Routledge.

Lammers, J. C., Magnifico, A. M., & Curwood, J. S. (2014). Exploring tools, places, and ways of being: Audience matters for developing writers. In K. E. Pytash and R. E. Ferdig (Eds.), *Exploring technology for writing and writing instruction* (pp. 186–201). Hershey, PA: IGI Global.

Luke, A. (1988). *Literacy, textbooks and ideology: Postwar literacy instruction and the mythology of Dick and Jane*. London, UK: Falmer Press.

Luke, A. (1993). Genres of power? Literacy education and the production of capital. In R. Hasan and G. Williams (Eds.), *Literacy in society: Applied linguistics and language study series*. London, UK: Longman.

Luke, A. (2008). Pedagogy as gift. In J. Albright and A. Luke (Eds.), *Pierre Bourdieu and literacy education* (pp. 68–91). New York, NY: Routledge.

Luke, A., & Dooley, K. T. (2009). Critical literacy and second language learning. In E. Hinkel (Ed.), *Handbook of research on second language teaching and learning* (pp. 856–868). New York, NY: Routledge.

Luke, C. (1994). Feminist pedagogy and critical media literacy. *Journal of Communication Inquiry, 18*, 30–47.

Luke, C. (1995). Childhood and parenting in popular culture. *Australian and New Zealand Journal of Sociology, 30*, 289–302.

McCarthey, S. J., Magnifico, A., Woodard, R., & Kline, S. (2014). Situating technology-facilitated feedback and revision: The case of Tom. In K. E. Pytash and R. E. Ferdig (Eds.), *Exploring technology for writing and writing instruction* (pp. 152–170). Hershey, PA: IGI Global.

Michaels, S. (1986). Narrative presentations: An oral preparation for literacy with first graders. In J. Cook-Gumperz (Ed.), *The social construction of literacy*. New York, NY: Cambridge University Press.

Michaels, S., O'Connor, M. C., & Resnick, L. (2002). *Accountable talk: Classroom conversation that works*. Pittsburgh, PA: Institute for Learning, University of Pittsburgh.

Michaels, S., O'Connor, M. C., & Richards, J. (1993). Literacy as reasoning within multiple discourse: Implications for restructuring learning. In *1993 Restructuring Learning: 1990 Summer Institute Papers and Recommendation* (pp. 107–121). Washington, DC: Council of Chief State School Officers.

Nakata, M. (1993). An Islander's story of a struggle for "better" education. *Ngoonjook: A Journal of Australian Indigenous Issues, 9*, 52–66.

Nakata, M. (1997). *The cultural interface: An investigation of the intersection of Western knowledge system and Torres Strait Islander positions and experiences*. (Doctoral dissertation). James Cook University of North Queensland, Townsville, Australia.

Nakata, M. (2007). *Disciplining the savages: Savaging the disciplines*. Canberra, Australia: Aboriginal Studies Press.

New London Group. (1996). A pedagogy of multiliteracies: Designing social futures. *Harvard Educational Review, 66*(1), 60–92.

O'Reilly, T. (2005, September 30). *What Is Web 2.0: Design patterns and business models for the next generation of software*. Retrieved from http://www.oreilly.com/pub/a/web2/archive/what-is-web-20.html

Olmanson, J., & Abrams, S. S. (2013). Constellations of support and impediment: Understanding early implementation dynamics in the research and development of an online multimodal writing and peer review environment. *e-Learning and Digital Media, 10*(4), 359–378.

Rose, M. (1993). *Authors and owners: The invention of copyright*. Cambridge, MA: Harvard University Press.

Shelby-Caffey, C. V., Caffey, R., Caffey, C. A., & Caffey, K. A. (2014). The promise of remix: An open message to educators. *Voices from the Middle, 21*(4), 47–53.

Widdicombe, B. (2016, March 19). What happens when Millennials run the workplace? *The New York Times*. Retrieved from http://www.nytimes.com/2016/03/20/fashion/millennials-mic-workplace.html?_r=0

Woodard, R., Magnifico, A. M., & McCarthey, S. (2013). Supporting teacher metacognition about formative writing assessment in online environments. *e-Learning and Digital Media, 10*(4), 442–470.

CHAPTER 3

Documenting and Transferring Meaning in the Multimodal World
Reconsidering "Transcription"

Katharine Cowan and Gunther Kress

Much has changed since the original New London Group (NLG) manifesto was produced 20 years ago, yet its central aims of valuing diversity and enhancing equity remain just as pressing today. To achieve that aim there is a need for tools that can bring meaning-making in all its multimodal forms into full view, giving clear accounts *of* all these forms, including those that have been difficult to document, and *for* how these forms work to create meaning. In doing this, it will become possible to accord *recognition* to all who are makers of meaning of all kinds.

That is our theoretical, pedagogical, and political aim, in both the broadest and in the most specific terms. Achieving it requires producing tools that bring all *means* for making meaning—*modes*—into "visibility," allowing us to document them in ways that permit work to be done with and on these means. That is, meanings, in their many and diverse material/modal forms, have to be turned into data. In the multimodal semiotic world one fundamental issue is to develop ways to provide a satisfactory account for meanings in any mode. That is an essential project for social semiotic approaches to multimodality. One central aspect of this task is the entirely common and frequent need to transfer meaning from one mode to another: to "move meaning across modes." That is the focus of this chapter.

TOOLS FOR DOCUMENTING MEANING-MAKING

Transcription seems to offer itself as the obvious model to think about in this matter. So we ask, "What *is* transcription?" "What is it used to *do*?" Above all we ask about the principles that inhere in the practice, and, most important for our aim, we ask whether these principles could, in some form, prove useful for achieving our aim.

50

Transcription, like all significant theoretical or methodological terms, acquired its meanings in a particular place and time. The American linguist Leonard Bloomfield, writing in the 1930s, suggested in his *Language* (1933) that while speech was the primary form of language, the alphabet made it possible for speech to be "fixed" as writing. He saw no particular implications for meaning in the change from (what was for him) one form of language to the other. For him, writing was speech transcribed by means of the alphabet, a process not regarded as a serious issue of "authenticity" or meaning. *Speech* transcribed *as* writing made research on language possible and easier.

From the earlier parts of the 20th century onward, transcription—of changing kinds of phenomena including sounds, stretches of speech, spoken interactions—has been seen as the process of "fixing" speech in/as writing. Inevitably aims and assumptions change over time, and vary with differing foci: on material change for instance, from sound to inscription on a surface; or a focus on meaning, keeping meaning "intact" in the change, more or less. The alphabet provided the means for the process of transcription.

Different kinds of research led to elaborations of both practice and "means," responding to questions posed in the various disciplines that relied on transcription. As the technologies of recording speech changed, the scope of potential data changed with them. The wax-cylinder of the very late 19th century gave a huge boost to phonetics and phonology, while the reel-to-reel tape recorder in the mid-1950s opened up research on extended stretches of speech, inaugurating text linguistics and discourse analysis.

There were serious challenges to naïve views of transcription, notably by Elinor Ochs (1979), who saw the process as theory-laden; that is, the conventions researchers use and what they choose to transcribe reflect particular theoretical perspectives that in turn shape their interpretations of the data. Yet the critiques did not, by and large, unsettle the foundations of mainstream transcription practices. Transcriptional methods and tools were modified: the boat repaired as it was crossing the ocean, so to speak. Various notational devices were added, each responding to specific demands posed by research needing differing kinds of data. If hesitation was deemed significant, or intonational or rhythmic features were seen as contributing to meaning, then necessary notational additions could be made to the set of tools. The practice remained buttressed by the solid assumption that language was the high road to meaning, and hence central for research in large areas of the humanities and social sciences.

In that context, the multiliteracies manifesto was groundbreaking. Its proposal that "all meaning-making is multimodal" (New London Group, 1996, p. 81) sent a clear signal that privileging language led to overlooking a rich, broad, and diverse range of means for making meaning. In social semiotic theory all modes are in principle regarded as of equal significance, so the proposal challenged notions of "peripheral" or "marginal" elements, which appeared in the transcriptional resources as "notational supplements" (e.g., the "extra-linguistic," "para-linguistic"), and which had kept modes other than speech and writing firmly on the margin of serious attention.

As it had been before, technology was instrumentally involved: this time as video-recording, first analog then digital. Video recordings made readily evident what the manifesto declared. The burgeoning interest in multimodality over the last two decades has referred to all the meanings apparent in such recordings; in particular, the meanings of hitherto "ephemeral" modes evident in video recordings: action, gesture, gaze, and movement. While previously these had been recognized, they had been difficult to record and hence to document prior to the wide availability of video. Video has made these modes incontrovertibly evident and researchable.

From the moment that we acknowledge the world of meaning as multimodal, transcription in its traditional sense and uses becomes fraught. For one thing, language no longer appears as unproblematically "central" in communicational settings as it had (seemed) before. The formerly marginal elements, the "extras-" and "paras-" of linguistic transcriptions, frequently appear as the traces or the presence of other modes, whose contribution to the meaning of the overall composition now needs to be fully recognized and acknowledged. The contemporary ubiquitous technology of digitally enabled screens not only shows the same phenomena; all those in possession of such screens can produce texts in which language, whether as speech or as writing, has the place that the maker of the text has designed for it, as part of a multimodal complex/composition.

The modally and conceptually larger frames of video recordings and of contemporary screens show speech as distinct, in different environments and with different functions from those of writing. A social semiotic approach to multimodality treats *speech* and *writing* as distinct modes. Distinct, because their materiality (speech as sound, writing as marks on surfaces) differs; distinct also due to their "logics" (speech governed by the logic of time; writing governed by the logic of space).

All this makes the notion of "preservation of meaning" in the process of transcription impossible to maintain. Transcription does not preserve meaning; we suggest it is one instance of the general phenomenon of *meaning transfer* between modes, an instance of the general process of *transduction*. In short this means that the methodologies and the tools that seemed to work for the monomodal world, the world dominated by the then mainstream views of language, are no longer fit for the multimodal world of meaning. Apt principles, and, with these, requisite tools, need to be developed.

It is essential to bear in mind that transcription dealt with the relation of two modes only, those of speech and writing. We keep this term, from here on, no longer as the overarching term for meaning transfer, but only for the mode-specific transfer of meaning between any particular mode and writing. In the process of transcription from speech to writing, meanings initially realized/made material in speech are newly realized/made material in writing. The entities of the mode of writing serve as the material means through which transcription happens: the alphabet ("script") as well as all other entities of the mode by and through which meaning is newly realized/re-materialized: words, sentences, clauses, text-types. These constitute, seen from a formal position (in this specific case, speech *to* writing) the notational resource for the process of transcription; and from a wider semiotic position, the resources for the transfer of meaning.

PRINCIPLES OF TRANSCRIPTION

What principles were and are embedded in transcription of the (more or less) traditional kind? Here we describe eight such principles:

1.   There are two modes, the first, in which meanings are made material (for example, speech), and the second, in which these meanings are re-constituted (for example, from speech to text).
2.   The elements of the second mode act as the *notational resources* in *meaning transfer*. For example, when transcribing speech into text, notational resources include symbols used to indicate pauses, how words are stressed, and so forth. The entities of the two modes are not identical, so that the process of transfer is never a simple process of "replication" but a process of "re-constitution" or "re-materialization." It is always the making of a new sign. For example, the International Phonetic Alphabet is a set of signs used in the transcription of speech to text.
3.   The process of transfer has two aspects: one formal, involving the notational resources; the other focused on meaning. The process of meaning transfer is *not* the exchange of one set of signs for another; it is the making of apt new signs. Thus, for example, transcribing speech into text requires notations that are not part of typical written language.
4.   The term transcription applies to any instance where the meanings of any mode are transferred (in)to script, that is, into the mode of writing. The term does not fit other instances

of meaning transfer. In the multimodally constituted world of meaning there are many instances of meaning transfer between any modes available in a community. Think, for example, of how interpretive dance might be used to tell a story. The notational resources of the second mode are never identical to or even similar to those of the first.

5. To move beyond this narrow conception of transcription, we need an account of what meaning transfer entails, both general and precise enough to account for all instances. The general term that covers all these instances is *transduction*, the transformation of one form into another.

6. The overarching aim in the process of meaning transfer is the documentation of meaning in a mode other than the originating one, capable of fixing meaning for a variety of purposes, with research being just one.

7. A further principle in the process of meaning transfer is that the resulting documentation be as full or as complete in meaning as possible in relation to the originating source text. "As full or complete in meaning as possible" refers to the aims and purposes of the agent who transfers meaning. It is her or his aims and purposes that shape meaning transfer and determine what constitutes full meaning. Given the always different materiality and the frequently different logics of the two modes involved, the entities of the first mode and the notational resource of the second mode used in the process are always nearly incommensurable. Consequently the achievement of fullness and completeness of meaning can only be an approximation.

8. This last principle suggests that the cultural and semiotic expectations and requirements of those involved, whether as audience, as participants, or as researchers, can and do provide an overriding rationale for the choice of the *transducting notational resource*, that is, the mode and corresponding sign system. In an art gallery, for instance, a brief account of a painting might best be done through writing; in this case, written language is the transducting notational resource. There is a choice about the receiving mode in transduction in most, perhaps all, cases. That choice is an effect of which mode and therefore which notational resources are most apt; it is also an effect of assumptions about potential recipients of the transferred meaning, and of the purposes for the newly created document.

The (re-)materialized meaning is a newly made sign: It is always a metaphor in relation to the meanings of the first mode. It is based on the "apt" relations of signifiers (the material means, the notational resources) realizing the signifieds (the originating meaning). In the transcription of speech into writing, for example, phonemes are rematerialized via graphemes. Whether from the perspective of "form" or "meaning" this process always leads to approximations—as an always more or less apt metaphor. "Aptness," here, as in all sign-making, is established by the interest of the person who does the rematerialization.

In the social semiotic approach to multimodality, speech and writing (in communities with alphabetic script systems) are treated as distinct (though weakly related) modes. They are connected at some points in lexis; weakly connected in some aspects of syntax; and weakly connected also through the vaguely matching categories of phoneme and grapheme.

As a brief interim review, we are suggesting that in the world of meaning recognized as multimodal, the issue of changes in meaning is crucial. We suggest that there are two major forms of changes: *transduction*, dealing with meaning transfer between two modes; and *transformation*, dealing with changes in arrangement within a mode. In the former case the entities in the two modes involved are not commensurate: The process of meaning transfer is a process of meaning being rematerialized in the transducting mode. Such changes, as well as frequent changes in "logics" (spatial to temporal) entail ontological changes. In the case of transformation the elements of the mode involved remain the same; the arrangements change. As a result there is always epistemological change, more or less far-reaching.

In transduction, the fact that modes and their elements are never commensurate means that the "agent of change" will need to find apt relations between signifiers (the notational/transducting resource) and the signifieds, the meanings of the original mode being transducted. The result of a transduction, as a new sign, is always also a metaphor. All this requires the principled application of *design*.

TRANSDUCTION: MOVING MEANING ACROSS MODES

In transduction/meaning transfer, we are addressing changes in meaning *associated with the move across modes*. Changes in meaning also take place *within a mode*, as the effect of *transformation*. We are not dealing with the latter in this chapter, nor with a multitude of other issues around meaning.

The distinction between transduction and transformation is highly significant. In transduction the elements of the two modes differ in materiality and commonly also in *logics*. That is, the elements from a mode founded on the logic of space may need to be rematerialized in a mode founded on the logic of time. As a consequence of the change in materiality and the change in logic the elements of the two modes will differ markedly. What is entailed in a change of elements, and certainly where a change of logics is involved as well, is a change in ontology. In transformations within a mode, the elements remain the same; there is a change in their arrangement. Ontology is not usually affected by such a change; epistemology is. As an example, the transformation of a sequence of two simple sentences to one complex sentence may have ontological effects or it may not, but it certainly has epistemological ones. The transformation of the written part of a text from the genre of *report*, say, to the genre of *recount,* is a change in epistemology. The two kinds of change and their different effects need to be carefully considered in the design of multimodal complexes.

For this domain of multimodality, meaning, and transfer of meaning, we propose a change in naming. We suggest that the term transcription can no longer serve as a general, overarching term to deal with changes in or transfers of meaning; so, as the new general, overarching term we propose the term *transduction,* as it is used in social semiotic theory. When the process is focused on meaning, we propose the term meaning transfer, for any mode involved. As the name for the material means involved in meaning transfer we use the term *notational resource,* and propose naming it in relation to the mode involved, for instance, the notational resource of image. In the transduction from writing to image the notational resources used are those of the mode of image; there is as yet no fitting single term. We are not in a hurry to invent names that might produce new problems: We would rather resort to a phrase such as "the notational resource of the mode of image." However, our change in naming does push the emphasis from "means" to "meaning," prioritizing the latter.

While in social semiotics the general, overarching term to describe the move of meaning from one mode to another is transduction, specific instances of meaning transfer between two modes will need to be given mode-specific names. For meaning transfer from any mode to writing we can keep the term tran*scription,* that is, "into" script. Meaning transfer from any mode to the mode of image has yet to be named, and that is the case for meaning transfer with all other modes.

Transduction has two aspects, one dealing with formal/material aspects: the "How is it done?" ("What are the notational resources?"); the other with meaning: the "What is moved?"("What are the meanings that are at issue?"). Formally and materially, in transcription (the transfer of meaning using the notational resources of script), elements of a mode are rematerialized by elements of the mode of writing. In the most usual case of speech to writing, phonic stuff, "sound," is rematerialized as graphic stuff; sounds, very loosely speaking, are rematerialized as letters; even more loosely speaking, phonemes are rematerialized as graphemes. In a process that is in no way straightforward, the meanings of a mode are rematerialized through the meanings of the mode of writing. The focus is meaning transfer. Searching for a metaphor for this set of metaphors, "purchasing power" (which is entirely about approximations in complex environments) might be better suited to this process than the seemingly straightforward one of "currency exchange."

Before attempting to generalize about the practice of meaning transfer among all modes, a brief comment on the category of "mode" is essential. In social semiotic theory *mode* is a socially shaped material resource for the realization of meaning. Multimodality refers both to the collection of modes available in a society and to the assumption that meaning is always realized by "collections" of modes, or multimodal complexes. Modes are characterized by *affordances*: by potentials and limitations for representation, hence for sign-making. Affordances are the joint effect of materiality and of the social work done in shaping the material of mode in the course of a society's history. Affordances shape a mode's capacity for making signs; hence affordance shapes a mode's capacity for transporting meaning. By definition all modes have the capacity to express meanings about social relations, to offer means to represent states of affairs in the world, and to offer means for producing semiotic complexes that are coherent internally and that cohere with a designed place in the world. Given their differing affordances, all modes, speech and writing included, offer partial means only for the materialization of meaning.

The New London Group (1996) was clear in signaling that privileging language leads to overlooking the rich, diverse range of means for making meaning. Most significantly, the NLG offered the potential to make evident the often unrecognized capacities of very many meaning-makers. The interest in multimodality since then has drawn attention to meaning made in many frequently "ephemeral" modes, for instance in speech, action, gesture, gaze, and movement. The methodology and the means that seemingly worked for the monomodal world are not fit for the semiotic work needed in the multimodal world of meaning. Apt requisite principles, such as those suggested here, need to be given consideration.

Fixing the Ephemeral: Documenting Meaning in a Game of "Chase"

To illustrate some of the issues we have raised, we present an example from a study of the multimodal meaning-making of 3- and 4-year-old children in an English nursery school. The example takes as its central focus a process that presented particular challenges for transcription: a group of children playing a game of tag or "chase" where one child is "it" and chases other children until they are tagged as "it." This was one of several instances of play video-recorded as part of the study (see also Cowan, 2014a). From a social semiotic perspective, the chasing games were equally significant, deliberate, and worthy of attention as activities that left more permanent traces, such as drawing or making models; yet they are a form typically overlooked or disregarded as "just running" (see Cowan, 2014b; Cowan & Berry, 2015).

The study sought possibilities for "fixing" the running game to widen the scope of what gets recognized as meaningful in young children's play. The specific challenge was that the play, involving a changing group of 2 to 5 children chasing one another around the outdoor area of the nursery, was fast and fleeting. Ephemeral modes the children drew upon included gesture, gaze, speech, and many features of movement (for example, speed, direction, distance, and body position). Video provided a record of the complex spatio-temporal unfolding of the game, but the research required more stable and permanent documentation to enable the play to be discussed and shared in publications. This necessitated consideration of how the three-dimensional running game might be documented in two dimensions.

Selecting notational resources for documenting the running play required consideration of the aptness of modes for representation. Interest in the multimodality of the play clearly made a traditional transcript unfit for the purpose. Attempts to describe the play as a written vignette also proved problematic as far as depicting the children's many rapid, changing movements and their complex use of the space. Central to the game was the children's placement in space over time, weaving around obstacles, zigzagging past one another and changing their direction and speed in response to each other's movements.

A map-like form was chosen as an apt means for documenting the play, making use of a spatial, visual layout for the best approximation of the original modes used by the children. Figure 3.1 visually represents just a short extract (about 35 seconds) of the children's running play, in which two boys, George and Billy (marked as "G" and "B"), end their chase. It depicts a bird's-eye view of part of the outdoor play area, with lines representing the movement of each child. The arrows along the lines indicate the direction of their running and are positioned at approximate one-second intervals to show when the children were moving slowly (the arrows closer together) or at speed (the arrows farther apart). While this map represents distance, direction, and speed, it less adequately represents sequentiality, and so multiple "fixings," or representations, were produced for different stages of the game. As stillness was significant as well as action, pauses were incorporated into the design using a circle with a number denoting the time (in seconds) that

Figure 3.1. Game of Chase

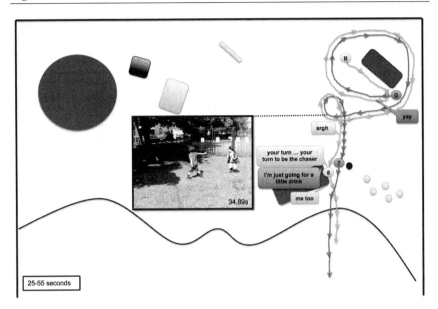

the children were still. The children's talk was incorporated by locating speech bubbles at the relevant points along their movement path. In this way, the notational resources were carefully selected as the most apt means for depicting salient features of the original episode.

Representing the dynamic running play in a static map form is an inevitable transduction. Characteristic of transduction, it involves both gains and losses (Kress, 2005). Through "fixing" ephemeral aspects of the play, certain features were foregrounded that had not been immediately obvious from the original video recording. The shift of perspective, and the act of mapping itself, drew attention to patterns and points of interest in the mapped representation, enabling scrutiny of movement and use of space as a crucial aspect of the play.

In this way, the process of *notation* supported certain *noticings*. It drew particular attention to George's movement in a circular direction accompanied by decreasing speed, which Billy mirrors just before the two children decide to go into the classroom. This pattern was not immediately evident when viewed from camera-level but was made more striking when re-presenting the movement as if looking from above. Taking this to be a particularly significant "rich point," the documentation incorporates a video still from this moment to support further scrutiny of modes working in combination. The video still makes visible George's strong outstretched arm gesture and the boys' gaze directions at this moment.

In combination, the video still, the speech bubbles, and the mapping enable close consideration of the way in which the play is efficiently stopped by George following their chase. This "closing down" is accomplished through George's subtle combination of movements, including decreasing his speed, changing direction and keeping Billy at a distance through an outstretched arm gesture. Billy mirrors these qualities in his own movement, following George's circular direction and slowing down, and does not attempt to catch George even though this would have been possible at slower speed and closer proximity. The play is successfully "wound up" by George before they discuss the reason for stopping, which ensures George avoids being caught or surrendering. The chase is paused and suspended, subtly communicating the message "truce" through multiple ephemeral modes.

A shift toward a multimodal social semiotic perspective on running play, supported by map-like multimodal documentation, reshapes how we conceptualize and interpret play of this kind. It gives clarity to an episode of play that may at first appear chaotic and disorganized, supporting the observer to look beyond the fast-paced, fleeting nature of such play and to consider the ways young children are subtly communicating and negotiating signals and messages. Such attention is rewarded with insights into ephemeral multimodal meaning-making occurring on the go and in the moment. Rather than seeing such activity as unfocused or unproductive, easily overlooked or disregarded, such "fixing" of ephemeral modes might support recognition of the *many* forms of meaning-making and the capacities of many meaning-makers.

CONCLUSION

With this example we return to our opening paragraph and our aims. We have chosen the chasing game to show meaning where it might not be looked for, seen or recognized; to show agency where it is not immediately apparent; to show the use of power in an unusual form; and to suggest how means for recognition come to play a part. Design is evident, we think, in these ephemeral modes, even if it is made in the moment. Design has to be a major feature of the theoretical means to be used. Without the assumption that there is design in the children's actions, the teachers' work of design and redesign is not possible.

The recognition of agency and design in each of the two children's actions—very differently and yet closely coordinated—is, we think, evidence that is useful for a teacher in getting a sense of each of the two children: a sense that might not be apparent, or as apparent, in much or any of the children's other semiotic work.

In this way, we hope the principles underpinning our discussion of documentation raise some possibilities and considerations for the tools that might be needed to account for multimodal meaning-making by means beyond language. We hope this goes some way toward revisiting, and contributing to, the NLG's enduring aims of valuing diversity and enhancing equity by suggesting some means for noting, noticing, and so recognizing meaning-making of all kinds, in all forms, by all meaning-makers.

References

Bloomfield, L. (1933). *Language.* Chicago, IL: University of Chicago Press.

Cowan, K. (2014a). Multimodal transcription of video: Examining interaction in early years classrooms. *Classroom Discourse, 5*(1), 6–21. doi:10.1080/19463014.2013.859846

Cowan, K. (2014b). Multimodality: Observing and documenting with video in nursery. *The Early Education Journal, 74,* 6–7.

Cowan, K., & Berry, M. (2015). 'Once there was someone who walked on the sky': Creativity in the early years. In D. Whitebread & P. Coltman (Eds.), *Teaching and learning in the early years* (4th Ed.) (pp. 246–267). London, UK: Routledge.

Kress, G. (2005). Gains and losses: New forms of texts, knowledge, and learning. *Computers and Composition, 22*(1), 5–22. doi:10.1016/j.compcom.2004.12.004

New London Group. (1996). A pedagogy of multiliteracies: Designing social futures. *Harvard Educational Review, 66*(1), 60–92.

Ochs, E. (1979). Transcription as theory. *Developmental Pragmatics, 10*(1), 43–72.

CHAPTER 4

Multiliteracies and Multilingualism in Action
An Intergenerational Inquiry Through a Poetry Translation Program

Jie Y. Park, Sarah Michaels, Elvis Arancibia, Saint Cyr Dimanche,
Deborah Diaz Lembert, Abby Moon, and Kevin Sanchez

In this chapter, we explore the ongoing relevance of the original New London Group's (NLG) ideas related to multiliteracies and their design metalanguage, as well as their pedagogical implications, through an examination of the innovative literacy program *Poetry Inside Out*. Our research team was comprised of university faculty, a group of youth researchers (high school seniors in one of the poorest secondary schools in Massachusetts), and undergraduate researchers. We focus in particular on the impact of this program on bilingual youth (what they learn about themselves and others), and the perspective they provide as researchers from the inside out. We hope to demonstrate the power and viability of youth-centered multiliteracies research as a means of engaging youth as well as adult researchers in the design of meaning, knowledge, and more inclusive social futures.

FROM THE NEW LONDON GROUP TO POETRY INSIDE OUT

In 1996, a group of diversely positioned researchers and educators came together to propose a new vision for literacy pedagogy "in which language and other modes of meaning are dynamic representational resources, constantly being remade by their users as they work to achieve their various cultural purposes" (New London Group, p. 64). In 2015, another group came together, drawing on different languages, perspectives, and social locations, and similarly interested in understanding the possibilities for transformative multiliteracies pedagogy. In this group, we were an intergenerational constellation of scholars: a senior researcher who was a member of the NLG, a junior scholar of literacy, an undergraduate studying linguistics and education, and five bilingual high school students who participated in an innovative multi-literacies-aligned curriculum in their school.

We spent the last two years together as an intergenerational group of practitioner-inquirers, working to document and theorize the nature and impact of an innovative multiliteracies-aligned program. The program is known as *Poetry Inside Out* (PIO), developed at the Center for the Art of Translation in San Francisco (http://www.catranslation.org). In PIO, participants translate poems from around the world into English from their original language (e.g., Spanish, Chinese). Students work with a partner and then in groups of four to discuss their translations and eventually they create their original poems for publication, often in their home language and in English.

In our research group, we produced new knowledge about PIO, and also developed a culture of productive talk that supported us in critically framing and transforming ideas about literacies, language, youth, and even research itself. Through a co-created data collection and analysis process, we developed five key themes that explain the "how" and "what" of PIO for bilingual high school youth. We theorized how PIO recruits students' conceptions of available designs, expands their multiple literacies, and supports the production of transformed designs (publishable multimodal texts of their own making).

Like the challenges faced by the NLG in creating a single text combining the voices of many, we too faced the challenge of writing this chapter from our different positions and discursive repertoires. Whose terms, phrases, or stylistic registers should be used when there are different and competing voices and possibilities? This is not trivial when the group is made up of experienced academics, undergraduates, and high school students. There were countless hours of behind-the-scenes deliberation, moments of consensus, wordplay, and experimentation with language. This 2-year-long process of co-generation of knowledge and authorship embodies the spirit of productive diversity, taking us to newfound and transformed ideas about what research can become when we, in the words of the NLG, "recruit, rather than attempt to ignore and erase the different subjectivities—interests, intentions, commitments, and purposes students bring to learning" (New London Group, p. 72).

In what follows, we try to make visible our different subjectivities through foregrounding different "voices" as we describe the project and our findings. We identify the lead authors in the heading of each section (i.e., Youth Researchers, All Researchers). After the introductions, the youth researchers took charge of describing PIO, providing a step-by-step process of PIO, as well as its goals and purposes. The "we" in this section, although inclusive, refers to the youth, who had free rein to describe PIO and narrate the story of our collective research. The text reflects their discourse style and word choice (e.g., describing the research group as "cool" or "beautiful"). In subsequent sections we summarize our research and findings.

INTRODUCING THE INTERGENERATIONAL RESEARCH GROUP AND *POETRY INSIDE OUT*

First we offer a brief introduction of our research group members. The five youth researchers included Elvis Arancibia, Saint Cyr Dimanche, Deborah Diaz Lembert, and Kevin Sanchez. Deborah was born in the U.S. and the other four are immigrants. All except for Saint Cyr speak Spanish as well as English; Saint Cyr is fluent in four languages and Kevin also speaks Quechua. Abby Moon was an undergraduate at Clark University, and before joining this research group, she co-facilitated an after-school program using the Poetry Inside Out framework. Jie Park, an assistant professor at Clark University, attended schools in South Korea and in the United States, which is how she developed a deep interest in linguistic and cultural navigations of immigrant youth. Sarah Michaels is a professor at Clark and was a member of the original NLG.

In addition to describing our research team, it is important to describe the context of our study. Claremont Academy is a public secondary school (grades 7–12) located in Worcester, MA, with approximately 500 students. About 89 percent come from low-income families, 80 percent of the students are students of color, and 41 percent are English language learners. While the Main South neighborhood, where Clark and Claremont are both located, is "poor," based on economic statistics, we see it as among the richest in the Commonwealth.

A STEP-BY-STEP SKETCH OF PIO (YOUTH RESEARCHERS)

In PIO, the teacher gives students a packet with the poem page and translator's glossary. In addition to the poem, the poem page includes a picture of the poet, and the poet's biography. The biography highlights the conditions of the poet's life and his or her perspectives. The translator's glossary provides a definition, information about the part of speech, and possible synonyms for every word in the poem.

First, students read the poet's biography, making connections with parts of the poem. Then several students take turns reading the poem in its original language. If it's written in a non-Roman script, there is a transliterated version. According to Elvis, in PIO anyone can read the poem, even when no one in the class speaks the language of the poem.

After reading the poem and biography, students in pairs work on a phrase-by-phrase translation of the poem into English. Next, two pairs come together and a group of four students work on the "make-it-flow," a translation that accounts for the poem's style, structure, and pattern (e.g., rhyme and repetition). When translating a poem written in a language that a student speaks at home, the "language expert" helps everyone in the group to understand the poem. Elvis noted that when translating Spanish poems, he helped his group to understand that a particular word in Spanish can mean many different things, not just what is listed in the translator's glossary. If there are other language experts in the group, they may have their own ideas about what words to use. These different ideas help everyone to understand not just the word, but also the poem, more deeply.

After the make-it-flow, each group presents its translation of the poem. Typically, one person reads the translation, but in some cases the group might perform the poem together. After listening, students discuss differences and similarities in the translations, ask each other why groups translated the same word or phrase differently, and what the poem might mean.

In the view of the youth researchers, the richest parts of PIO are students working to make the poem flow, sharing translations in front of the class, and discussing the poem's possible meanings. When they work to make the poem flow, students bring out and share ideas they have inside. It is a mixing of ideas. When they work to understand the meaning of the poem, students notice specific words, connections to the biography, and repetition and patterns. When students share, they discuss why they chose a word and who chose it. The translations are similar, but there is always a difference, even just one word. It takes three or four class sessions to fully complete the process.

After translating different poems, students create their own poem pages, with biographies, self-portraits, and translator's glossaries if the poem is written in one of their home languages, all modeled after PIO poem pages. If their poem is written in a language other than English, they also provide an English translation. They present the poem in front of the class in both the language it is written in, and in English.

GOALS OF *POETRY INSIDE OUT* (YOUTH RESEARCHERS)

As a research group, we discussed the goals and purposes of PIO. For example, Deborah believes that students gain leadership skills, gain more confidence in themselves, and develop academic skills including translating, debating an opinion or view, and reflecting on learning. PIO helps students appreciate what others have to say. Elvis believes that the goal of PIO is to improve classroom cultures. According to Elvis, in PIO students need help from their classmates to translate a poem. Everyone has to share their ideas, and talk with others. Some of us observed that before PIO students tended to talk with others who spoke the same language. In PIO, students worked with others who speak different languages and come from different countries. At the end of the year, students knew their entire class, could talk to anyone, and knew more about others' ways of thinking, culture, and background.

In PIO there is no right or wrong answer. However, students are expected to defend their translation, using evidence that includes the biography, their knowledge of language, and their personal experiences and worldviews. The teacher can see what the students are trying to understand in the poem and how they are working together. This helps the teacher see the cultural and linguistic strengths of their students, listen carefully to their ideas, and in some cases, change the way they teach and approach the students individually. PIO shifts the dynamic where students actively participate and teachers listen more.

POETRY INSIDE OUT IN A 12TH-GRADE ENGLISH CLASS (YOUTH RESEARCHERS)

Our research took place in Lori Simpson's 12th grade English class. The class consisted of 22 students; all but two were English language learners. The languages spoken were English, Spanish, Vietnamese, French, Arabic, and patois. PIO was a consistent part of the course, taking place every 2 weeks. Over the year the class translated six to seven poems and created their own poem pages, presenting them at a final poetry reading. Spanish was the most common language used by students in the class. Ms. Simpson embraced PIO and youth research, creating a space for the research group to work. She was committed to full participation among her students and fostered an atmosphere where everyone's opinion mattered and students felt safe to speak their minds.

Whenever PIO took place, the youth researchers brought their audio recorders and notebooks to record small-group and whole-class discussions. Outside of class, youth researchers conducted interviews with selected classmates using the interview protocol the group developed. In the next section we describe the intergenerational research team, focusing on the ways we learned to learn together, and listen to one another.

YOUTH RESEARCH TEAM AND RESEARCH PROCESS: THE BEGINNING

Our research began in September of 2014 when Jie invited every student in Ms. Simpson's first-period class to join a research team. Six students joined the group. We met once a week after school in Ms. Simpson's classroom.

Five of the six youth had participated in PIO during their junior year. In the first few meetings, we discussed PIO and our experiences with it. We talked about our identities—where we came from, what life was like there, and how the education there is different from here. Cultural and linguistic diversity was a beautiful and interesting part of our group, because our backgrounds and cultures influenced a great part of our work. Jie and Sarah handed out recorders and research notebooks and asked students to start audio-recording and writing down what was happening during PIO. We read articles by members of the NLG, including Jim Gee and Courtney Cazden, and other scholars.

We began each meeting with a focused free-write, where everyone wrote for 10 minutes in response to a prompt. This was designed to activate our knowledge and ideas about PIO and research. The expectation was that some of our writing would be shared publicly within our meetings. When we wanted to understand a concept more completely, the youth instituted the practice of examining a word in each of our home languages (for example, words like *context*).

Because the youth researchers are bilingual, and Claremont is a predominantly bilingual school, we wanted our research to focus on the experiences of bilingual youth. Over many sessions of discussion and writing, we developed the following research questions:

- How does PIO help bilingual high school students understand more about themselves and others?
- What do bilingual high school students gain from participating in PIO?

In addition to the adults' recordings of each class session, the youth researchers began to audio-record themselves and their classmates during PIO. When we met in the research group, we listened to some of the recordings and looked at transcripts. Each youth prepared to interview a classmate. We negotiated and reached consensus on a set of questions to ask these classmates.

THE "HOW" AND THE "WHAT" OF *POETRY INSIDE OUT* (ALL RESEARCHERS)

Our approach to data analysis was eclectic. We worked from transcripts of sessions that struck any of us as interesting, puzzling, or significant. Jie transcribed most of the classroom segments, but the youth, particularly Deborah, transcribed when multiple languages were in play. Sarah and Jie transcribed several episodes of the research group meetings, and the youth transcribed their own interviews. These transcripts became our data corpus from which to search for patterns, themes, and evidence for claims. From multiple readings, annotations, and discussion of the data, we developed five themes: safe and open communication, confidence in our voices, discussion about meaningful yet taboo topics, deep focus on language, and special listening. Due to space limitations, here we focus on one theme, special listening.

Special Listening: "How" and "What"

This theme, special listening, is unusual. The other four themes focus on the use and production of language for communication. In contrast, listening is typically thought of as silence and something that goes on inside an individual's head. In contrast, we view listening as an active, collaborative accomplishment. This theme serves as a foundational "what" and "how" for PIO. It is, in our view, at the core of *how* PIO works to promote learning across differences, and it is also a critical capacity (a valued *what*) that is engendered in participants.

By special listening we mean a kind of listening that is different from what typically counts as listening in everyday lifeworlds, as well as in conversation analysis, sociolinguistics, and classroom discourse literatures (Schiffrin, Tannen & Hamilton, 2008; Schultz, 2003). It means more than just listening with one's ears—that is, taking in what someone else is saying. It means listening with ears, eyes, mind, one's history, culture, languages, and actively and interactively trying to see behind what the person is saying. Yet still it's more than that. The listener also must want to develop her own ideas further. It's an interested kind of listening. You want to hear and understand what the other person is saying because you want to learn from him, and build a better understanding of what he thinks, but also about what you think.

Special listening is a capacity that you develop over time. But it is not an individual (inside the head) process. Special listening requires interaction between two or more people (minds) and it requires that more than one person is both speaking and listening. Here are some dimensions that distinguish special listening from what we typically associate with listening:

- Special listening starts with having an idea, some kind of meaning that one wants to share (or grow).
- Special listening assumes that you are listening with interest, because you want to understand someone else's ideas to make your idea clearer or bigger.
- To practice special listening, you must have knowledge, a

position, or a perspective first. You can't do special listening without key elements of a context or framework in place.

- When you practice special listening, you get something more than just what the other person says. You learn about the other person, her background, or why she has this to say.

While looking through our transcripts, we realized that something unusual was going on in terms of the ways students were listening to each other and asking for clarification. We started to talk about this kind of listening, but we didn't know what to call it. One of the youth suggested we simply call it special listening. Some of us like the term; some of us are dissatisfied because "special" is so vague.

We identified episodes that stood out as particularly interesting, often ones where students worked in and across multiple languages successfully, or engaged in extended struggle and then made what seemed like breakthroughs. The one we focus on here took place in the spring of 2014, as the class translated a Polish poem by Wisława Szymborska. This particular segment (3 minutes of a 35-minute recording) took place during the first day of the make-it-flow translation, the third day that the students had been working on this poem. Deborah and Elvis were in a group with three other classmates, Bobby, Rudy, and Marbella. The group was working on a shared translation of the first line and stanza of the poem. This is what they eventually agreed on: "When I say the word future, the first syllable already belongs to the past."

To illustrate the process of special listening, next we provide a detailed description of a segment of this group's conversation. At the beginning of the segment, each student has a "Phrase-by-Phrase" translation as well as a "Make-it-Flow" page. Deborah looks at the papers on the table, then refers to her paper, which has the words "starts the syllable, belongs to the past." She asks the group (in Spanish) if they should go with this or change it, finishing her turn by shifting to English, and asking if there's anything they want to "add in or challenge." There's silence, with Bobby looking at the two pages in front of him, moving his lips, reading silently. He utters something under his breath and begins to write on the "Make-it-Flow" page. Elvis and Rudy look at their own papers and at the others. Deborah initiates a focus on the word "belongs," and Bobby says, "Belongs already to the past." Deborah says "already," and asks the others in Spanish what they think. As the others talk, Bobby very softly reads, "When I say the word future, start syllable belongs already to the past." He then nods his head and loudly says, "Mmmmm," as if he finally got it. The entire group orients to Bobby. Deborah says, "What does that mean, 'already'?" and, speaking over Elvis, says "I want to, like, understand what he means." This begins a long segment of Bobby trying to explain to Deborah what he means, trying to give an example ("So for example, when you're reading this"—pointing to the paper and reading—"When I say the word future, the start syllable is already in the past." He continues, "Now if you look in the past, what word is in the past? He pauses and looks Deborah in the eye, with a questioning expression, and says, "Past." Deborah says she doesn't think she's getting it. Bobby then shifts modalities. He says, "Look it, look it, look, look, look," and grabs two pencils, a yellow highlighter, and a pink cell phone from the table.

He lines them up in a row, and says the words, "When I—say—the word—future," pointing to each object in turn on the beat. And then he follows with the words, "it already belongs to the past," moving his hand out past the objects, as if down the road in time.

Now that he's established the movement of words in time, a time-line of sorts, he moves his hand dramatically back, returning to the pink cell phone (which was standing in for the word "future,") and points to it. He says, "And back here (in time) is what?" using the intonation of a teacher testing. Deborah says, "The past?" Bobby confirms, saying, "The past." He then reviews, continuing to motion forward and back in time: "So when I say this word" (hands cupped over the cell phone), "It already belongs to the past once I've said it."

Deborah and the entire group, quite joyously, demonstrate that they get it, in both Spanish and in English. Deborah has engaged in spe-cial listening, which in turn helped Bobby explicate a complicated and counterintuitive idea, unpacking his understanding through word, ges-ture, and a staged performance with objects, to a multilingual audience.

The youth researchers, not the university professors, first identified and worked hard over months to explicate the notion of special lis-tening. It's perhaps because the youth were new to academic work on classroom discourse, and were not steeped in traditional analytic cate-gories separating speakers and listeners or steeped in the emphasis of "within the head" thinking that is dominant in much academic writing on reasoning. We have come to see for ourselves the value of youth perspectives on what counts as data, what counts as knowledge, and where our standard categories for classroom discourse and educational curricula need to expand.

THEORIZING MULTILITERACIES FROM YOUTH RESEARCH (JIE AND SARAH)

We end by asking two questions: (1) What is the significance of the NLG's ideas for our work with PIO and the inclusion of youth research-ers? and (2) What is the significance of our work for the vision and ideas—the "what" and "how" of a pedagogy of multiliteracies and pro-ductive diversity—put forward by the NLG, 20 years later?

We see the NLG manifesto's greatest contribution in providing a metalanguage and framework for talking with practitioners, colleagues, and students about PIO and other educational programs and practices. Here we mean both the constructs and terms relating to design (available designs, designing, and redesign) as well as the framework around pedagogy (situated practice, overt instruction, critical framing, and transformed practice). With the multiliteracies metalanguage, we now see PIO as a design space where students-as-translators use their available designs of meaning, along with the poem itself and the translator's glossary, "in the process of shaping emergent meaning [that] involves representation and recontextualization" (New London Group, 1996, p. 75). We also see youth research, with opportunities for youth to engage in a sustained practice around research. We see youth receive, at times, overt instruction from more knowledgeable adults about research tools and analytic approaches. We see them critically frame their educational experiences and learning. We see them generate new knowledge, as a form of multiliteracies pedagogy. Multiliteracies practice in the youth research group inspired, and then cultivated, youths' interest in, and imagination around, special listening.

The value of these constructs grows out of and persists as a result of the productive diversity the group brought together.

> The role of pedagogy is to develop an epistemology of pluralism that provides access without people having to erase or leave behind different subjectivities. This has to be the basis of a new norm. (New London Group, 1996, p. 72)

While it is far more common today to hear about "recruiting" or "leveraging" diversity as assets (Lee, 1993; González, Moll, & Amanti, 2006; Park, Simpson, Bicknell, & Michaels, 2015), we find ourselves writing this conclusion (in the summer of 2016) when these views are still questioned, publicly denounced, and rejected by leaders and private citizens in tweets and blogs across the media-sphere. The youth voices and the work we did together stand as a strong counter-voice to these leaders and private citizens, lending support to the manifesto's argument that productive diversity is possible, generative, and a viable means to writing new social futures.

It is our hope that youth-centered multiliteracies research will continue not only to impact the youth involved (and us), but also to add dimensions to the construct as it was conceived 20 years ago. The perspectives brought forward by the youth and the themes they constructed from their research add texture and color to a set of theoretical terms and programmatic principles. Therefore, in closing, we want to make the case for the value and power of youth-led practitioner inquiry. As designers of meaning and knowledge, youth-as-practitioner inquirers remake themselves and expand their social futures, and in the process, help adult researchers who work with them or who read their work do the same.

REFERENCES

González, N., Moll, L. C., & Amanti, C. (Eds.). (2006). *Funds of knowledge: Theorizing practices in households, communities, and classrooms*. New York, NY: Routledge.

Lee, C. D. (1993). *Signifying as a scaffold for literary interpretation: The pedagogical implications of an African American discourse genre*. Urbana, IL: National Council for Teacher Education.

New London Group. (1996). A pedagogy of multiliteracies: Designing social futures. *Harvard Educational Review, 66*(1), 60–92.

Park, J. Y., Simpson, L., Bicknell, J., & Michaels, S. (2015). "When it rains a puddle is made": Fostering academic literacy in English learners through poetry and translation. *English Journal, 104*(4), 50–58.

Schiffrin, D., Tannen, D., & Hamilton, H. E. (Eds.). (2008). *The handbook of discourse analysis*. New York, NY: John Wiley & Sons.

Schultz, K. (2003). *Listening: A framework for teaching across differences*. New York, NY: Teachers College Press.

PART II

CONTEMPORARY VOICES ON MULTILITERACIES

CHAPTER 5

Around and Around We Go

Layering Turns into the Multiliteracies Framework

Jennifer Rowsell and Julianne Burgess

The meeting of the New London Group (NLG) nearly 25 years ago signaled an important union of linguistics with semiotics that filled a gap at the time for more expansive definitions and frameworks for literacy teaching and learning. As a result of their intellectual work, the group radicalized literacy studies by asking researchers and educators to think about literacy as multimodal, and as culturally and linguistically plural, moving the focus away from enacting literacy through one mode, mostly words, to enacting literacy through a variety of available modes that people design and redesign. The central argument put forth by the NLG (1996) is that communication involves more than one mode at a time and that design is a (more) apt and contemporary term for meaning-making because it situates literacy within present-day realities.

This chapter approaches the NLG's manifesto from a layered perspective by enfolding other theories within the multiliteracies framework to fill in cracks that inevitably materialize over time when a conceptual paradigm comes of age. Our argument rests on a belief that modern-day multiliteracies are far more layered and variegated than the original manifesto rendered them. By extension, contemporary communication practices are most effectively analyzed by activating a range of interlocking theories that are spatial, affective, emotional, temporal, and posthuman, and the strength of combining the multiliteracies manifesto with these turns, or paradigm shifts, unlocks doors to understanding modern meaning-making.

The concept of design in the multiliteracies framework tends to eclipse the concept of pedagogy, which acknowledges and incorporates cultural and linguistic diversity (Collier & Rowsell, 2014). What the emphasis on cultural plurality adds to the manifesto is an appreciation that there are people and subjectivities behind designs and that we live in political, contested landscapes. Over the past 20 years, some of the original mission of the NLG has been fractured. To fill in some cracks, we combine multiliteracies with other theories that have emerged with time and circumstances to show that the field has moved on, and to show how complicated literacy is as a lived practice. In this chapter we will describe these turns that have taken place in literacy studies, then illustrate each turn through data from a research study with adult language learners. We will conclude the chapter by looking ahead to the future of multiliteracies.

THEORETICAL TURNS AS TOOLS FOR MULTILITERACIES RESEARCH

In order to examine ways to conceptualize multiliteracies coupled with other turns in literacy studies, we present a research study with vestiges of each turn and with a central multiliteracies focus. The central theory of multiliteracies focuses on the three main tenets of the manifesto: available design, design, and redesign. That is, adult language learners had at their disposal various modal choices in terms of not only what to depict in their body maps, but also forms and methods of depiction, colors, placement, framing vectors, etc. We taught the unit of study using the language of multiliteracies and talking about existing designs and ways of reframing or redesigning these designs.

The research featured in this chapter took place over 6 weeks in May 2015 at a community college in southern Ontario where Julianne teaches in the Language Instruction for Newcomers to Canada (LINC) program. One of the reasons that we feature this specific research study is that it is non-digital and, as such, the research relies more on the linguistic diversity and contested landscape dimension of multiliteracies, which we feel has been neglected.

LINC is a free program, funded by Citizenship and Immigration Canada, providing settlement English classes to adult newcomers who are permanent residents or Convention refugees (people who are outside their home country or the country where they normally live, and who are unwilling to return because of a well-founded fear of persecution). The LINC Youth program targets youth aged 18 to 25; the focus is English for academic study in a post-secondary setting (Ontario Council of Agencies Serving Immigrants, 2016). In recent years, the learners in the LINC program have come primarily from Iraq and other Middle Eastern countries, as well as from Colombia.

The research design involved Julianne's development of lessons around the idea of body maps (Griffin, 2014, 2015). Students used digital photography to produce a poster in which their languages were mapped onto their self-portraits. What this entailed was drawing maps on 11" x 17" sheets of paper, with colored pencils and markers. As they worked, they were encouraged to use colors, symbols, and labels in their home languages. The guiding question in this body mapping inquiry was: Where is home? Is it a place, an object, or something we carry inside ourselves? They were also asked a series of questions to help stimulate ideas for their artwork, including: Where are you from? How do you feel about being here? Draw a recent experience of home, a favorite memory of home, a sad memory of home (a sensitive question that students could choose to ignore). And, where is home—is it the place your parents come from, or where you grew up? Is it a location, a person, an artifact, a feeling you carry within yourself?

Jennifer attended many of Julianne's sessions, interacted with students, drew her own body maps, and debriefed with Julianne after lessons. We took detailed field notes in the tradition of Wolcott (2001) and Geertz (1993), with a specific focus on cultural meanings and symbolic meanings embedded within multimodal artifacts. At the end of the unit of study we interviewed all the participants about the research and what they derived from designing body maps. In this chapter we focus on four case study learners (matched up with each turn) as telling examples of our population.

Part of our analytic lens relied on getting to know participants—speaking with them, observing their design and production practices, watching the group interact, reflecting on our own reflexivity, and conducting post-research interviews. A consideration of how ethnographic insights can inform multimodal analysis played a key role for us in conducting the research. The 6-week study therefore combined ethnographic perspectives (Green & Bloome, 1997) with multimodality. Research at the intersection of multimodality and ethnography is research that combines a fine-grained, contextually rich account of ethnography with a focus on modal choice and the material qualities of texts. A consideration of how ethnographic insights can inform multimodal analysis continues to be pertinent within the field of education, as researchers trace the journeys of young people's meaning-making practices across sites (Pahl, 2014).

For data analyses, we visually analyzed (Albers, Frederick, & Cowan, 2009) multimodal features of each student's body map. We would like to stress that we interpreted the turns within multimodal artifacts and that students did not actively layer in or embed them. Together we examined how illustrations exhibit connotative and denotative qualities, ideological perspectives such as sociopolitical or cultural perspectives (Youngs & Serafini, 2013), and structural and design features. Reading the drawings several times, we began to recognize visual narratives that combine different theoretical turns. We did notice that participants exaggerated some design features, privileging some aspects of identity over others. In the next few sections we break apart these ideologies and discourses in conjunction with thick description about our case study learners and we illustrate how rich it is to combine multiliteracies with theoretical turns. There is a tacit point within the case studies depicted here that disrupts a more static view of design that signals diversity, pluralism, and a variety of modes (multiliteracies version), encouraging more of an assembled version of design that layers and folds in histories, ways of knowing, emotions, bodies, and posthuman worlds.

BODY MAPPING AS A CRITICAL MULTILITERACIES APPROACH

Albers (2011) promotes the use of critical multimodality in educational settings to create a space for the analysis and interrogation of texts, to encourage students to better understand how language and power work, and for learners to see the potential for their creative work to shift, to transform, and to break down barriers and turn the spaces in their world inside out. Certainly what we both find is that multiliteracies pedagogy in ESL classrooms is a natural fit; it allows teachers to privilege diverse and marginalized voices and perspectives (Rogers & Schaenen, 2014).

Multiliteracies projects, such as this mapping one's home project, allow English learners to transcend the barriers imposed by their limited mastery of English. Multimodality promotes communication across and between modes, or synesthesia (Cope & Kalantzis, 2000), creating more powerful forms of communication that do not require fluency in English. In addition, by recruiting learners' linguistic and cultural resources, their design work in the second language classroom becomes transgressive (hooks, 1994); when learners use home language and culture in imaginative and subversive ways, they contest and defy narrow, state-mandated definitions of what constitutes literacy in ESL contexts.

Through the process of designing multimodal projects, individuals are changed; their work makes a contribution to the social world, which then reflects back to the individual. As Rogers and Trigos-Carillo (this volume) explain, "transformation (learning) extends its reach from the individual to the collective and back again" (p. 176). Using this activist frame, we can revisit our students' body maps.

Farah's body map, for example, highlights the tensions of gender and culture in her lived experience as an Arab woman. Her artwork clearly articulates her message: *"I am a strong woman who lives alone"* in Canada. Farah's design proudly reflects her ability to contest traditional gendered cultural expectations, signifying her individualism, ambition, and independence, as a young unmarried Arabic woman. Farah's feminist stance is projected through local circles within the school community and the local Arabic community, and globally, as she communicates on social media with family and friends in the Middle East and beyond.

We have seen how multiliteracies teaching practices, and our learners' multilingual, multimodal design work, can collectively challenge injustice in small but powerful ways, helping to fulfill the transformative potential of multiliteracies. Rebecca Rogers and Lina Trigos-Carrillo (this volume) call on scholars to reconsider the promise of design and transformation in the multiliteracies project. She argues critical social theory has been relegated to the background in the enactment of multiliteracies, with multimodal assemblage taking center stage. The resulting emphasis on the possibilities of design obscures the lack of attention paid to issues of power and injustice, which were built into the equity agenda articulated in the original multiliteracies manifesto.

COMBINING MULTILITERACIES WITH TURNS

When we returned to the visual data from the 6-week project, we realized that simply focusing on available designs and redesigns limited our interpretative frame. Stepping back from these multimodal productions, we decided to excavate linguistic, cultural, identity-laden memory work that the participants portrayed in their body maps through design and other conceptual turns. Activating a range of turns (one for every visual artifact) opened up our analyses to more interlocking concepts and prompted us to see the artifacts as complex, entangled multimodal productions. To avoid imposing turns, although admittedly there is a degree of imposition, we relied on interview data for references to turns such as the materiality of texts (Yung), or time and memory and text (Farah), and we aligned the multimodal production with these respective turns.

MULTILITERACIES AND THE DESIGN TURN

One of the first turns that is clearly associated with the multiliteracies pedagogy is the design turn. Recognizing the limitations of monomodality as *the* defining nature of literacy, the NLG argued for design as fundamental to future understandings of literacy. But how does one learn and teach through design? The notion of design and attendant theorizing that the NLG performed relied so heavily on design choice: image or word; sounds or music with moving images; Times New Roman or Calibri as fonts; pastel shades or bold colors, and the list of design and production choices goes on and on. So many research studies have telescoped in on design choices and the associated affordances and constraints that they imply. Within our body mapping research, for instance, design played a key role in how learners mediated their identities onto body maps. We draw on the story of Aadi as an example.

Aadi is a 24-year-old from Nepal. His family is originally from Bhutan, but Aadi identifies as Nepali after spending most of his life in a refugee camp in the eastern part of the country. He is married and is the father of a 2-year-old girl. As a result of a United Nations resettlement initiative, Aadi's family members and those of his wife are scattered across the United States, Norway, the Netherlands, and Canada.

In a journal reflection on his body map (see Figure 5.1), Aadi wrote: "When I drew this picture I forgot about Canada because my mind and body are in Nepal. In my heart are all my friends and our neighbors and cousins." "*Yo mann to mero Nepali ho*" means "My heart belongs to Nepal."

From what he expressed to both of us, in the forefront of Aadi's mind is designing a map that features camaraderie, friendship, and community. A visual of linked figures holding hands in a circle appears on Aadi's t-shirt with Aadi at the center. Aadi wears the Nepalese flag on his hat and is surrounded by visual anchors that embody his figured worlds (Holland, Lachicotte, Skinner, & Cain, 1998). Aadi is quiet and soft-spoken, and he gets misty-eyed when he talks about Nepal. However, through the course of our conversations with him, he revealed that Nepal was not, in fact, his birthplace. "Bhutan is my motherland. When I was 1 year old I left my first country because Bhutan government killed (some of) my family and my family was afraid. Nepal was my second country. I want study in Nepal and I had lots of friends in Nepal. I stayed in Nepal 25 year. But Nepal government did not give citizenship. After that I want to process to Canada. Canada is my 3rd country in my life. In this country I do not have lots of friend because I new immigrant." Aadi's fondness for Nepal is palpable. There were many moments over the course of the research when he could be found doodling pictures of the Nepalese flag or of stick figures dancing, and these moments crystallized something key about his character. Music, talk, and dancing were consistently vital in Aadi's design and every visual on his map showcased places like his house, the community square where he met with friends and family, and the local school. When Jennifer spoke with Aadi, he spoke most about "dwelling places," that is, he wanted his map design to privilege gatherings and places where he would sit, talk, dance, and sing with his friends and family. So it is on his map that you see people dancing; you see a covered building in the top right corner where he would have picnics with his community. There is his house in the top left corner; he was popular amongst his friends for hosting impromptu parties. On the right side of his map near the central figure's shoulder, Aadi drew a group singing and dancing—once again reminding the viewer about the convivial nature of his life in Nepal. Aadi's

Figure 5.1. Aadi in Nepal: A Self-Portrait

design is a motivated sign (Kress, 1997) and clearly shows how motivated he is by community, celebration, talk, and connection more broadly. As a learner, Aadi was one of the clearest and most resolute about what his design would look like. In this way, Aadi's body map is a contested artifact that strongly benefits from a multiliteracies interpretation.

MULTILITERACIES AND THE TEMPORAL TURN

The work of Compton-Lilly (2014, in press) and of Lemke (2000) stand out as illustrations of temporal research that accounts for how subjectivities and objects carry with them epistemologies, ideologies, and associations that circulate and dominate over time and people's histories;

this can both afford and constrain individuals and their life trajectories. Compton-Lilly talks about how time exists like chronotopes (Bakhtin, 1981) and that chronotopes of time exist in classrooms. That is, institutional classroom routines, discourses, and spaces honor certain histories over others, and these histories are often rooted in White middle-class models that cut out other model—ones that carry the stamp of time as children come of age at school and exist within these temporally-laden schooling patterns (Compton-Lilly, 2014). So, how is time depicted within in a multiliteracies framework? Interwoven into both the semiotic and linguistic strands are historical lineages about design and how designs are informed by cultures, lived histories, and diversities riven into objects and symbols that we value. Viewing Farah's map through a multiliteracies lens allows us to recognize the meticulous deliberateness of her choices that depict phases of her history. The map intricately presents her timeline of the past 5 years and the emotional story that it tells.

To contextualize it, Farah is an independent 21-year-old economics student from Iraq. Her family fled the unrest in their homeland and ended up in a refugee camp in Turkey. Because she has Crohn's disease, Farah was selected by the United Nations High Commissioner for Refugees (UNHCR) to come to Canada to receive urgent medical treatment. She was forced to leave her parents and brother behind and suffered from homesickness during her first months in Canada. As her health has improved, Farah has discovered an inner strength and tremendous pride in her ability to live on her own and take care of herself; she is a rarity in Arabic culture. Farah's body map (see Figure 5.2) shows two faces: her sick, unhappy self in Iraq, and her happy, healthy self in Canada. She has illustrated the disease in her intestines, bombs falling on her neighborhood in Iraq, and tents under a hot sun in her refugee camp. She has also written in Arabic the verse to a favorite song, and she's drawn her apartment in Canada, noting, "My life here began to move forward."

In her written reflection Farah states, "When I drew my body map I felt joy, because I like a lot of things in my life, happy and sad. There were a lot of ideas in my mind. I thought about my family; and now, I am happy: Farah is a strong woman. She lives alone and learns a lot of things in her new life here. I love my life no matter where I live."

In some ways her map demonstrates design, affect, temporal, and spatial turns all together—it is so intricately laden with parts of herself that it was hard to think where to start. But the moment that you meet Farah, it is clear that her health, specifically Crohn's, has presided over her life and history for a long time. She recounted her story to us through the timescale (Lemke, 2000) of her Crohn's. Lemke talks about shorter and longer timescales, with shorter ones carrying much less significance than longer ones. It is for this reason that we saw her design

Figure 5.2. Farah in Iraq: A Self-Portrait

as imbued with temporality and the passage of time from the severity of her illness in Iraq to its abatement in Canada.

The temporal unfolding of Farah's story begins in the upper left corner of her map with bombs dropping on her home city of Mosul. Farah talked about sitting in her parlor room reading and looking out at soldiers with guns fixed on civilians. Her depiction is not entirely solemn, inflected with happier moments like her two friends, playing music, a map of her country, Arabic script, and a butterfly. As her visual narrative moves on, the central figure of Farah in the center shows her two faces—one happy and one stricken with pain—and her intestinal system coupled with an airplane to Canada and her treatment. In the bottom left and right corners, Farah has been in Canada now for a year, she has an apartment, which she loves, new friends, and a new language. She has built a life now in Canada and enough time has passed that she thinks fondly of home and familiar things like her favorite food, her language, and culture. "When I come to Canada I feel sad because in my mind I think my home is not here. My home (is) in Iraq. But you know, after 2 month, I see a lot of things is so good in here. In my country I have big house but in here I live in studio (apartment). But I feel that house (the studio) is safe. When I put my head on the pillow I feel safe. Here is a small house, but the freedom that I live in Canada now let me see this house is beautiful paradise."

The map is a site of self with colors signaling strong feelings like red for pain and blood and signifiers like flags betokening belonging. Designing the map, Farah emphasized her past, present, and future. Time exists here as what Lemke (2000) describes as a social semiotic practice.

Together, the modes in her drawing have a dizzying effect on the spectator. Yes, there is culture. Yes, there is linguistic diversity. Yes, there is design—in abundance. But to us what is profound for Farah is the mapping of her agency and story *over time*. Zigzagging down the body map, there is a marked movement from guns, violence, anxiety, and fear to the bottom of the visual with a butterfly, her Canadian apartment building and her favorite food, which she could not eat at home. As a chronotope, Farah's time in the LINC classroom has allowed her to represent her previous life with less fear, anxiety, and angst, and although clearly her life in Mosul carries a far longer timescale, her short stay in Julianne's classroom has borne witness to her blossomed transformation, which can be seen in her design and production work.

Multiliteracies and the Spatial Turn

Space and spatial research couple well with the multiliteracies framework because the formal and informal spaces that people inhabit inform the kinds of communicational practices that they engage in; people exist in socio-cultural-political diasporas that equally shape understandings of literacy and communication. In seeing space as something not given, but made, it is possible to interrogate space as having more or less power. That is, space is semiotically constructed through discourses and practices. Scholars examining space as an interpretative lens for practice tend to question the ways in which people define space and how space is constructed. Leander and Sheehy (2004), for example, argued that spaces where meanings are constructed generally draw on both perceived and conceived senses of space. From a spatial turn came a temporal turn—seeing time as shaping memories and subjectivities. There have been studies that account for time and history as pivotal to literacy lives. As with the previous turns, though, what does space have to do with multiliteracies?

Abdullah is a soft-spoken 25-year-old university graduate from Yemen. He and his mother fled to Canada after his activist father was forced into hiding. Abdullah had been dreaming of a life in Canada for a long time. He explains this in his journal:

> When I draw my body map I made a mix about my future and my past, but I was trying to explain to everybody how I am. In the past I had friends, family, goals and dreams. I attained my goal of finishing college and I sat thinking how I can attain my dreams? My dream was I wanted to go to another country. I want to search about good country, because I want continue my goals. I was thinking about going to an Arabic country, because Canada is just a dream in my life. But I broke all the limits and I insisted on going to Canada and I attained my dream. Actually I take a long way, but I know I become happy when I reached Canada because I wanted the make new friends, new home and I will continue with my goals, but I will use my new language.

Abdullah was the comedian in the class, teasing his classmates, and he seldom became serious—unless he was talking about Yemen. As with other visuals, there are images of murders and killings and strife outside of his home. The Yemeni flag is on prominent display, and a gradual trail almost like footprints leads to Canada. Although the visual does not depict an expansive space, the map centrally deals with space: (1) moving spaces; (2) shifting destinations from other Arab nations or Canada; and (3) movements to familiar spaces. In the map, there is a sense of a wide gap between Yemen and Canada and footprints between the two. It is difficult to see, but there are practices and discourses that inform Abdullah's sense of space such as local sites or hubs, a cistern, and farmland. Mills and Comber (2015) describe "a social and spatial stratification of literacy practices, power and economy" (p. 93) that certainly plays out in Abdullah's map, with the left side of the visual narrative showing dead bodies and the right side representing a space of freedom with birds carrying the Canadian flag. The design of the map (see Figure 5.3) relies on space as a practice with fallen bodies and gunfire in front of Abdullah's home and then yellow lines charting his voyage with his family. When we spoke with Abdullah, he said that the distance from Yemen to Canada felt immense before the journey, but as time passed, the distance between Canada and Yemen shrank. Drawing and discussing his body map allowed Abdullah to reconsider what it means to be at home in the world. He explained, "The home is not where I was born or where my father is born. The home is where I

Figure 5.3. Abdullah in Yemen: A Self-Portrait

find myself. At home it's where I built myself. My home is where I can feel comfortable and at peace."

MULTILITERACIES AND THE POSTHUMAN TURN

With an increased focus on modes, materials, and technologies in literacy research came posthuman work by researchers like Kuby (2013; Kuby & Gutshall Rucker, 2015) who look at children's material worlds in sophisticated ways, theorizing through new materialism and embodiment with the work of Barad (2007) and Deleuze and Guattari (1987). Such research explores what humans do *to* and *with* materials in literacy learning. Posthuman research examines designs or end products that humans create as well as the in-the-moment becoming with materials (Leander & Boldt, 2013) that happens with the increasing presence of screens and converged devices. Building on multimodality as a popular field of inquiry and scholarship (and a key component of multiliteracies), posthumanism in literacy studies strives to move away from language to focus more on objects and the materials used to produce and think through objects.

Yung is 19 years old, and he has lived with his mother and brother in Canada for 4 months. Yung is an enthusiastic learner and presents an innocence and a sense of wonder at the world around him. His demeanor conceals the fact that Yung was devastated by his father's death in a car accident 8 years ago. His struggle with depression left him unable to finish his secondary school education in China. He feels that he has been given a fresh start in Canada and he is eager to make up for lost time.

Describing his body map (see Figure 5.4), Yung writes,

> This beautiful picture has a pretty house on his face. Both his two hands have two things. What are they? One is the tallest tower in China. In the tower there is a Ferris wheel and a rotating restaurant. On the other hand, it is my favorite food. It is made up of rice and meat and you add some soy and oil. What is the popular wall in China? It is the Great Wall.

Thinking about this excerpt from his written narrative, Yung recounts the creation of his body map/beautiful picture as a series of visual and artifactual anchors—the Great Wall, the Ferris wheel, the rotating restaurant. We spoke at length with Yung as he drew his body map and we both found that Yung talked in terms of things and places in Beijing and much less about relationships or about feelings or about culture. It is for this reason that we decided to interpret his illustration through a coupling of multiliteracies with temporality.

When Yung described his body map, he described it in relation to artifacts and locations—food, mountains, a tower, a temple, and his home—the stuff of his old life. Unlike other maps, there was little affect and fewer subjectivities embedded within the visual. Instead, it is a simple, pure celebration of things that he prizes and if he had his way, he would have added in more objects. The visual is a form of becoming through materials, objects and posthuman worlds. As he told us about his map he laughed about all of the food that he featured and he exhibited such pride about the historical monuments in and near Beijing, such as the Temple of Hope, the Great Wall, and the Forbidden City. For a poetry poster he completed as part of the mapping home project, he chose butterflies to celebrate the diversity within the classroom. *"We found beautiful pictures of butterflies because butterflies have a lot of colors in their wings. It (is) like our class, have a lot of languages and we are in one body in the butterfly."* Yung and the objects that he values are entangled together. They literally depict him and his figured worlds (Holland et al., 1998). Combining design with posthuman principles, albeit not consciously adopting posthuman principles, Yung shows how objects are agentive for him and he exhibited this conviction as he produced his visual.

Figure 5.4. Yung in Beijing: A Self-Portrait

Concluding Remarks

When we completed the research we looked at each other and asked: What did we learn about multiliteracies research? As scholars committed to applying the notions of available designs and redesign and the attendant framework of situated practice, overt instruction, and critical framing, we knew that there was something more at work in the research. The maps emoted, spatialized, charted histories, and exposed an Ariadne's thread between material and physical worlds. As our lens for teaching and learning language, there was little doubt that design was central to the thinking and production processes. But design alone did not do justice to the myriad of ideas and discourses that circulated within student body maps. These learners had diverse histories, emotional dispositions, stark spatial differentials and understandings, strong material, artifactual and experiential connections that seeped through their maps as fractures of habitus and journeys.

Probing deeper, these language learners needed to work through their struggles with the loss of their own culture and homeland, family, close friendships, advanced studies for some, careers for others. What was palpable to us was pain and politics embedded in most of the maps. Julianne made a connection between the language learners' identity work and negotiations with Gee's (2007) concept of projected identity. As Julianne articulates it, these learners have to visualize themselves as competent English users, working, studying, playing, and living in English, in their new homeland. What this means for Julianne, as an English language teacher, is that she has to help learners build that bridge to their projective identity. When students discover their projective identity, Gee says, *"magic happens."* From her experience, body mapping is a way to help students with their personal project of building a bridge to their projective identities. Griffin (2014) maintains that body maps are transformative. Through the project, students considered notions of home and their lived experiences in new ways, using their intellect, culture, language, and imagination: aspects of their identity. Their body maps act as a mirror, reflecting their past, present, and future selves, at once, in their new homeland. They can see who they are, where they've come from, and where they are going.

Thinking about data collected for this project that had a stated aim of applying multiliteracies in an adult literacy environment, it was clear to us that there was far more than meets the eye. Certainly design, available design, and redesign played roles in resultant maps, but these emotionally, temporally, and spatially laden multimodal artifacts require a theoretically entangled, fluid, and variegated framing. Multiliteracies, as a fluid mobility in motion for nearly 25 years now, has the strong appeal of diversifying literacy through multimodal orientations to communication and meaning-making, coupled with an account of cultural diversity and cosmopolitanism. To live on and flourish, in our view, it must align with the deeper grooves and undulations of larger social theories that explain the human condition.

References

Albers, P. (2011). Double exposure: A critical study of pre-service teachers' multimodal public service announcements. *Multimodal Communication, 1*(1), 47–64.

Albers, P., Frederick, T., & Cowan, K. (2009). Features of gender: An analysis of the visual texts of third grade children. *Journal of Early Childhood Literacy, 9*(2), 234–260.

Bakhtin, M. M. (1981). *The dialogic imagination: Four essays* (C. Emerson & M. Holquist, Trans.). Austin, TX: University of Texas Press.

Barad, K. (2007). *Meeting the universe halfway: Quantum physics and the entanglement of matter and meaning.* Durham, NC: Duke University Press.

Collier, D. R., & Rowsell, J. (2014). A room with a view: Revisiting the multiliteracies manifesto, twenty years on. *Fremdsprachen Lehren und Lernen, 43*(2), 12–28.

Compton-Lilly, C. (2014). Temporal discourse analysis. In P. Albers, T. Holbrook, and A. Seely Flint (Eds.), *New methods of literacy research* (pp. 40–55). New York, NY: Routledge.

Compton-Lilly, C. (in press). *Reading students' lives: Literacy learning across time.* New York, NY: Routledge.

Cope, B., & Kalantzis, M. (2000). Multiliteracies: The beginning of an idea. In B. Cope & M. Kalantzis (Eds.), *Multiliteracies: Literacy learning and the design of social futures* (pp. 3–8). London, UK: Routledge.

Deleuze, G., & Guattari, F. (1987). *A thousand plateaus: Capitalism and schizophrenia* (B. Massumi, Trans.). Minneapolis, MN: University of Minnesota Press.

Gee, J. P. (2007). *What video games have to teach us about language and literacy.* New York, NY: Palgrave.

Geertz, C. (1993). *The interpretation of cultures.* London, UK: Fontana Press.

Green, J., & Bloome, D. (1997). Ethnography and ethnographers of and in education: A situated perspective. In J. Flood, S. B. Heath, & D. Lapp (Eds.), *Handbook of research on teaching literacy through the communicative and visual arts* (pp. 181–202). New York, NY: Macmillan.

Griffin, S. M. (2014). Meeting musical experience in the eye: Resonant work by teacher candidates through body mapping. *Visions of Research in Music Education, 24,* 1–28.

Griffin, S. M. (2015). Shifting from fear to self-confidence: Body mapping as a transformative tool in music teacher education. *Alberta Journal of Educational Research, 61*(3), 261–279.

Holland, D., Lachicotte, W., Skinner, D., & Cain, C. (1998). *Identity and agency in cultural worlds.* Cambridge, MA: Harvard University Press.

hooks, b. (1994) *Teaching to transgress: Education as the practice of freedom.* New York, NY: Routledge.

Kress, G. (1997). *Before writing: Rethinking the paths to literacy.* New York, NY: Routledge.

Kuby, C. R. (2013). *Critical literacy in the early childhood classroom: Unpacking histories, unlearning privilege.* New York, NY: Teachers College Press.

Kuby, C. R., & Gutshall Rucker, T. (2015). Everyone has a Neil: Possibilities of literacy desirings in writers' studio. *Language Arts, 92*(5), 314–327.

Leander, K. M., & Boldt, G. M. (2013). Rereading "a pedagogy of multiliteracies": Bodies, texts, and emergence. *Journal of Literacy Research, 45*(1), 22–46.

Leander, K., & Sheehy, M. (Eds.). (2004). *Spatializing literacy research*. New York, NY: Peter Lang.

Lemke, J. (2000). Across the scales of time: Artifacts, activities, and meanings in ecosocial systems. *Mind, Culture, and Activity, 7*(4), 273–290.

Mills, K. A., & Comber, B. (2015). Socio-spatial approaches to literacy studies: Rethinking the social constitution and politics of space. In J. Rowsell & K. Pahl (Eds.), *The Routledge handbook of literacy studies* (pp. 91–103). London, UK: Routledge.

New London Group. (1996). A pedagogy of multiliteracies: Designing social futures. *Harvard Educational Review, 66*(1), 60–92.

Ontario Council of Agencies Serving Immigrants. (2016). What is the language instruction for newcomers to Canada (LINC) program? Retrieved from http://settlement.org/ontario/education/english-as-a-second-language-esl/linc-program/what-is-the-language-instruction-for-newcomers-to-canada-linc-program/

Pahl, K. (2014). *Materializing literacies in communities: The uses of literacy revisited*. London, UK: Bloomsbury Academic.

Rogers, R., & Schaenen, I. (2014). Critical discourse analysis in literacy education: A review of the literature. *Reading Research Quarterly, 49*(1), 121–143.

Wolcott, H. (2001). *Writing up qualitative research* (2nd ed.). Newbury Park, CA: Sage Publications.

Youngs, S., & Serafini, F. (2013). Discussing picturebooks across perceptual, structural and ideological perspectives. *Journal of Language and Literacy Education, 9*(1), 185–200.

CHAPTER 6

Intersecting Intellectual Trajectories
Multiliteracies and Critical Discourse Analysis

Rebecca Rogers and Lina Trigos-Carrillo

The New London Group (NLG) report was published at a time when neoliberal policies made multinational expansion around the globe a reality. Anglophone countries were questioning how to "manage" diversity to account for an economy that was shifting to one based in service. Corporations appropriated discourses of diversity to gain new markets (which were culturally and linguistically diverse) rather than using a discourse of equity and transformation as had been espoused in social movements decades earlier. Occurring in tandem, educational policy and practice also reflected market and managerial frames, and emphasized standards, choice, and competition. The New London Group (1996) included critical discourse scholars Allan Luke, James Gee, Norman Fairclough, and Gunther Kress, who read this landscape and issued a warning:

> Fast capitalism, notwithstanding its discourse of collaboration, culture, and shared values, is also a vicious world driven by the barely restrained market. As we remake our literacy pedagogy to be more relevant to a new world of work, we need to be aware of the danger that our words become co-opted by economically and market-driven discourses, no matter how contemporary and 'post-capitalist' these may appear." (p. 67)

These very issues—the increasing interaction across cultural and linguistic boundaries, the increasing tendency of texts to be modally dense, and equity—were at the heart of the NLG's efforts a little more than 20 years ago. This chapter shows how critical discourse analysis (CDA) has contributed to the multiliteracies project and points out what contributions it still has to make. It uses critiques that have developed, many coming from multiliteracies scholars, in ways that might strengthen the multiliteracies project. It reflects on three aspects of the work—the "multi" in multiliteracies, design/critique, and learning. It begins with an overview of the intersecting intellectual trajectories of CDA and multiliteracies.

The NLG report, as others in this volume have pointed out, outlines a theoretical overview for an approach to literacy pedagogy concerned with access and critical engagement with multiple routes of meaning-making. Positioning people as designers rather than recipients of meaning-making rang true for educators who were witnessing children and youth using global technologies to accomplish social practices they deemed important. As people interact with modes (linguistic, visual, gestural, auditory) in creative ways, they transform meanings and are, themselves, transformed in the process. The theoretical overview was brought to life through four overlapping components of literacy pedagogy that include: situated practice, overt instruction, critical framing, and transformed practice (NLG, 1996).

The NLG's multiliteracies report contributed to a shift that was occurring in the field of literacy studies, from an autonomous to an ideological model of literacy: from literacy events to literacy practices (Heath, 1983; Street, 1985). Many of the authors of the report brought sociological frames to bear on understandings of discourse and society. Indeed, a critical analysis of discourse practices was woven into the fabric of the report. A thread through the report was the idea that literacy pedagogy was not connecting to the multimodal resources that children, especially marginalized children, were using in their families and communities, and an urgency that interventions needed to be responsive, relevant, and transformative. However, for people with an equity agenda, transformation needs to extend from the individual to collectives, from schools to broader social reform. This is a promise that has not yet been realized.

SURVEYING THE LANDSCAPE OF CRITICAL DISCOURSE ANALYSIS

Critical discourse analysis (CDA) has roots in critical social theory, critical linguistics, sociocultural studies, and critical pedagogy. The term critical language awareness emerged in the early 1990s when a group of researchers in northern England used it in a series of articles about power issues in the context of literacy and language instruction (Clark, Fairclough, Ivanic, & Martin-Jones, 1990). The more formalized tradition of CDA emerged in 1991. It was during this time that a group of scholars (Norman Fairclough, Gunther Kress, Teun van Dijk, Theo van Leeuwen, and Ruth Wodak) gathered for a symposium in Amsterdam to discuss the theories and methods of CDA. A set of papers that stemmed from this meeting were published in a special issue of *Discourse & Society* in 1993.

Just a year later, the NLG met and included two of the five scholars who met in Amsterdam (Fairclough and Kress). Its report, the multiliteracies manifesto, published in 1996, provided a pathway for CDA to become seeded in the context of literacy studies. It was a theoretical overview and pedagogical initiative that positioned people as critical analysts of meaning-making systems. What it did not include (because it was not the charge) was a methodological link for a fine-grained semiotic analysis of how power is enacted, resisted, and transformed. CDA offered this link and provided theoretical and methodological routes for tracing the relationships between texts, discourse practices, and social wide processes.

Steadily, literacy scholars engaged with CDA. Allan Luke's comprehensive essay (1995) devoted to CDA and educational research called "Text and Discourse in Education: An Introduction to Critical Discourse Analysis" helped to spur the recognition of CDA in learning sciences. By 1997, scholars in literacy studies were drawing on Norman Fairclough's books. Bloome and Talwalker (1997) published a book review essay in *Reading Research Quarterly* that synthesized four of his books. Around the turn of the century, the *Language, Power, and Identity* working group, which included North Atlantic scholars Jan Blommaert, James Collins, Monica Heller, Ben Rampton, and Stef Slembrouck, met regularly. Their work focused on multilingual spaces, power, and identity (Blommaert, 2005; Collins & Blot, 2003; Heller, 2001). James Gee's influence on the presence of critical discourse analysis in literacy studies cannot be understated (1990, 1999). In 2000, the *Handbook of Reading Research*, one of the premier guides for theory and research in literacy education, included a chapter by Gee that emphasized the convergence of discourse studies and sociocultural studies of literacy. During this time, the empirical work published in literacy studies that used CDA was slowly appearing (Rogers, Malancharuvil-Berkes, Mosley, Hui, & Joseph, 2005). Cope & Kalantzis's edited book *Multiliteracies: Literacy learning and the design of social futures*, an extension of the 1996 NLG report, was published in 2000. These early developments had a cumulative influence on literacy scholars who were consistently turning to CDA. Indeed, there was a spike in CDA scholarship in the field of literacy after 2000 (Rogers & Schaenen, 2014; Rogers et al., 2016). Studies of critical literacy, which flourished in Australia and South Africa, were synergistic spots of CDA work (Alford & Jetnikoff, 2016; Comber & Cormack, 2011; Janks, 1997; Kettle, 2005). Diverse research networks and collaborations have resulted in journals, conferences, networks, and pedagogical interventions (see Rogers et al., 2016 for a review of these efforts).

Literacy researchers who came of age with the multiliteracies project have consistently turned to CDA as a tool for describing, interpreting, explaining, and intervening in relations between texts, practices, and social practices. Interesting questions, critiques, and tensions have arisen. To reflect on these points, we draw on two literature reviews that together represent three decades of CDA in literacy studies (Rogers et al., 2005; Rogers et al., 2016). In these reviews, we included scholarship that self-identified as CDA versus critical approaches to discourse analysis; the latter would include a much broader array of scholarship. We learned that the presence of CDA in literacy studies has deepened and broadened. In 2005, we reported on just 18 articles between 1983 and 2004, compared with 76 articles in just the following 9 years (2005–2014). Perhaps more interesting than the increase in quantity of literacy scholarship using CDA are the ways in which the research has contributed to the agenda of the NLG.

Intersections between Multiliteracies and Critical Discourse Analysis

The New London Group (1996) provoked the field of literacy studies to think about how the concept "multi" might be a frame for understanding the changing nature of literacy practices and processes. They wrote,

> First, we want to extend the idea and scope of literacy pedagogy to account for the context of our culturally and linguistically diverse and increasingly globalized societies, for the multifarious cultures that interrelate and the plurality of texts that circulate. Second, we argue that literacy pedagogy now must account for the burgeoning variety of text forms associated with information and multimedia technologies. (p. 61)

This charge was effective. Indeed, in the past several decades, there is a proliferation of documented literacies and inquiry into how to prepare teachers for cultural and linguistically diverse contexts. Yet we also see deep and permanent racism, xenophobia, sexism, and classism. Perhaps because of this, literacy scholars have consistently turned to CDA to describe, interpret, and explain the reproduction and resistance of inequities. The following sections explore CDA's enactment of "multi."

Multiple Semiosis

Like multiliteracies, CDA draws from systemic functional linguistics (SFL), a social theory of meaning-making based on function, rather than rules (Halliday, 1978). It is also oriented to the choices people make when they are communicating with others. The basic idea is that every meaning unit (utterance, image, or gesture) functions in three ways simultaneously: It organizes the interaction as a particular kind of genre of social practice (textual function); it represents ideas (ideational function); and it construes relationships (interpersonal function). Each of these functions can be realized through any range of semiotic forms: linguistic, visual, spatial, gestural, temporal, or auditory. This is what the NLG referred to as available designs.

As our ideas about discourse expanded and included the multimodal semiotics included in any interaction and, at the same time, classrooms became increasingly diverse, attention to multimodality within CDA continued to rise. With respect to multimodality, in the original 2005 review of CDA in literacy research, analysis of multimodal interactions was nearly absent. This included scholarship from 1983–2004. CDA scholars were primarily focusing on written and spoken texts. By contrast, the 2014 review, which included scholarship from 2005–2014, demonstrated that 29% of the articles included some level of multimodal analysis. This demonstrates the flexibility of CDA frameworks to respond to modally dense social practices.

For example, Wohlwend (2012) set out to study young children's enactment of gender expectations during classroom play. She drew on Gee's (1999) approach to critical discourse analysis and "moment-by-moment discourse analysis to examine physical actions— including the interaction sequence, gestures, and manipulation of objects—as well as the social effects of speech" (p. 10). Her transcript included a record of verbal exchanges and physical actions. Her findings demonstrated that as children play with dolls they mediate gender identity texts that circulate through global media. Children's mediation of hetero-normative gender roles was accomplished through their embodied performances.

Rogers and Mosley (2008) present a case study of teachers learning about racial literacy through book clubs. Drawing on an integrated CDA framework (Fairclough, 1992; Kress, 2000; van Leeuwen, 2008), we traced the presence of racial literacy across multiple modes (visual, linguistic, gestural, spatial) as the teacher education students participated in a book club discussion about racial justice. We presented a detailed coding system that presents how the metafunctions (textual, ideational, and interpersonal) are accomplished across semiotic systems. We documented the increase in modal density as teacher education students worked through complex ideas such as taking action to disrupt White privilege.

Jacobs (2013) argued that multiliteracies research has been limited in its somewhat narrow focus on digital technology and popular media and has not included the multiplicity of modes and contexts in which meanings are made. Written texts, for example, are multimodal in the layout of print on the page or the inclusion of images. Speakers make choices about their intonation, pausing, and cadence as they talk. Combining the emphasis from the multiliteracies project on modally dense, quickly changing, digital literacies with CDA's emphasis on power, context, and transformation could be quite synergistic. The point here is that CDA is aptly prepared to describe, interpret, and explain modally dense interactions in real time and in virtual contexts.

Multiperspectival

For literacy scholars committed to creating access and critical engagement with codes of power, "multi" also means multiperspectival. The NLG (1996) wrote, "the role of pedagogy is to develop an epistemology of pluralism that provides access without people having to erase or leave behind different subjectivities" (p. 73). Yet there were skeptics who questioned the extent to which a project initiated by academics in the global North could transcend a scholarship of privilege. From South Africa, Newfield and Stein (2000) wrote,

> We did initially have reservations about its top-down nature and whom it claimed to be representing. For while it had ambitiously established itself as a global project it then comprised only academics from Australia, the USA, and Britain; all post-industrial societies with massive resources. However, simply to dismiss the Project as another form of neo-colonialism which we, in the developing world, were in danger of being sucked into, would have been too negative a response to a very positive initiative. (p. 292)

Literacy scholars from around the world have been influenced by the multiliteracies project and are using CDA as a tool in their research: in South Africa (Janks, 2010; Kapp, 2004), Australia (Nichols, 2002), and Spain (e.g., Martín Rojo, 2010, 2014). Scholars in Latin America have steadily integrated multiliteracies and CDA (e.g., Alvarez Valencia, 2016; Farías, 2015; López-Bonilla & Pérez Fragoso, 2010; Mora, 2015). Much of this scholarship is available in Spanish and presents key multiliteracies concepts from a Latin American perspective characterized by a focus on discourse and social conflict (Trigos-Carrillo & Rogers; manuscript in preparation).

Troubling the European roots of CDA, literacy scholars bring a diverse range of theoretical frameworks such as critical race theory (Rogers & Mosley, 2008), Chicana feminist theory (Martinez-Roldan, 2005), and queer theory (Moita-Lopes, 2006). They have created a more robust set of multicultural frameworks that moves beyond Western epistemologies of individualism, the primacy of the speaker's goals, and a separation of mind and body (Ladson-Billings, 2003; Resende, 2010; Shi-xu, 2009).

Marshall & Toohey's (2010) study is a good example of a multicultural theory of discourse infused into a multiliteracies classroom. The authors used van Leeuwen's (2008) approach to CDA and examined educators' efforts to incorporate funds of knowledge from the communities and families of Punjabi Sikh students in a Canadian elementary school. Using MP3 players, students first recorded and then translated their grandparents' stories of life in India into picture books to serve as cultural resources in their school community. In retelling their grandparents' stories, students drew on a multiplicity of ancestral, globalized, and Western discourses in their textual and pictorial illustrations. The authors used CDA to examine what happens when the funds of knowledge that students bring to school contradict normative, Western understandings of what is appropriate for children.

CDA's attention to multiple levels of analysis also contributes to the NLG's goal of creating an "epistemology of pluralism." CDA often includes multiple levels of analysis, which means that the analysis itself creates a multiperspectival context. Fairclough (2000) wrote, "The critical discourse analysis of texts can be conceived of as linking together or mapping on to one another three different sorts of analysis: linguistic (semiotic) analysis of text, intertextual analysis of text, and sociocultural analysis of discursive event" (p. 175). An example of this multistaged analysis can be seen in Comber & Cormack's (2011) study, which showed how principals in local school contexts interpreted neoliberal assessment policies imposed by the state. Their analysis demonstrated that the discourses of accountability "reach deep into the lives of formerly semiautonomous professionals" (p. 85). Thus, "multi" also means tracing literacy practices across time, space, and contexts. This holds great potential for centering marginalized voices.

THE ROLE OF CRITIQUE AND DESIGN IN THE MANIFESTO

Critique and design were major concepts in the multiliteracies manifesto. Different scholars in the NLG placed different emphases on these concepts. Kress (2000), for example, thought that critique was a backward-looking endeavor, and that emphasis in a world infused with multiliteracies should be placed on design. He wrote,

> Critique and Design imply deeply differing positions and possibilities for human social action; and deeply differing potentials for human subjectivities in social and economic life. The likely shape of the near future is such that the facilities of Design rather than those of critique, will be essential for equitable participation in social, economic, and cultural life. (p. 161)

Yet critique might be thought of as a kind of design. Fairclough (2000) also saw the enormous potential of casting meaning-making through the concept of design and wrote,

> In centering the concept of Design, we are suggesting that meaning-making
> is a creative application of existing resources for meaning . . . in negotiat-
> ing the constantly shifting occasions and needs of communication. . . . In
> this process of Designing, the resources for meaning are themselves trans-
> formed. (p. 162)

Fairclough did not, however, see the practicality of disregarding
critique in favor of only focusing on the assemblage of new meanings. Indeed, the word critique stems from the Greek word *kritikós*,
"of or for judging, able to discern." Critique might be thought of as an
appraisal that can be positive or negative. It might also be thought of
methodologically and theoretically. Methodologically, in Fairclough's
version of CDA, the analysts focused on *crisis* or *cruces*, which are
turning points in social change or transformation (which may be positive or negative). Theoretically, the idea of critique in CDA connects
social practices with critical social theory, offering possible interpretations of why certain configurations, or *designs*, of meaning are privileged more than others.

Multiliteracy scholars have taken up the tensions between critique
and design introduced in the NLG's work (e.g., Janks, 2005; Pahl &
Rowsell, 2005). Leander & Boldt (2013), for example, critique the struc-
turalist overlay of systemic functional linguistics that is assumed with
multiliteracies *and* CDA. They argue that bodies and interactions cannot
be reduced to functions, nor complex actions accounted for solely with
an eye toward the future. They point out the importance of attending
to emerging social practices, those that are improvisational and embodied. However, this might not be read as a constraint of the framework
itself. Indeed, the New London Group's (1996) program called attention
to both structure and creativity. They wrote, "we are both inheritors
of patterns and conventions of meaning and at the same time active
designers of meaning" (p. 65). It is important, though, to reflexively
evaluate the promise of "design" and "transformation" as it has been
articulated through the multiliteracies project. That is, have the possibilities of "designing" eclipsed the material consequences of injustices?
As literacy educators and researchers escaped the determinism of the
written word, we may have entered into a system of signification that
has endless possibilities but fails to make a material difference. This
valorizes individuals' agency in the design of new meanings but fails to
recognize the deep-rooted social and cultural conditions through which
individuals are entrapped. Indeed, children and youth may be proficient
with media literacy but not have access to genres of power required by
social institutions (Mills, 2006).

Anderson and Wales (2012) ask "Can you design for agency?" prob-
lematizing the orchestration of agentive opportunities for youth when

the social milieu in which they live and learn is shaped heavily by static and narrowly bounded discourses of literacy and learning. Perhaps critique—in all of its fullness—has been de-emphasized for too long. Siegel and Panofsky (2009) pointed out that studies of multimodality have backgrounded power and history and foregrounded the multimodal assemblage. Yet critique and design are intimately connected and one without the other will not do. This is inherently what critical discourse analysts understand and one of the ways in which CDA can continue to contribute to the multiliteracies project.

POWER AND LEARNING

For too long, power has been conceptualized as top-down and oppressive. Indeed, early studies of CDA demonstrated how racism, sexism, and classism were reproduced in classrooms (Rogers et al., 2005). In a follow-up review, we learned that literacy researchers are casting their gaze on episodes of learning, transformation, agency, and liberation—constructive forms of power and positive discourses (Rogers & Schaenen, 2014). In turn, this focus broadens our view of power from power *over* to power *with* and *through*. It stretches us to think of power as generative and constructive without forgetting the enduring presence of social structures (Boltanski, 2011).

For example, Dutro (2010) presents a CDA of third graders' experiences reading and responding to a story about a Depression-era farm family's economic hardships from the district-mandated reading curriculum. Her CDA demonstrates how middle-class privilege is reproduced through the curriculum. Many analysts would have stopped at describing the reproduction of ideologies. Dutro does not. She recognizes the difficulty in disentangling structure and agency, the epistemic and ontological stronghold of commercially produced and mandated reading materials and the lived experiences of children living in urban poverty. She turns toward the "positive," which means shining light on the *struggle* toward liberation. Just as the story set in the 1930s obscures poverty, her students bring their present-day experiences with poverty into the dialogue. And, while the teacher's guide urges the teacher to focus on overcoming poverty, the third graders' writing reveals the enduring dimensions of living in poverty. In this way, Dutro's analysis does not deny the structural constraints of poverty reinforced through mass-produced curricular materials, but neither does it underestimate the power of children and teachers to make room for themselves in the world by naming their own class-based realities. Dutro takes the reader with her as she imagines different scenarios with the curriculum—what she refers to as "imagined revisions" (p. 285).

Over the past 20 years, in part influenced by the NLG, literacy re-searchers have documented asset-based approaches in multilingual and literate environments. Methodologically, the focus has been on learning, becoming, and transformation. However, theoretically the field has not kept up. Expansive studies of learning rooted in Cultural Historical Ac-tivity Theory can be considered part of a turn in critical social theory ori-ented to transformation (e.g., Stetsenko, 2012; Kontopodis, 2014). This theory of learning focuses on collective and interacting activities, activist stances, and social transformation. Stetsenko (2012) proposes the idea that "human development is an activist project" (p. 147). When some-one contributes to the world—with, say, a digital storytelling project in a high school classroom—they do so from a goal-oriented position. Through our contributions we are changed, which, in turn, contributes to our becoming, as a human being, and to the transformation of the social world more generally. In this view, transformation (learning) ex-tends its reach from the individual to the collective and back again. This emphasis on the constructive aspects—on the positive contributions be-ing made by multiliteracies work—does not preclude an analysis of oppressive varieties of power but strengthens our ability to learn from literacy pedagogy that is making a difference in individual lives and in the social world.

LOOKING FORWARD

The theme of the 2016 conference of the Literacy Research Associa-tion, *Mobilizing Literacy Research for Social Transformation,* reflects the enormous influence of the NLG's scholarship. The NLG report was part of a network that linked literacy scholarship with CDA and influenced and inspired a generation of educators and scholars. It is easy to imagine all of the ways in which this work—work that crosses theoretical and methodological boundaries—has impacted the lives of children, youth, families, and educators. Looking forward, there are some cautionary issues and opportunities that stem from this reflexive look at the field.

The multiliteracies project grew up within a neoliberal context that emphasizes corporations over states, profit over people, and a shrink-ing public sector. The very concept of design has morphed into neo-liberal terms such as innovation that are used to justify the closing of traditional public schools and the opening of charter schools. The skepticism raised by Newfield and Stein (2000) about the neocolonial danger of multiliteracies work should be remembered as a cautionary note. Moving forward, multiliteracy scholars might reflexively draw on critical social theories to buttress their examination of social systems through which multiliteracies flow. Indeed, a sociological analysis of the neoliberal contexts in which educators work is necessary to imagine social futures that rely on collective accomplishments and contributions and push toward equity. Further research should investigate the multiliteracies scholarship that has taken place in the global South, particularly Latin America, alongside the NLG work documented in this book.

In the name of designing social futures, critique has been backgrounded and interpreted mainly as deconstructive and not as the project of constructing new meanings. The multiliteracies project needs better theorizations of the horizontal and generative nature of power and associated conditions of learning. Expansive studies of learning such as these offer generative potential to educators who wish to fulfill the original equity agenda of the NLG. Likewise, we need to reinvigorate the "critical" framing component that the NLG proposed. Teachers need a healthy dose of critical social theory—indeed, need to see themselves as theorizers—to connect the dots between capitalism, militarism, racism, and environmental destruction. Perhaps we should reconsider Carmen Luke's (2000) term "critical multiliteracies," which emphasizes the dual focus on power, history, and context and multimodal assemblages.

The pedagogical framework proposed by the NLG is still quite relevant for thinking about the demands on students as readers and writers in 21st-century schools. The very notion of *reading* has been marginalized, and it need not be. Students need to be able to communicate across digital platforms but they also need to decode printed text, whether hyperlinks or tables of content (Carmen Luke, 2000). We need more efforts to integrate critical multiliteracies with accelerative literacy practices, especially for students who find reading and writing difficult (Dozier, Johnston, & Rogers, 2005).

The combined efforts of scholars practicing CDA within a multiliteracies tradition has raised awareness of the multiple resources that children/youth call on to accomplish social goals, the diverse perspectives that exist, and also the gross inequities that are reproduced through texts, institutional processes, and social policies. It has also shown the possibilities of the literacies that emerge from efforts to create more socially just classrooms, schools, and communities. Extending our gaze to connect what happens inside classrooms with the broader world of social change and movements can help fulfill the transformative potential of multiliteracies.

REFERENCES

Alford, J. H., & Jetnikoff, A. (2016). Orientations to critical literacy for English as an additional language or dialect (EAL/D) learners: A case study of four teachers of senior English. *Australian Journal of Language and Literacy, 39*(2), 111–123.

Álvarez Valencia, J. A. (2016). Social networking sites for language learning: Examining learning theories in nested semiotic spaces. *Signo y Pensamiento, 35*(68), 66–84.

Anderson, K., & Wales, P. (2012). Can you design for agency? The ideological mediation of an out-of-school digital storytelling workshop. *Critical Inquiry in Language Studies, 9*(3), 165–190.

Blommaert, J. (2005). *Discourse: A critical introduction.* Cambridge, UK: Cambridge University Press.

Bloome, D., & Talwalker, S. (1997). Critical discourse analysis and the study of reading and writing. *Reading Research Quarterly, 32*(1), 104–112.

Boltanski, L. (2011). *On critique: A sociology of emancipation.* Cambridge, UK: Polity Press.

Clark, R., Fairclough, N., Ivanic, R., & Martin-Jones, M. (1990). Critical language awareness. Part I: A critical review of three current approaches to language awareness. *Language and Education, 4*(4), 249–260.

Collins, J., & Blot, R. (2003). *Literacy and literacies: Texts, power, and identity.* Cambridge, UK: Cambridge University Press.

Comber, B., & Cormack, P. (2011). Education policy mediation: Principals' work with mandated literacy assessment. *English in Australia, 46*(2), 77–86.

Cope, B., & Kalantzis, M. (2000). *Multiliteracies: Literacy learning and the design of social futures.* New York, NY: Routledge.

Dozier, C., Johnston, P., & Rogers, R. (2005). *Critical literacy/critical teaching: Tools for preparing responsive teachers.* New York, NY: Teachers College Press.

Dutro, E. (2010). What "hard times" mean: Mandated curricula, class-privileged assumptions and the lives of poor children. *Research in the Teaching of English, 44*(3), 255–291.

Fairclough, N. (1992). *Discourse and social change.* Malden, MA: Polity Press.

Fairclough, N. (2000). Multiliteracies and language: Orders of discourse and intertextuality. In B. Cope & M. Kalantzis (Eds.), *Multiliteracies: Literacy learning and the design of social futures* (pp. 162–181). South Yarra, Australia: Macmillan.

Farías, M. (2015). Análisis crítico multimodal y percepción del discurso homofóbico en el paisaje sociosemiótico de Santiago de Chile. In D. García da Silva & M. L. Pardo (Comps.), *Pasado, presente y futuro de los estudios en América Latina.* Retrieved from: https://www.researchgate. net/publication/299283246_Analisis_critico_multimodal_y_percepcion_ del_discurso_homofobico_en_el_paisaje_sociosemiotico_de_Santiago_ de_Chile

Gee, J. P. (1990). *Social linguistics and literacies: Ideology in discourses.* London, UK: Falmer Press.

Gee, J. P. (1999). *An introduction to discourse analysis: Theory and method.* London, UK: Routledge.

Gee, J. P. (2000). Discourse and sociocultural studies in reading. In M. Kamil, P. Mosenthal, P. D. Pearson, & R. Barr (Eds.), *Handbook of reading research* (pp. 195–208). Mahwah, NJ: Erlbaum.

Halliday, M. A. K. (1978). *Language as a social semiotic: The social interpretation of language and meaning.* Baltimore, MD: University Park Press.

Heath, S. B. (1983). *Ways with words: Language, life, and work in communities and classrooms.* New York, NY: Cambridge University Press.

Heller, M. (2001). Critique and sociolinguistic analysis of discourse. *Critique of Anthropology, 21*(2), 117–141.

Jacobs, G. (2013). Reimagining multiliteracies: A response to Leander and Bolt. *Journal of Adolescent and Adult Literacy, 57*(4), 270–273.

Janks, H. (1997). Critical discourse analysis as a research tool. *Discourse: Studies in the Cultural Politics of Education, 18*(3), 329–342.

Janks, H. (2005). Language and the design of texts. *English Teaching Practice and Critique, 4*(3), 97–110.

Janks, H. (2010). *Literacy and power.* London, UK: Routledge.

Kapp, R., 2004, "Reading on the line": An analysis of literacy practices in ESL classes in a South African township school. *Language and Education, 18*(3), 246–263. doi:10.1080/09500780408666878

Kettle, M. (2005). Agency as discursive practice: From "nobody" to "somebody" as an international student in Australia. *Asia Pacific Journal of Education, 25*(1), 45–60.

Kontopodis, M. (2014). *Neoliberalism, pedagogy, and human development: Exploring time, mediation, and collectivity in contemporary schools.* London, UK: Routledge.

Kress, G. (2000). Multimodality. In B. Cope & M. Kalantzis (Eds.), *Multiliteracies: Literacy learning and the design of social futures* (pp. 182–202). London, UK: Routledge.

Ladson-Billings, G. (2003). Racialized discourses and ethnic epistemologies. In N. K. Denzin & Y. S. Lincoln (Eds.), *The landscape of qualitative research: Theories and issues* (pp. 398–432). Thousand Oaks, CA: Sage Publications.

Leander, K., & Boldt, G. (2013). Rereading "A pedagogy of multiliteracies": Bodies, texts, and emergence. *Journal of Literacy Research, 45*(1), 22–46.

López Bonilla, G., & Pérez Fragoso, C. (2010). *Discursos e identidades en contextos de cambio educativo.* Madrid, Spain: Editorial Plaza y Valdés/ Benemérita Universidad Autónoma de Puebla.

Luke, A. (1995) Text and discourse in education: An introduction to critical discourse analysis. *Review of Research in Education, 21*(3), 1–48.

Luke, C. (2000). Cyber-schooling and technological change: Multiliteracies for new times. In B. Cope & M. Kalantzis (Eds.), *Multiliteracies: Literacy learning and the design of social futures* (pp. 69–91). New York, NY: Routledge.

Marshall, E., & Toohey, K. (2010). Representing family: Community funds of knowledge, bilingualism, and multimodality. *Harvard Educational Review, 80*(2), 221–241.

Martín Rojo, L. (2010). *Constructing inequality in multilingual classrooms.* Berlin, Germany: De Gruyter Mouton.

Martín Rojo, L. (2014). Occupy: The spatial dynamics of discourse in global protest movements. *Journal of Language and Politics, 13*(4), 583–598.

Martinez-Roldan, C. M. (2005). Examining bilingual children's gender ideologies through critical discourse analysis. *Critical Inquiry in Language Studies: An International Journal, 2*(3), 157–178.

Mills, K. (2006). Discovering design possibilities through a pedagogy of multiliteracies. *Journal of Learning Design, 1*(3), 61–72.

Moita-Lopes, L. P. (2006). Queering literacy teaching: Analyzing gay-themed discourses in a fifth-grade class in Brazil. *Journal of Language, Identity, and Education, 5*(1), 31–50.

Mora, R. A. (2015). City literacies in second languages. *Journal of Adolescent & Adult Literacy, 59*(1), 21–24.

New London Group. (1996). A pedagogy of multiliteracies: Designing social futures. *Harvard Educational Review, 66*(1), 60–92.

Newfield, D., & Stein, P. (2000). The multiliteracies project: South African teachers respond. In B. Cope & M. Kalantzis (Eds.). *Multliteracies: Literacy learning and the design of social futures* (pp. 292–310). New York, NY: Routledge.

Nichols, S. (2002). Parents' construction of their children as gendered, literature subjects: A critical discourse analysis. *Journal of Early Childhood Literacy, 2*(2), 123–144.

Pahl, K., & Rowsell, J. (2005). *Literacy and education: The new literary studies in the classroom.* London, UK: Sage.

Resende, V. M. (2010). Between the European legacy and critical daring: Epistemological reflections for critical discourse analysis. *Journal of Multicultural Discourses, 5*(3), 193–212.

Rogers, R., Malancharuvil-Berkes, E., Mosley, M., Hui, D., & Joseph, G. O. (2005). A critical review of critical discourse analysis. *Review of Research in Education, 75*(3), 365–416.

Rogers, R., & Mosley, M. (2008). A critical discourse analysis of racial literacy in teacher education. *Linguistics & Education, 19*, 107–131.

Rogers, R., & Schaenen, I. (2014). Critical discourse analysis in literacy education. *Reading Research Quarterly, 49*(1), 121–143.

Rogers, R., Schaenen, I., Schott, C., O'Brien, K., Trigos-Carrillo, L., Starkey, K., & Chasteen, C. (2016). Critical discourse analysis in educational research: A review of the literature, 2004–2012. *Review of Educational Research, 86*(4), 1192–1226.

Shi-xu. (2009). Reconstructing Eastern paradigms of discourse studies. *Journal of Multicultural Discourses, 4*(1), 29–48.

Siegel, M., & Panofsky, C. (2009). Designs for multimodality in literacy studies: Explorations in analysis. *58th Yearbook of the National Reading Conference*, 99–111.

Stetsenko, A. (2012). Personhood: An activist project of historical becoming through collaborative pursuits of social transformation. *New Ideas in Psychology, 30*(1), 144–153.

Street, B. (1985). *Literacy in theory and practice.* Cambridge, UK: Cambridge University Press.

Trigos-Carrillo, L., & Rogers, R. (in press). *Latin American influences on multiliteracies: Toward epistemological diversity.*

Van Leeuwen, T. (2008). *Discourse and practice: New tools for critical discourse analysis.* Oxford, UK: Oxford University Press.

Wohlwend, K. (2012). "Are you guys girls?" Boys, identity texts, and Disney princess play. *Journal of Early Childhood Literacy, 12*(3), 3–23.

CHAPTER 7

A Multimodal Perspective on Touch, Communication, and Learning

Carey Jewitt

Two decades ago, the New London Group's (NLG) manifesto *A Pedagogy of Multiliteracies* (1996) argued for the need to better connect literacy with the changing social environment facing students and teachers and called for more understanding of the diversity of representational forms available within the communicational environment. A key tenet of the NLG manifesto is that the requirements of each social and cultural epoch, of which technologies are a part, are intimately connected to the shape, use, and design of communicational modes within a community:

> Designing will more or less normatively reproduce, or more or less radically transform, given knowledges, social relations, and identities, depending on the social conditions under which Designing occurs . . . producing new constructions and representations of reality. . . . [through which] people transform their relations with each other, and so transform themselves. (NLG, p. 12)

As has been evidenced by the immense changes in the digital landscape since the NLG paper was published, the social conditions of design can change rapidly and in significant ways. The once radical call of NLG to focus on the importance of an "increasing multiplicity and integration of significant modes of meaning making, where the textual is also related to the visual, the audio, the spatial, the behavioral, and so on" (NLG, 1996, p. 64) has now become standard and accepted against the advanced technologies of the contemporary moment. The primary focus of the NLG on "linguistic design," "visual images," and "written word" and their changing relationships reflected the digital environment of the 1990s, which consisted of "desktop publishing" and "mass media, multimedia and electronic hypermedia," and where whole-body and touch interfaces were a feature of science fiction books and film.

Over the past decade digital advances have freed learners from the desk and the classroom in ways that newly foreground the bodily and spatial aspects of pedagogic interaction, through interactive physical-digital games (Burn, 2014), mobile devices (Sakr, Jewitt, & Price, 2015), and tangible technologies (Price & Jewitt, 2013). While the NLG paper mentions "Gestural Meanings (body language, sensuality)" as a design element in the meaning-making process, this was not in focus.

In this chapter I intend to touch on an emergent communicational form that is coming into focus through the effects of changing social communication requirements. Notably, a new wave of digital sensory technologies that draw on touch capacities highlights the need to better understand the role and potential of touch for communication, learning, and literacies (Bezemer & Kress, 2014; Crescenzi, Jewitt, & Price, 2014; Walsh & Simpson, 2014). I draw on the literature to present a brief sketch of the place of touch in communication and pedagogy. I then focus in to address three questions. First, why does touch matter in the contemporary moment? Second, can touch be thought of as a mode? Third, what is the effect of the digital on touch? Through the chapter I build the argument that touch is an act of communication and a pedagogic resource, and that digital environments involve a complex exploitation of touch in which touch-response-feel sequence is an aspect of encounters between humans and the digital. Thinking of touch in this way I bring three interconnected aspects of communication into focus: the production of communicative digital touch artifacts; their interpretation; and their use to engage with others. I conclude the chapter by looking forward to tentatively consider the potential implications of digitally mediated touch for the communicational and pedagogic landscape.

THE PLACE OF TOUCH IN THE COMMUNICATIONAL AND PEDAGOGIC LANDSCAPE

Touch is frequently referred to as a neglected sense (Field, 2001). Indeed, touch appears to have passed under the radar of the academic (Classen, 2005), and despite being a "complex and effective channel [touch] seldom receives any serious attention in accounts of communicating" (Finnegan, 2014, p. 197). While a review of the literature shows that touch may not be much spoken about in the fields of communication and pedagogy, it provides people with significant information and experience of the world. Touch is the first sense through which humans encounter their environment and it is central to our development; it is crucial for object recognition, manipulation, and tool use (Fulkerson, 2014). Although touch is often underestimated, we are able to process large amounts of abstract information through touch, a capability that it has been suggested can reduce the risk of visual and auditory overload (van Erp & Toet, 2015).

While tactile communication is often "below the level of conscious awareness" and difficult to research (Finnegan, 2014, p. 176)—perhaps one reason for its low profile—touch is central to communication: "Just as we 'do things with words' so, too, we act through touches" (Finnegan, 2014, p. 208). Indeed, knowing how to infer meaning from touch is considered to be the very basis of social being (Dunbar, 1996). Touch can take many social forms in our daily lives, such as greetings—shaking hands and embracing; intimate communication—holding hands, kissing, cuddling, and stroking; and in correction and punishment—restraining, hitting, and beating (Linden, 2015). Touch has been shown to be as effective as facial expression and voice at communicating a range of emotions (Field, 2001).

In a study in which participants were allowed to touch an unacquainted partner on the whole body to communicate distinct emotions, for example, fine-grained coding documented specific touch behaviors associated with different emotions, and the person being touched decoded the intended emotions (anger, fear, disgust, love, sadness, happiness, gratitude, and sympathy) at greater than chance levels (Hertenstein, Holmes, McCullough, & Keltner, 2009). Touch has been shown to have a role in communicating complex social messages of trust, receptivity, and affection, as well as nurture, dependence, and affiliation (Field, 2001; Linden, 2015; McLinden & McCall, 2002). It is perhaps unsurprising that touch is an effective means of influencing people's attitudes and creating bonds with people and places (Field, 2001; Krishna, 2010).

In clinical and professional situations, for example, interpersonal touch has been shown to improve information flow and to result in a more favorable evaluation of communication partners and to increase compliance. Finnegan (2014) argues that "establishing tactile contact is an act of communication" (p. 201).

Touch is largely neglected in pedagogy in comparison with other forms of communication. It has received some attention as a "compensatory mode" with reference to tactile interaction and sign-systems for the visual and hearing-impaired. Much of this research is concerned with understanding (and training) learners' exploratory strategies using hand movement, tactile manipulation, and touch to communicate and to learn, such as mapping tactile features (e.g., vibration, texture, shape, hardness/softness, elasticity etc.) and the functions of touch (e.g., to control, to convey information, express emotion, to bond, to protect), (McLinden & McCall, 2002).

Touch is also recognized as a primary form of interaction for very young children. It forms part of our multimodal sensory systems and has been shown to be important for child development (Smith & Gasser, 2005). In general, touch has been argued to be important in extending children's understanding and knowledge of the world through its specific sensory functions, for example, experiencing texture, shape, and weight, as well as contributing to learners' classification skills. Here I focus on how touch has been taken up in museum education to point to some of the more general potentials of touch for pedagogy.

The "sensory turn" of the past decade together with the activism of advocates for the visually impaired and blind communities, has led to some contemporary museum educators rethinking the role of touch for museum learning. This development links with the history of the museum as a cultural space. In the late 17th and 18th centuries, visitors to great museums such as the Ashmolean Museum and the British Museum were allowed to rub, pick up, shake, and even taste the artifacts on display (Classen, 2014). This tactile and sensory engagement with museum objects was gradually restricted to museum conservators. Today the museum shop has become the primary space where touch is permitted and, as a result, where visually impaired visitors have commented they have done most of their learning (Levent & McRainey, 2014).

The sensory turn to touch has been used as a way to include visually impaired communities otherwise excluded from the ocular-centric experience of art galleries and museums. A new focus on directly experiencing the properties of things (Dudley, 2012) has emerged, and studies have shown the social and learning benefits that touch can have in the museum, for instance in relation to object handling, engagement, and aesthetic tactile pleasure, understanding through the tactile acquisition of knowledge, and information retention and recall (Levent & Pascual-Leone, 2014). Some museums are newly driven by the idea that "feeling" is linked with "feelings" (Chatterjee, 2008), and that touch establishes an essential connection. This has prompted the establishment of touch rooms and artifacts such as the Hands On project at the British Museum (London), the Touch Gallery at the Louvre (Paris), and the Please Touch Museum in Philadelphia, PA, as well as other museums that allow visitors to handle touchable artifacts from their collections. While other galleries incorporate touch into exhibits, the Treasures Gallery in London's Natural History Museum, for example, presents a series of treasures exhibited in glass cabinets alongside 3D digitally printed replicas that can be touched by visitors.

THE IMPORTANCE OF TOUCH IN NEW TIMES

The centrality of touch to areas of the law, religion, medicine, and family activities in earlier societies, e.g., in the European Middle Ages (Classen, 2012), is well recorded. As is the lessening role of touch in the past centuries, due to a complex set of social, political, economic, and technological changes including changing relationships to distance and travel, kinship relations, the rise of the notion of the individual, health-related "tactophobia" and the "contamination" of touch against a backdrop of the plague and other epidemics, changing religious rituals, and the emergence of optic and print technologies.

By the beginning of the 20th century touch had been "ousted" by the visual, as "vision become an ever-more important sensory avenue for acquiring knowledge about the world" (Classen, 2012).

Over the past two decades the possibilities for touch communication realized by the portability, connectivity, and power of the digital and their effects on communication is again changing the communicative and pedagogic role of touch. This can be understood as a response to changing societal interests and needs. The design of touch technologies has emerged in response to the need to manage shifts in how social relations, both personal and work-related, are conducted. For example, technologies that support touch connection at a distance enable people to connect and reconnect with one another, objects, and environments. Digital devices and platforms are increasingly creating new sensory devices and experiences, interfaces, and environments that push at, and remake, the boundaries of touch.

Today, touch is at the center of a reimagining of digital sensory communication. There is a new wave of technologies and devices that rely on touch sensation interfaces and use touch to create the illusion of shape and textures that enable users to feel a variety of virtual objects and control remote manipulators (e.g., the haptic Phantom). The rise of touch has been accompanied by growing interest in re-evaluating the roles of all senses within education studies, and the social sciences more generally, and a desire to move beyond a vision-centric approach (Howes & Classen, 2014). From a multimodal perspective, modes and semiotic resources are shaped by the social functions they are used to realize they are fluid and changing in character rather than fixed. It follows that as the social usage of touch changes, so does its function in the production of knowledge, social relations, and identities—and people themselves change. Touch matters *now* as contemporary social requirements appear to be changing the place of touch in the communicational landscape. There is an ever-closer relationship between the semiotics of touch, technology, and communication. As society and technology turn to touch, so must multimodal researchers. Multimodal work on touch is at a very early stage. At a time of significant social and technological change in which touch is becoming ever more central to communication, understanding what touch is and might be is essential.

Touch as a Mode

The NLG manifesto reference to "Gestural Meanings (body language, sensuality)" as a design element in the meaning-making process is indicative of the exploratory character of the multiliteracies project and its ability to set a new agenda. It also provides some insight into subsequent developments, debates, and theorization within multimodality—and the move away from the terminology of "languages" to the terminology of modes; the rethinking of "body language" as discrete but interconnected modes of gesture, movement, gaze, and posture in a theory of learning (Bezemer & Kress, 2016); and distinctions between concepts of mode, sense, and affect (see Kress, 2014).

For my purpose in this chapter two relevant questions are prompted: Can we distinguish between gesture and touch? Can touch be thought of as a mode? I argue that we can distinguish between the modes of gesture and touch, and that it is useful to do so to get at the granularity and specifics of interaction. I understand *gesture* to refer to integrated "non-contact" sets of movements of hands, fingers, arms, and facial expression that are received through sight (Bezemer, 2013), while I take *touch* to refer to the contact of the maker of the sign— usually through hands or fingers (and the mouth in the case of very young learners)—with "another" (I will expand on this "another" later in this section).

For something to count as a mode it needs have a set of semiotic resources and organizing principles that are recognized within a community as realizing meaning. For example, the resources of gesture have been semiotically shaped into communicative modes to serve a diverse range of communities (e.g., hearing-impaired communities, visually and hearing-impaired people, ballet dancers). For a particular set of semiotic resources for making meaning to be considered a mode, it needs to meet the requirements of Halliday's theory of meaning. He developed three metafunctions to describe the functions of language: the "ideational" (subject matter), the "interpersonal" (enactment of social relations and creation of a stance to the world), and the "textual" (organization to create coherence).

The metafunctional principles are adopted to understand the functionalities and underlying organization of semiotic resources and to investigate the ways in which semiotic choices interact to create meaning in multimodal texts and interaction. One test for whether or not a set of resources counts as a mode is to ask if the three Hallidayan metafunctions (Halliday, 1978) are realized. Definitions of mode continue to be refined and developed. However, it is important to note that what a mode is continues to be subject to debate. One response to this debate is that definitions of mode are dependent on what are counted as well-acknowledged regularities within any one community. Using these criteria it is clear that touch is already a mode for certain social groups: People who use the "tactile sign" system are likely to have a secure grasp of the range and potentialities of touch, whereas this might not qualify as a mode among others who may not have access to and knowledge of these resources and their affordances.

Using Halliday's concept of mode, Bezemer and Kress (2014) suggest that touch becomes effective as a mode when the following three conditions are met:

- Touch communicates something (e.g., tapping on a person's shoulder may mean "well done" or "can I have your attention please"): This meets Halliday's ideational metafunction.
- Touch is designed for one or more specific persons, and someone is addressed (e.g., a handshake): This meets Halliday's interpersonal metafunction.
- Touch is coherent with signs made in the same and other modes in forming a complete semiotic entity, an interaction (e.g., a handshake accompanied by saying "nice to see you again"): This meets Halliday's (inter)textual function.

For touch to be considered a mode it should be able to realize meanings in the three metafunctions. Bezemer and Kress suggest:

> We can distinguish between communities in which touch is weakly developed, has limited semiotic reach or 'communication radius,' and communities in which touch has been developed into a mode which is highly articulated, with extensive reach. (p. 80)

The concept of communication is essential to the NLG manifesto, and here I turn to the question of whether or not it is possible to discuss touch as a form of communication. Bezemer and Kress (2014) suggest that for touch to be considered a communicative mode it needs to be (a) designed as a message, (b) addressed to a community, and (c) treated as having meaning to be interpreted. For Bezemer and Kress touch as mode *always* involves tactile means of addressing another human:

> Where two or more participants are involved, touch often relies on a dual materiality: visible and tactile. Each of these materialities has distinctly different potential. When both materialities are 'exploited' to communicate, as in shaking hands, or when only the tactile materiality is 'exploited', as in tactile signing, touch can develop into mode. (p. 82)

Other commentators within multimodality, however, work with a broader conception of mode and touch communication and suggest that meaning is communicated through "our tactile interaction with other beings and objects in our world" (Cranny-Francis, 2011, p. 465). Norris (2012), for example, includes the potential of touch communication with people, objects, and animals. In a multimodal ethnographic study of horse riding she observes lessons in which a rider communicates with a horse primarily through the mode of touch. A key aspect of learning to ride is learning how to touch the horse and how to feel the horse's response to the rider's touch. Norris explores touch via a focus on foot, leg, and hand movement within the broader multimodal frame of interaction in the horse-riding lesson. This highlights that touch is a mode that can involve the whole body. She shows a sequence in which the riding instructor demonstrates both the incorrect and the correct "touch-response-feel" expected. Norris distinguishes between acts of "touch," "response," and "feel." She notes that a sequence of touch-response-feel happens between two social actors, and she suggests that a social actor may be either another human or an object.

I want to argue here that it is not the object that is "acting," rather it is the social intentions of the object's designer imbued in the object. The programming of digital touch technologies raises questions about what interaction is and how an object can "act." For example, some digital clothing or devices vibrate to give a player physical feedback in specific contexts. The idea of "responsive objects" is a feature of Cranny-Francis's work on technology and touch (2013). She suggests that meanings are potentially activated when we touch objects, although the nature of the particular interaction determines which meanings are deployed and to what ends. She goes on to suggest that "by exploring those meanings we are able to map the potentials that are available in every tactile encounter and how they might be mobilized to create the most effective and/or rich interaction" (p. 465). This notion connects with the multimodal understanding of artifacts as material traces of the work of those who made them. That is, the object itself is not seen as agentive, but rather full of meaning potentials that can be activated via interaction.

This exploration of touch as a mode connects with the NLG paper and other early multimodal explorations that set out to map the modal qualities, materiality, and semiotic potential of emergent modes, and to investigate whether, and under what conditions, they fulfilled the criteria of being a mode. In the case of sound (van Leeuwen, 1999) and color (Kress & van Leeuwen, 2001), the answer was that in some social contexts of usage color and sound were fully articulate modes; in others they exhibited "mode-like" qualities and potentials when used in combination with other modes. More recently the resources of sound and color have been extended and used in some new ways, particularly in combination with digital mediation. The same appears to be the case for touch, at least at the moment of writing.

Touch can be a mode, an act of communication, and a pedagogic resource. Touch can refer to contact that is human-to-human, human-to-animal, and human-to-object/digital. Touch in digital environments involves a complex exploitation of touch including the potential for digital touch feedback that leads to felt responses—suggesting in other words that a touch-response-feel sequence is an aspect of encounters between humans, humans and animals, and humans and digital artifacts. Thinking of touch in this way brings three interconnected aspects of communication into focus:

1. The production of communicative digital touch artifacts: The process of producing the device itself is understood as a communicative one, the device is seen as designed with an imagination of its communicative context and user, and the traces of the designer's work are embedded in the design of devices as a set of meaning potentials that are a part of shaping communication.

2. Their interpretation: The ways in which people *interpret* these digital touch devices—what it is possible and not possible to communicate via them—is an aspect of communication.

3. The use of a device to engage with others: that is, how a user's engagement with a touch device is constrained and shaped though not determined by its design, by its user's interests and purpose, and the context of use.

KEY DEVELOPMENTS IN THE DIGITAL MEDIATION OF TOUCH AND ITS EFFECTS ON TOUCH

Touch is being drawn into and mediated by a wide range of technologies, including tangible, haptic, wearable, and material technologies. In this section I provide a brief overview of key developments in the terrain of touch as it is digitally mediated with a focus on communication and pedagogy in the broadest sense. The examples below are presented to help point to some of the varieties of interaction and texts that touch technologies will enable and in the style of NLG raises some questions, as yet unanswered—perhaps an agenda—for what these might mean for literacy and the negotiation of a multiplicity of discourses. The touch developments outlined below make new dimensions and designs of meaning available, and can be exploited for pedagogy, in the context of NLG's concern with changing working lives, public lives, and private lives.

Haptic technologies rely on sensory or motor activity based on touch and kinesthetic sensation to create the illusion of shape and textures. These blur the boundaries between people, objects, and environments, shifting communication from co-present human-to-human interaction to activating surfaces that provide tactile feedback. For instance, in vibro-tactile technologies, "tixels" (or tactile pixels) can create new felt sensations, textures, and differently intense tactile experiences (Hoggan, 2013). It has also been used to create interactive museum display cases in which users can feel an object's texture without actually touching it by sliding their finger on the glass. In other words, the digital can be used to supplement a lack of touch or to heighten touch. The investigation of sensory engagement and authenticity in the provision of touch experiences in museums has been a feature of research on the design and use of digital technologies, notably the potential of digital touch technologies to extend and enhance sensory engagement in a museum using touch experiences. This shifts the learner from a passive visitor to an active participant, and has the potential to reconfigure one's emotional and physical distance from museum artifacts, which in turn raises new potentials for visitors to encounter tactile experiences of the material qualities of the past as well as questions of authenticity and experience (Hurcombe, Dima, & Wright, 2014).

Tangible technologies are "graspable" technologies that depend on the physical manipulation of physical objects embedded with computational power and wirelessly linked to various forms of digital representation (Price, 2013, p. 307). Tangible technologies can extend or reconfigure the semiotic features of touch, deploying touch for new communicative purposes where people and technologies are co-located. Tangible technologies can also be used to supplement and extend remote (i.e., at a distance) digital touch communication. The inFORM device is a shared tangible surface that three-dimensionally changes shape (Leithinger, Follmer, Olwal, & Ishii, 2014). It enables learners to interact with digital content remotely, to manipulate, tweak or radically transform objects virtually across distance, even experience the sensation of holding hands with a person hundreds of miles away.

The role of physical actions in learning has fostered enthusiasm for developing novel learning representations using emerging technologies such as tangibles. The ability to integrate technology into physical objects makes the importance of understanding how, or even if, these materials help children learn, and understanding how different forms of touch interaction will affect children's conceptual development (Manches & Price, 2011).

Advancements in material and wearable technologies draw the skin, the body's largest organ and the sensory receptor for touch, into the realm of communication and learning. Textile sensors can be designed to supplement the loss of touch. The "Touch Glove" integrates a textile pressure sensor into a glove for people who have lost their tactile sensation to enable differences in pressure to be made visible by being translated into light patterns embedded at the wrist of the glove. Wearable devices can also heighten touch and extend it into new domains: Buzzwear (Lee & Starner, 2010) is a tactile display worn on the wrist that can transmit different tactile patterns that users can accurately identify. Such technologies can extend touch to communicate connection across distance. Such devices make use of existing face-to-face touch practices *and* herald new digital touch practices and semiotic affordances.

Technologies such as those outlined above draw different tactile resources and capacities into play and intensify how the sensorium itself is utilized and mediated (Jones, 2007). Just as the NLG called for us to understand the technological and organizational changes brought about by the visual, this chapter calls for a focus on the potentials of touch as it is digitally mediated for communication and pedagogy.

Concluding Remarks

Building on the arguments of the NLG, I have argued that the changing social environment means that touch matters in a new way in the contemporary moment. I have shown that these changing conditions provide a basis from which to suggest that, at least sometimes, touch can be thought of as a mode. I have also shown that new digital developments are serving to supplement, heighten, extend, and reconfigure the resources and practices of touch. Using the NLG concepts of materiality, modal affordance, and semiotic resource, we can ask how the sensory, material, and physiological aspects of touch are drawn into, shaped, and given social meaning. Multimodality can help us to explore the effects this reimagining and remaking of touch in digital environments might have on the semiotic resources of touch—to explore the new potentials for who touches, what and how people touch, against a backdrop of digital globalized social relations.

At a time of significant social and technological change, when digital touch is becoming ever more central to communication, an investigation of digital touch, what it is and might be, how it may newly constitute our experience of communication with close and distant others, is timely and essential.

References

Bezemer, J. (2013). Gesture in operations. In C. Jewitt (Ed.), *Handbook of multimodal analysis* (2nd ed., pp. 354–364). London, UK: Routledge.

Bezemer, J., & Kress, G. (2014). Touch: A resource for making meaning. *Australian Journal of Language and Literacy, 37*(2), 77–85.

Bezemer, J., & Kress, G. (2016). *Multimodal learning and communication: A social semiotic frame*. London, UK: Routledge.

Burn, A. (2014). The case of rebellion: Researching multimodal texts. In C. Jewitt (Ed.), *Handbook of multimodal analysis* (pp. 151–178). London, UK: Routledge.

Chatterjee, H. (Ed.). (2008). *Touch in museums: Policy and practice in object handling*. Oxford, UK: Berg.

Classen, C. (Ed.). (2005). *The book of touch*. New York, NY: Berg.

Classen, C. (2012). *The deepest sense: A cultural history of touch*. Urbana, IL: University of Illinois Press.

Classen, C. (2014). Touching the deep past: The lure of ancient bodies in nineteenth-century museums and culture. *The Senses and Society, 9*(3), 268–283.

Cranny-Francis, A. (2011). Semefulness: A social semiotics of touch. *Social Semiotics, 21*(4), 463–481.

Cranny-Francis, A. (2013). *Technology and touch*. London, UK: Palgrave Macmillan.

Crescenzi, L., Jewitt, C., & Price, S. (2014). The role of touch in preschool learning. *Australian Journal of Language and Literacy, 37*(2), 86–95.

Dudley, S. (2012). *Museum objects: Experiencing the properties of things*. London, UK: Routledge.

Dunbar, R. (1996). *Grooming, gossip and the evolution of language*. London, UK: Faber and Faber.

Field, T. (2001) *Touch*. Cambridge, MA: MIT Press.

Finnegan, R. (2014). *Communicating*. London, UK: Routledge.

Fulkerson, M. (2014). *The first sense: A philosophical study of human touch*. Cambridge, MA: MIT Press.

Halliday, M. A. K. (1978). *Language as social semiotic*. London, UK: Edward Arnold.

Hertenstein, M., Holmes, R., McCullough, M., & Keltner, D. (2009). The communication of emotion via touch. *Emotion, 9*(4), 566–573.

Hoggan, E. (2013) Haptic interfaces. In S. Price, C. Jewitt, & B. Brown (Eds.), *The Sage handbook of digital technology research* (pp. 342–358). London, UK: Sage.

Howes, D., & Classen, C. (2014). *Ways of sensing: Understanding the senses in society*. London, UK: Routledge.

Hurcombe, L., Dima, M., & Wright, M. (2014) Touching the past: Haptic augmented reality for museum artefacts. *Virtual, Augmented and Mixed Reality. Applications of Virtual and Augmented Reality, 8526*, 3–14.

Jones, C. A. (Ed.). (2007). *Sensorium: Embodied experience, technology and art*. Cambridge, MA: MIT Press.

Kress, G. (2014). What is mode? In C. Jewitt (Ed.), *Handbook of multimodal analysis* (2nd ed.) (pp. 60–75). London, UK: Routledge.

Kress, G., & van Leeuwen, T. (2001). *Multimodal discourse*. London, UK: Arnold.

Krishna, A. (2010). *Sensory marketing: Research on the sensuality of products*. London, UK: Routledge.

Lee, S. C., & Starner, T. (2010). Buzzwear: Alert perception in wearable tactile displays on the wrist. In *Proceedings of the SIGCHI conference on Human factors in computing systems* (pp. 433–442). New York, NY: ACM.

Leithinger, D., Follmer, S., Olwal, A., & Ishii, H. (2014). Physical telepresence: Shape capture and display for embodied, computer-mediated remote collaboration. In *Proceedings of the 27th Annual ACM Symposium on User Interface Software and Technology* (pp. 461–470). New York, NY: ACM.

Levent, N., & Pascual-Leone, A. (Eds.). (2014). *The multisensory museum: Cross-disciplinary perspectives on touch, sound, smell, memory and space*. Lanham, MD: Rowman and Littlefield.

Levent, N., & McRainey, L. (2014). Touch and narrative in art and history museums. In N. Levent & A. Pascual-Leone (Eds.), *The multisensory museum: Cross-disciplinary perspectives on touch, sound, smell, memory and space* (pp. 36–61). Lanham, MD: Rowman and Littlefield.

Linden, D. (2015). *Touch: The science of hand, heart and mind*. London, UK: Random House.

Manches, A., & Price, S. (2011). Designing learning representations around physical manipulation: Hands and objects. In *Proceedings of the 10th International Conference on Interaction Design and Children* (pp. 81–89). New York, NY: ACM.

McLinden, M., & McCall, S. (2002). *Learning through touch: Supporting children with visual impairments and additional difficulties*. London, UK: David Fulton Publishers.

New London Group. (1996). A pedagogy of multiliteracies: Designing social futures. *Harvard Educational Review, 66*(1), 60–92.

Norris, S. (2012). Teaching touch/response-feel: A first step to an analysis of touch from an interactive perspective. In S. Norris (Ed.), *Multimodality in practice* (pp. 2–19). London, UK: Routledge.

Price, S. (2013). Tangibles: Technologies and interaction for learning. In S. Price, C. Jewitt, & B. Brown (Eds.), *The Sage handbook of digital technology research* (pp. 307–325). London, UK: Sage.

Price, S., & Jewitt, C. (2013). A multimodal approach to examining "embodiment" in tangible learning environments. In *Proceedings of the Seventh International Conference on Tangible, Embedded and Embodied Interaction* (pp. 43–50). New York, NY: ACM.

Sakr, M., Jewitt, C., & Price, S. (2015). Mobile experiences of historical place: A multimodal analysis of emotional engagement. *Journal of the Learning Sciences, 25*(1), 51–92.

Smith, L., & Gasser, M. (2005). The development of embodied cognition: Six lessons from babies. *Artificial Life, 11*(1–2), 13–29.

van Erp, J., & Toet, A. (2015). Social touch in human–computer interaction. *Frontiers in Digital Humanities, 2*(2), 14.

Van Leeuwen, T. (1999). *Speech, music, sound*. London, UK: Routledge.

Walsh, M., & Simpson, A. (Eds.). (2014). Special issue on touch. *Australian Journal of Language and Literacy, 37*(2), 96–102.

CHAPTER 8

Designing Pedagogies for Literacy and Learning Through Personal Digital Inquiry

Julie Coiro, Carita Kiili, and Jill Castek

New opportunities created by culturally and linguistically diverse individuals as well as an increasing diversity of text forms (New London Group, 1996) not only inspire but demand a broader vision of literacy and learning in a globalized digital world. Teaching in this context has become "less about delivering a body of knowledge and skills that will be good for life and more about forming a deeply knowing kind of person" (Kalantzis & Cope, 2012a, p. 71). Literacy and learning should embody "the skills of seeking knowledge as needed, collaborating, abstracting, and discerning patterns while navigating large bodes of knowledge" (p. 315). To that end, we believe effective educators are those who actively involve students in deep, authentic, and personally relevant learning experiences that foster academic achievement, reflection, and civic engagement. In this chapter we introduce a multidimensional framework of Personal Digital Inquiry (PDI) that seeks to help educators envision how to design curriculum-based pedagogies that integrate personal inquiry, online research, and digital tools in ways that empower all learners to fully participate in society. This framework draws on thinking about how to design learning spaces that encourage multifaceted ways of reading the world.

UNDERSTANDING THE PEDAGOGIES OF PERSONAL DIGITAL INQUIRY

The essence of our framework for Personal Digital Inquiry (PDI) is built on a set of problem-solving practices during which students do the following: 1) wonder and discover; 2) collaborate and discuss; 3) create and take action; and 4) analyze and reflect. While connected to familiar literacy practices supported by theory and research, the PDI framework also integrates classic and contemporary principles of multiliteracies

(Cope & Kalantzis, 2015; New London Group, 1996) and new literacies (Leu, Kinzer, Coiro, Castek, & Henry, 2013) with elements of connected learning (Ito et al., 2013). Before outlining our vision of PDI, we briefly summarize key tenets of work in these areas and explain how each informs our framework.

Multiliteracies

Generally, multiliteracies represents the multiple modes of meaning-making that require diverse ways of reading, thinking, and communicating (New London Group, 1996). These differences, which reflect the increasing diversity of people and of texts in an information age, introduce new challenges associated with how we work, play, and learn with others in a range of local and global communities (Kalantzis & Cope, 2012b). Our vision of PDI incorporates elements of multiliteracies pedagogy framed as the process of designing learning activity sequences that focus on action (what we do to gain knowledge) rather than cognition (what we know) (Cope & Kalantzis, 2015). That is, our framework draws on thinking about how to design learning spaces that encourage four multifaceted ways of reading the world (New London Group, 1996): *situated practice*, which involves experiential learning and opportunities to actively build personally relevant connections to a certain perspective and knowledge base; *overt instruction,* through which students develop explicit ways of thinking and talking about meaning-making conventions in different contexts; *critical framing*, which involves contextualizing and critically interrogating ideas from multiple perspectives; and *transformed practice*, in which learners, informed by their personal goals and values, design new ways of demonstrating and transferring their knowledge to new contexts.

Components of our PDI framework also encompass more recent iterations of multiliteracies pedagogy, described by Cope and Kalantzis (2015) as "reflexive pedagogy" that engages students in a range of learning activity types, or "different things you do to know." These activities are contextualized in a balance of academic and real-world practices designed to address specific learning goals while responding to learners' changing needs, interests, and emotions in localized contexts. Thus, designing instruction in any discipline involves carefully broadening ways of teaching with activity sequences that engage students in four overlapping knowledge processes: *experiencing* (immersing in known and new experiences while engaged in metacognitive reflections), *conceptualizing* (developing and classifying disciplinary schemas and mental models), *analyzing* (interpreting text functions and the interests of people in relation to knowledge purposes), and *applying* (using and representing knowledge in new and creative ways). Our attraction to a pedagogy grounded in multiliteracies is the emphasis on designing learning sequences that encourage students to move beyond building a body of knowledge to using and acting on that knowledge in personally and socially relevant ways.

New Literacies

A second body of work informing our vision of PDI covers new literacies (Coiro, Knobel, Lankshear, & Leu, 2008). Broadly conceived, a new literacies perspective argues that the nature of literacy and learning is rapidly changing and transforming as new technologies emerge. While there are many perspectives associated with the term *new literacies* (e.g., Cope & Kalantzis, 2000; Hull & Schultz, 2002; Kress, 2000; Lankshear & Knobel, 2003; 2006; New London Group, 1996; Street, 1998), a theoretical review of this work (Coiro et al., 2008) concluded that most share a set of common assumptions: (1) new skills, strategies, dispositions, and social practices are required by new technologies for information and communication; (2) new literacies are central to full participation in a global community; (3) new literacies regularly change as their defining technologies change; and (4) new literacies are multifaceted and benefit from multiple points of view. Results from investigations framed in a new literacies perspective have challenged existing classroom practices and pedagogies.

Within this broader context of changing workplace cultures, new social relationships, and rapidly emerging technologies, a new literacies perspective of online research and comprehension frames online reading as a self-directed problem-solving process that involves constructing texts and knowledge while engaged in at least five sets of important online practices (Leu, Kinzer, Coiro, & Cammack, 2004; Leu et al., 2013). They include reading, discussing, and writing in order to (1) define important questions; (2) locate relevant information; (3) critically evaluate information for accuracy, reliability, purpose, and perspective; (4) compare, contrast, and synthesize information across multiple sources; and (5) communicate ideas with and for others. Research points to evidence suggesting these practices require additional literacy skills and strategies over and above those required when reading and learning from printed books (see Afflerbach & Cho, 2009; Cho & Afflerbach, 2015; Coiro, 2011; Coiro & Dobler, 2007; Hartman, Morsink, & Zheng, 2010; Zhang & Duke, 2008). Consequently, our PDI framework is designed to incorporate activity sequences that offer regular opportunities for learners to successfully engage in authentic online research and comprehension practices across disciplines as part of full and equitable participation.

Designing Social Change Through Inquiry and Connected Learning

Two additional areas of work loosely inform our vision of PDI. First is the notion that all learners (both educators and students) are active designers of meaning, with the power to redesign their social futures in schools, workplaces, and communities (New London Group, 1996). Our vision of PDI encourages educators to design offline and online learning spaces that invite others to value varied experiences, languages, ways of thinking, and ways of representing knowledge as productive resources for inquiry and learning. As such, we believe that teachers are responsible for building a culture in which students with different experiences and perspectives become empowered to interact with and learn from each other as they develop creative solutions to real-life, relevant problems.

Similarly, our vision reflects principles of connected learning (Ito et al., 2013), which "advocates for broadened access to learning that is socially embedded, interest driven, and oriented toward educational, economic, or political opportunity" (p. 4). More specifically, connected learning proposes "a set of design features that help build shared purpose, opportunities for production, and openly networked resources and infrastructure" (p. 5). These features include specific *contexts* (peer-supported, interest-powered, academically oriented); *properties* (production centered, shared purpose, openly networked); *supports* (fostering engagement and self-expression; increasing accessibility to knowledge and learning experiences; expanding social supports for interests; expanding diversity and building capacity); and *design principles* (everyone can participate, learning happens by doing, challenge is constant, everything is interconnected). Like proponents of connected learning, we seek to capitalize on digital and networked media in ways that enable learners to "access a wealth of knowledge as well as be participants, makers, and doers engaged in active and self-directed inquiry" (p. 6). As such, we seek to explore what happens when experienced practitioners design flexible learning spaces that connect learners with authentic problems and intentional opportunities to break down barriers through active participation, global citizenship, critical thinking, and creative representation.

Personal Digital Inquiry

Our Personal Digital Inquiry framework weaves together and expands pedagogies for learning by linking dimensions of multiliteracies, connected learning, new literacies, and online reading to elements of engagement, inquiry-based learning, connectivity, and active participation in social change. We believe that instruction, within a framework of four sets of core pedagogies (see Figure 8.1), can actively involve students in deep, authentic, and personally relevant learning experiences while also fostering academic achievement, learner agency, reflection, and civic engagement.

At the core of our PDI framework are inquiry-based opportunities for learners to wonder broadly and discover new ideas. Bruce and Bishop (2008) define inquiry as "learning that starts with lived experience . . . where people actively shape their own learning as they work on real problems within their own communities" (p. 704). We, too, believe that learners grow and change with opportunities to identify problems in their community, generate personal wonderings, engage in collaborative dialogue around these problems, and apply their new knowledge by acting out solutions that transform thinking. Offering learners space to generate their own wonderings about these problems helps them connect their own interests to real life in ways that can lead to real change (Alberta Learning, 2004; Hobbs & Moore, 2013). In turn, opportunities for purposeful, self-directed inquiry become personally fulfilling learning experiences (Pink, 2009). Valuing and negotiating the diverse perspectives and experiences of others as part of these personal inquiries can advance learning for all students.

Figure 8.1. Core Pedagogies of Personal Digital Inquiry (PDI)

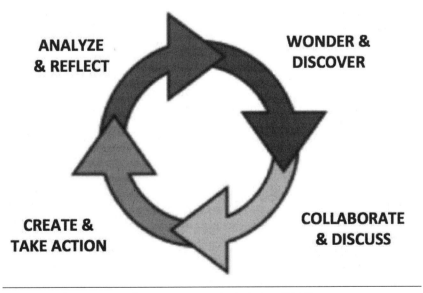

Adapted with permission from Coiro, Castek, & Quinn (2016)

The other components of our PDI framework call attention to several interconnected practices that enable students to merge the Internet's networking and knowledge-building resources with the problems they seek to solve. A focus on collaboration and discussion is prompted by research that suggests today's learners prefer and expect opportunities to collaboratively construct meaning and support each other's thinking in ways that lead to action (Schofield & Honore, 2010). These collaborative meaning-making experiences provide students with much needed practice in developing "the capacity to speak up, to negotiate, and to be able to engage critically with the conditions of their lives" inside and outside of the classroom (New London Group, 1996, p. 67). In turn, students learn through face-to-face and online interactions how to engage productively in building shared solutions, despite differences in their individual perspectives (Dillenbourg & Traum, 1996). Our PDI framework seeks to envision collaboration and discussion in ways that enable students to learn about themselves, each other, and the world around them through the inclusion of multiple voices, perspectives, and ways of expressing their ideas.

Ideally, inquiry leads to action, through both creation and participation, which Casey (2013) argues is the ultimate goal of learning. When students investigate personally meaningful problems within their community, they often want to build awareness and make positive changes by creating a digital product to share with others (Hobbs, 2010; Jenkins et al., 2009). Through participation, individuals assert their autonomy and ownership of learning; in turn, their inquiry becomes more personal and engaging (Pink, 2009; Zhao, 2009). Further, opportunities to explicitly connect home, school, and community in meaningful ways can help build social networks and stronger bonds between academic content and student interests (Ito et al., 2013). Ultimately, as inquiry shifts from "learning about" to "learning-to-be" (Brown, 2005; Dewey, 1938/1997), students become more active designers of meaning, and thus, designers of their socially constructed futures and their role(s) in them.

The final element in our PDI framework involves analysis and reflection, which can also be viewed as the beginning of inquiry. While inquiry is associated with the search for a comprehensive answer, ideally inquiry should also lead to a student's next burning question (Thomas & Brown, 2011). Reflecting on action enables students to reframe problems, identify gaps in their knowledge, and decide what additional inquiries may be necessary (Casey & Bruce, 2011). Reflection also challenges students to deeply consider the social and ethical impacts of their creations and ideas (Hobbs, 2010). And finally, guiding students to reflect on how to best tap into the varied cultural, linguistic, and multimodal resources in their interconnected world builds richer and more equitable learning spaces for everyone (Cope & Kalantzis, 2000).

Enacting Multiliteracies and New Literacies in the Context of Personal Digital Inquiry

In their introductory chapter describing the evolution of Learning by Design, Cope and Kalantzis (2015) explained their hopes of extending literacy teaching and learning from "a pedagogy of Multiliteracies" to "a pedagogy of communication and knowledge representation for all subject areas" (p. 15). With this aspiration in mind, we revisited our previously conceived notions of PDI and saw the potential of overlapping multiliteracies and new literacies practices to inform inquiry-based teaching and learning within any discipline and across multiple disciplines.

Figure 8.2 provides an overview of how components of multiliteracies and new literacies may help teachers of any discipline enact theoretically informed instructional practices, knowledge processes, and online research and comprehension practices aligned to phases of PDI. Each of the four components of PDI listed in the left column of the figure articulates student actions in that phase of the inquiry process, informed by work in multiliteracies and new literacies.

In the middle column of the figure, we reframed the New London Group's (1996) four ways of reading the world (the first bulleted item in each middle cell) as four instructional contexts through which educators might teach learners as they move back and forth between phases of PDI (e.g., teaching with situated practices, teaching with overt instruction, etc.). The second bulleted item in each middle cell aligns with one of Cope and Kalantzis's (2015) four knowledge processes (experiencing, conceptualizing, application, and analysis) to remind educators of how students should be actively engaging with new knowledge in each learning context and phase of inquiry. The right column of Figure 8.2 includes one or more online research and comprehension practices that students are likely to engage with as they interact with others in each learning context and phase of inquiry. These likely interactions pose explicit opportunities to model and/or scaffold the development of online reading skills and strategies as authentic practices are woven into personally relevant digital inquiry experiences.

Optimally, teachers in any discipline should strive to design learning activity sequences that immerse students in opportunities to inquire, collaboratively discuss, create, take action, analyze, and reflect for the purposes of experiencing, conceptualizing, analyzing, and applying their

Figure 8.2. Four Pedagogies of Personal Digital Inquiry

Components of Personal Digital Inquiry (PDI) Framework	Elements of a Multiliteracies Pedagogy	Elements of a New Literacies Perspective of Online Research and Comprehension
INQUIRY: Actively build personally relevant connections to a certain perspective and knowledge base or culture; these engagements prompt interest and personal wondering	• Teaching through Situated Practice (to foster experiences with authentic practices) • Learning through Experiencing	
COLLABORATION & DISCUSSION: Facilitate ways of talking about, examining, listening, and discussing underlying concepts that help build connections across different disciplines, modes, and perspectives	• Teaching through Overt Instruction (to foster depth of understanding) • Learning through Conceptualization	Reading, discussing, and composing to: • Define important questions; • Locate relevant information; • Critically evaluate information for accuracy, reliability, purpose, and perspective; • Compare, contrast, analyze and synthesize information across multiple sources; and • Communicate ideas with and for others
CREATION & PARTICIPATION: Engage in making, creating, performing, composing, interpreting, and explaining as diverse forms of constructing new knowledge	• Teaching through Transformed Practice (to foster knowledge transfer) • Learning through Application	
REFLECTION: Compare and contrast different contexts, purposes, and perspectives while coming to know whose interests a specific text, product, or solution serves best	• Teaching through Critical Framing (to foster breadth of understanding) • Learning through Analysis	

new knowledge to solve authentic, personally relevant problems in their local and global communities.

ENCOURAGING DIVERSE REPRESENTATIONS OF UNDERSTANDING AND PARTICIPATION

In this final section, we offer some illustrative examples of the kinds of pedagogical moves and learning activity sequences that we have seen engage a range of learners in personal inquiry, reflective thinking, critical reasoning, and civic participation—the core practices of personal digital inquiry—while increasing learners' understanding of and participation in a complex digital world.

Fostering a Culture of Curiosity, Reflection, and Creativity

As Dewey (1938/1997) proposed almost a century ago, when curriculum is built around a learner's instincts to talk, investigate, construct meaning, and express new discoveries with others, meaningful and transformative learning happens quite naturally. Intentional opportunities to wonder and think deeply about issues that matter can be incorporated into digital pedagogies for learners of all ages. One of the simplest ways we have seen teachers prompt curiosity and reflection begins with a mystery photo activity that provides opportunities for all learners, regardless of linguistic differences or reading ability. Smaller portions of a larger digital photograph are displayed to reveal key features within the image but not enough to give away what the object is. Students are invited to look at the smaller photo and think about what the image might be. Discussion and creative ideas emerge quite naturally as learners are asked to share what evidence in the picture supports their thinking.

For older students, digital photos or videos depicting discrepant events, or information that conflicts with students' prior knowledge, can create a similar state of perplexity wherein "the learner is prompted to search for questions that can guide him or her in the quest to resolve the discrepancy" (Ciardiello, 2003, p. 229). Once the mystery image or event is revealed, additional resources are made available to inspire or address further questions about things in the photograph or video. A more critical stance might focus on empowering students to critique, transform, or otherwise reflect on what is missing from the images or what could be imagined instead. While viewing these resources, students become intrigued and want to read, watch, and talk about what they have experienced with their classmates. These thought-provoking experiences, in turn, foster a mutual appreciation of different views, multiple ways of representing ideas, and feelings of student agency and belonging among a community of learners and creative thinkers.

As curiosity and creativity become valued practices in their learning community, we have seen students pursue personal wonderings that can lead to interdisciplinary connections and multimodal representations of their new knowledge and reflective thinking (see Coiro, Castek, & Quinn, 2016; Coiro, Dobler, & Pelekis, in press). For example, Ms. White engaged her 4th and 5th graders in a 6-week investigation into human body systems organized within a personal digital inquiry framework. Students were guided through personal explorations that dovetailed with science topics they learned about as a class. Ms. White guided her students' choices in developing inquiry topics framed by researchable (yet manageable) student-developed questions and introduced them to a range of digital tools and technologies with which to represent their learning. Inspired by their personal wonderings, students collected resources, created interactive diagrams, built multimodal websites, composed scripts, and used screencasting tools to reflect on both their design choices and new understandings.

We have also seen how personal inquiry organized around creating shared multimodal products fosters university students' engagement and creative knowledge building (Kiili, Mäkinen & Coiro, 2013; Smith, Kiili, & Kauppinen, 2016). In one university education course, small groups of students were asked to prepare a digital video focused on effective ways of teaching digital literacies in schools or in some other educational context. Students worked in three phases. First, they engaged in ideation for finding a video topic. Then, they composed an argumentative essay informed by their inquiry. The final phase was dedicated to digital video composition where students transformed ideas presented in their traditional academic essays to representations that utilized multiple modes of meaning (see Kress, 2000; New London Group, 1996).

Similar to the younger students' inquiry projects introduced above is the long-term nature of knowledge advancement processes (cf. Paavola, Lakkala, Muukkonen, Kosonen, & Karlgren, 2011) with work distributed across a period of 11 weeks. These multimodal inquiry projects tapped into both collaborative and creative processes. Sharing the projects and reflecting on the learning process with a learning community were powerful aspects of this instructional approach. Long-term processing around shared objects and the sequencing of complex tasks into manageable phases also makes space for multiliteracies pedagogies of experiencing, conceptualizing, analyzing, and applying. Researchers found that both mediums—written essays and digital videos—seemed to possess unique modal affordances for building knowledge based on their genres and modes of communication (Smith, Kiili, & Kauppinen, 2016). While written essays supported conceptualizing, analyzing, and critical argumentation, digital videos provided opportunities to transmediate written ideas to an audience in creative, flexible, and affective ways. Students created their videos by hybridizing and utilizing intertextuality (see New London Group, 1996, p. 82). Hybridization refers to students' articulation of academic content in new ways that remix modes, genres, and conventions. Intertextuality was also observed in many videos as students incorporated elements from narratives and popular culture.

Developing the Ability to Visualize, Critically Reason, and Deliberate Complex Ideas

Given the globalization of our economy and almost every other system affecting society—where cultures, values, disciplines, and ways of thinking and being are mixed—the Personal Digital Inquiry framework can be used to provide space for students to recognize and negotiate differences (Cope & Kalantzis, 2000; New London Group, 1996). For example, while adolescents are using the Internet to explore a controversial social issue, the newly developed Online Inquiry Tool (Kiili, Coiro, & Hämäläinen, 2016) creates space for them to take into account different perspectives and form their own positions on the issue after careful deliberation. The online tool itself seems to foster the conceptualization of the phenomena under exploration and collaborative work with the tool supports engagement in critically evaluating online sources (Coiro et al, 2014). While students in these studies were asked to represent their thinking about controversial issues with traditional essays, we believe the visualized results of personal digital inquiry may also stimulate the creation of different kinds of shared objects, such as multimodal products, panel discussions, or role-plays allowing students to use a broader range of cultural resources that foster more personally relevant connections (New London Group, 1996).

Expanding Access to Civic Participation for Children, Youth, and Adults

The ascent of science, technology, engineering, and mathematics (STEM) curricula, makerspaces, and innovation labs offers opportunities to leverage digital texts, tools, and multimodal representations for design, creation, play, and problem solving. Central to these learning environments are literacy practices that incorporate ways of learning and sharing knowledge from fields such as math, science, engineering, and history (Manderino & Castek, 2016). Digital literacy practices are not confined, however, to school settings or school-aged children. Libraries and other community settings offer public spaces for informal, self-directed learning. For example, the Library As Incubator Project (www.libraryasincubatorproject.org), the Exploratory (www.theexploratory.com), and The Makery (www.nycmakery.com) are innovative spaces where learners across the lifespan gather to compile online resources while interacting with each other; they also explore, design, prototype, and create works while collectively sharing their expertise. Such efforts call for a reimagining of collaborative and cognitive apprenticeship models (e.g., Greenleaf, Schoenbach, Cziko, & Mueller, 2001). In these learning spaces, all participants actively co-construct knowledge and participate in a culture that respects variations in how different individuals participate and actively contribute. Such learning spaces welcome learners from all backgrounds and offer spaces where critical dialogue around which the "emerging pluralistic forms of citizenship and different lifeworlds" can take place (New London Group, 1996, p. 73).

This kind of making culture invokes a spirit of innovation that begins with inquiry and incorporates a range of both analog and digital tools. However, digital tools are not used simply for the sake of technology. Rather, they offer multiple avenues for creativity and self-expression. Exchanging ideas in digital spaces is a shared value that sparks innovation, iteration, and continual improvement (Tucker-Raymond, Gravel, Wagh, & Wilson, 2016). Digital literacies are acquired that can be leveraged for personal goal fulfillment while also expanding opportunities for civic participation and learning beyond the walls of schools, post-secondary institutions, and formalized learning spaces.

CONCLUSION

Today's learning environments require a better understanding of how to design instruction that builds on, and consolidates, what we know about literacy practices, disciplinary learning, digital tools and technologies, student agency, and connected learning. In addition, we must take into consideration learners' changing needs while flexibly adjusting to the inevitable changes associated with increasingly diverse texts and the current range of cultural, linguistic, and digital practices. The Personal Digital Inquiry framework can guide instructional design decisions that bridge varied forms of in- and out-of-school learning. Through this framework, inquiry approaches to learning and problem solving are foregrounded so that digital literacies are not positioned simply as learning tasks to be mastered but rather as tools that help individuals construct knowledge and solve intellectual, real-world problems.

REFERENCES

Afflerbach, P., & Cho, B. (2009). Determining and describing reading strategies: Internet and traditional forms of reading. In H. S. Waters & W. Schneider (Eds.), *Metacognition, strategy use, and instruction* (pp. 201–225). New York, NY: Guilford Press.

Alberta Learning. (2004). *Focus on inquiry: A teacher's guide to implementing inquiry-based learning.* Retrieved from www.teachingbooks.net/content/FocusOnInquiry.pdf

Brown, J. S. (2005). *New learning environments for the 21st century.* Retrieved from www.johnseelybrown.com/newlearning.pdf

Bruce, B. C., & Bishop, A. P. (2008). New literacies and community inquiry. In J. Coiro, M. Knobel, C. Lankshear, & D. Leu, (Eds.), *The handbook of research in new literacies* (pp. 699–742). New York, NY: Routledge.

Casey, L. (2013). Learning beyond competence to participation. *International Journal of Progressive Education, 9*(2), 45–60.

Casey, L., & Bruce, B. C. (2011). The practice profile of inquiry: Connecting digital literacy and pedagogy. *E-learning and Digital Media, 8*(1), 76–85.

Cho, B.-Y., & Afflerbach, P. (2015). Reading on the Internet: Realizing and constructing potential texts. *Journal of Adolescent & Adult Literacy, 58*(6), 504–517.

Ciardiello, V. (2003). To wander and wonder: Pathways to literacy and inquiry through question finding. *Journal of Adolescent and Adult Literacy, 47*(3), 228–239.

Coiro, J. (2011). Predicting reading comprehension on the Internet: Contributions of offline reading skills, online reading skills, and prior knowledge. *Journal of Literacy Research, 43*(4), 352–392.

Coiro, J., Castek, J., & Quinn, D. J. (2016). Personal inquiry and online research: Connecting learners in ways that matter. *The Reading Teacher, 69*(5), 1–10.

Coiro, J., & Dobler, E. (2007). Exploring the comprehension strategies used by sixth-grade skilled readers as they search for and locate information on the Internet. *Reading Research Quarterly, 42,* 214–257.

Coiro, J., Dobler, E., & Pelekis, K. (in press). *Planning for personal digital inquiry in grades K–4.* Portland, ME: Stenhouse.

Coiro, J., Kiili, C., Hämäläinen, J., Cedillo, L., Naylor, R., O'Connell, R., & Quinn, D. (2014, December). *Digital scaffolds for reading multiple online sources and writing argumentative texts.* Paper presented at the annual Literacy Research Association Conference, Marco Island, FL.

Coiro, J., Knobel, M., Lankshear, C., & Leu, D. J. (Eds.). (2008). *Handbook of research in new literacies.* Mahwah, NJ: Erlbaum.

Cope, B., & Kalantzis, M. (Eds.). (2000). *Multiliteracies: Literacy learning and the design of social futures.* London, UK: Routledge.

Cope, B., & Kalantzis, M. (2015). The things you do to know: An introduction to the pedagogy of multiliteracies. In B. Cope & M. Kalantzis (Eds.), *A pedagogy of multiliteracies: Learning by design* (pp. 1–36). Basingstoke, UK: Palgrave Macmillan.

Dewey, J. (1997). Experience and education. In J. A. Boydston (Ed.), *John Dewey: The later works, 1938–1939 (Vol. 13).* Carbondale, IL: Southern Illinois University Press. (Original work published 1938)

Dillenbourg, P., & Traum, D. (1996). Grounding in multi-modal task-oriented collaboration. In P. Brna, A. Paiva, & J. Self (Eds.), *Proceedings of the European Conference on Artificial Intelligence in Education* (pp. 401– 407). Lisbon, Portugal.

Greenleaf, C., Schoenbach, R., Cziko, C., & Mueller, F. (2001). Apprenticing adolescent readers to academic literacy. *Harvard Educational Review*, *71*(1), 79–129.

Hartman, D. K., Morsink, P. M., & Zheng, J. (2010). From print to pixels: The evolution of cognitive conceptions of reading comprehension. In E. A. Baker (Ed.), *The new literacies: Multiple perspectives on research and practice* (pp. 131–164). New York, NY: Guilford Press.

Hobbs, R. (2010). *Digital and media literacy: A plan of action.* Washington, D.C.: John S. and James L. Knight Foundation and Aspen Institute.

Hobbs, R., & Moore, D. C. (2013). *Discovering media literacy: Teaching digital media and popular culture in elementary school.* Thousand Oaks, CA: Corwin.

Hull, G., & Schultz, K. (Eds.). (2002). *School's out! Bridging out-of-school literacies with classroom practice.* New York, NY: Teachers College Press.

Ito, M., Gutiérrez, K., Livingstone, S., Penuel, B., Rhodes, J., Salen, K., . . . Watkins, C. (2013). *Connected Learning: An agenda for research and design.* Irvine, CA: Digital Media and Learning Research Hub.

Jenkins, H., Purushotma, R., Weigel, M., Clinton, K., & Robison, A. J. (2009). *Confronting the challenges of participatory culture: Media education for the 21st century.* Cambridge, MA: MIT Press.

Kalantzis, M., & Cope, B. (2012a). *Literacies.* New York, NY: Cambridge University Press.

Kalantzis, M., & Cope, B. (2012b). *New learning: Elements of a science of education.* New York, NY: Cambridge University Press.

Kiili, C., Coiro, J., & Hämäläinen, J. (2016). An online inquiry tool to support the exploration of controversial issues on the Internet. *Journal of Literacy & Technology, 17*(1–2), 32–52. Retrieved from www. literacyandtechnology.org/uploads/1/3/6/8/136889/_jlt_sp2016_killi_ coiro_hamaianen.pdf

Kiili, C., Mäkinen, M., & Coiro, J. (2013). Rethinking academic literacies: Designing multifaceted academic literacy experiences for pre-service teachers. *Journal of Adolescent & Adult Literacy, 57*(3), 223–232.

Kress, G. (2000). *Multiliteracies: Literacy learning and the design of social futures.* South Yarra, Australia: Macmillan.

Lankshear, C., & Knobel, M. (2003). *New literacies.* Maidenhead, UK: Open University Press.

Lankshear, C., & Knobel, M. (2006). *New literacies* (2nd ed.). Maidenhead, UK: Open University Press.

Leu, D. J., Kinzer, C. K., Coiro, J. L., & Cammack, D. W. (2004). Toward a theory of new literacies emerging from the Internet and other information and communication technologies. *Theoretical models and processes of reading, 5*(1), 1570–1613.

Leu, D. J., Kinzer, C. K., Coiro, J., Castek, J., & Henry, L. A. (2013). New literacies: A dual-level theory of the changing nature of literacy, instruction, and assessment. In R. B. Ruddell & D. Alvermann (Eds.), *Theoretical models and processes of reading* (6th ed.) (pp. 1150–1181). Newark, DE: International Reading Association.

Manderino, M., & Castek, J. (2016). Digital literacies for disciplinary learning: A call to action. *Journal of Adolescent and Adult Literacy, 60*(1), 79–81.

New London Group. (1996). A pedagogy of multiliteracies: Designing social futures. *Harvard Educational Review, 66*(1), 60–92.

Paavola, S., Lakkala, M., Muukkonen, H., Kosonen, K., & Karlgren, K. (2011). The roles and uses of design principles for developing the trialogical approach on learning. *Research in Learning Technology, 19*(3), 233–246.

Pink, D. (2009). *Drive: The surprising truth about what motivates us.* New York, NY: Riverhead Books.

Schofield, C. P., & Honore, S. (2010). Generation Y and learning. *The Ashridge Journal,* Winter 2009–2010, 26–32.

Smith, B. E., Kiili, C., & Kauppinen, M. (2016). Transmediating argumentation: Students composing across written essays and digital videos in higher education. *Computers & Education, 102*, 138–151.

Street, B. (1998). New literacies in theory and practice: What are the implications for language in education? *Linguistics and Education, 10*(1), 1–24.

Thomas, D., & Brown, J. (2011). *A new culture of learning: Cultivating the imagination for a world of constant change.* Lexington, KY: CreateSpace.

Tucker-Raymond, E., Gravel, B., Wagh, A., & Wilson, N. (2016). Making it social: Considering the purpose of literacies to support participation in making and engineering. *Journal of Adolescent and Adult Literacy, 60*(2), 207–211.

Zhang, S., & Duke, N. K. (2008). Strategies for Internet reading with different reading purposes: A descriptive study of twelve good Internet readers. *Journal of Literacy Research, 40*(1), 128–162.

Zhao, Y. (2009). *Catching up or leading the way: American education in the age of globalization.* Alexandria, VA: ASCD.

CHAPTER 9

Video Games, Distributed Teaching and Learning Systems, and Multipedagogies

Jeffrey B. Holmes

This chapter addresses the changing nature of teaching and learning in the modern, digital world by extending the work of the New London Group (NLG) and introducing the concept of "multipedagogies" to account for the variety of people and things that teach and all the places, digital and analog, where teaching and learning happen.

In addition, the chapter outlines two important dimensions of multipedagogies. First, many different people and many different tools can teach. Second, teaching can happen outside of any particular, traditional educational institution. To illustrate these dimensions in action, I will provide a case study of the videogame *Dota 2*. In particular, *Dota 2* acts as a distributed teaching and learning system (Holmes, 2015) where teaching and learning happen through designed and emergent resources across a range of sites within and around the game. Such a system allows us to see how multipedagogies, especially around a deep problem, can extend to many different people and to many different sites that can be organized and rearranged by a learner to fit their own needs. In other words, multipedagogies can be enacted through these distributed teaching and learning systems to be dynamic, robust, adaptable, and open—open to all kinds of places where teaching can happen, and all kinds of people who engage in teaching, and they can even empower learners to design their own learning pathways. Finally, through the concept of multipedagogies, we can begin to think about ways to improve learning experiences through quality pedagogical practices wherever they happen.

THE ORIGINAL CONCEPT OF MULTILITERACIES

One key contribution of the NLG's original manifesto was its argument for new ways of thinking about the "what" and "how" of literacy pedagogy. Its notion of multiliteracies captured the "multiplicity of communications channels and media, and the increasing saliency of cultural and linguistic diversity" (New London Group, 1996, p. 63). Multiliteracies framed diverse texts, practices, and modes of representation as valid sites of literacy and opened these sites to analysis and incorporation into more traditional literacy pedagogy.

This connection to traditional literacy pedagogy, however, reveals an important limitation of the NLG's manifesto in the way it ties pedagogy so closely to schools and other settings usually associated with *formal* education. A major concern of the NLG was how to prepare learners to enter work and civic life, and contemporary public schooling is often the site where young people begin to gain access to and prepare to engage with these domains. Indeed, the NLG argues directly that schools "provide access to a hierarchically ordered world of work [and] shape citizenries" (New London Group, p. 72), so schools and the kinds of education programs they provide have historically been powerful sites for shaping the lives of learners.

In the 20 years since the NLG manifesto, research into *informal* educational environments, in particular digital spaces, has shown how people teach and learn in their everyday lives decoupled from any formal settings—in museums, workplaces, and homes and in old and new media of all sorts (Bennett, 2012). While public school remains a primary site where learning is credentialed and certified, informal environments are increasingly viewed as places where learners develop both key 21st century knowledges and noncognitive skills like mathematics, scientific reasoning, coding, systems thinking, problem solving, determination, cooperation, and collective intelligence (see, for example, Davidson & Goldberg, 2009; Ito, Baumer, & Bittani, 2009; Jenkins et al., 2009). These spaces are filled with acts of teaching, sometimes explicitly, as in a museum or a jobsite, sometimes rather tacitly, as in a videogame or on a playground, and sometimes as a mixture of both—done by a range of people and tools not traditionally considered "teachers" who are tied to no particular educational institution.

Such research in informal learning environments suggests that *where* teaching and learning happen and *who* (or *what*) teaches are increasingly important considerations in the evolving landscape of education in the 21st century. Just as the NLG developed "multiliteracies" to account for the shifting nature of texts and acts as literacy, we can extend a similar frame to teaching of all kinds as well. If teaching happens through multiple channels and media and not just in schools, and there are many types of teaching that include "cultural and [stylistic] diversity" around various subjects and interests beyond school-like content areas, then it is possible to think of a multiplicity of teaching, of what we can term *multipedagogies*. These multipedagogies may include traditional approaches to teaching, certainly, but also teaching in other contexts as well. It can account for diverse forms and "styles" of teaching. And it can account for many different people who engage in teaching, from teachers in traditional school settings but also parents, coaches, media designers, and many other people who engage in acts of teaching.

CHANGING TEACHING AND LEARNING

There are several reasons for addressing the "where" and "who" of pedagogy. For one thing, current reports of educational effectiveness suggest contemporary public educational institutions are failing to prepare learners to enter those things the NLG were concerned with, namely, work and civic lives, and in particular as economies and technologies change rapidly (Cappelli, 2014; see also Bessen, 2014). What people learn in their everyday lives outside of any educational institution is also important and even essential to their engagement with work and their civic lives (see, e.g., Falk & Dierking, 2010; Jenkins, 2009).

Nevertheless, discussions of teaching often center on school and formal educational settings. Indeed, even the term "pedagogy" has had deep ties to formal educational settings such as schools for more than a century; such discussions were particularly influenced by Dewey and later expanded by other critical educational theorists. We readily talk about and critique the pedagogical practices of classroom teachers; rarely do we refer to the pedagogy of a master auto mechanic training an apprentice or an expert soccer coach coaching her team. Pedagogy is often conflated with the identity of a "teacher" who is a trained, professional expert and has been certified through a formalized process to operate in a specific social institution (i.e., school). In other words, teachers teach *in school*. And, since teachers are found primarily in schools, so too is teaching.

What happens in informal spaces where people learn must be something different. Indeed, we have many names for teaching in other contexts: "apprenticing," "mentoring," "guiding," "training," "showing," "helping," "participating," "sharing," "demonstrating," "coaching," "telling," and so on. There is room for nuance here, of course, and these terms reflect some subtle variations in how teaching happens and who is involved. But more than just a problem of terminology, such euphemisms instead reflect a general bias against seeing this work as "teaching." Since it is not done by certified teachers, and it is not happening in school, it *must* be something other than teaching.

If, as research on informal learning environments suggests, we also consider the work done by these *teachers* outside of any school setting as *teaching*, then we have a clearer picture of the contours of these spaces and activities, a language and method for addressing those people who seek to increase what people learn and improve how they do so, regardless of where it happens. We also have the means to improve their teaching to realize these goals. The concept of multipedagogies, by focusing on the "where" and "who" of teaching, addresses these issues.

TEACHING BEYOND INSTITUTIONS

Informal learning is typically differentiated from school-based education as an institutionally backed organizing force (see Schugurensky, 2000; Sefton-Green, 2004; Marsick, 2009). Another key difference is the nature of the instruction related to informal learning. While not always the case, formal instruction is often set up as didactic and structured (such as lecturing), while informal learning is often contextually situated and experiential. Further, formal instruction is usually oriented toward top-down content delivery, whereas informal instruction changes the nature of the participants (learners and teachers) from rigid, often unidirectional relationships to shifting, reciprocal relationships where people learn through experts and peers alike as well as through their own participation.

In the broadest sense, informal learning is often contrasted with formal education (particularly school) and set up as a kind of alternative—an alternative *process* and an alternative *environment* (Jenkins, 2006). Claims about the nature of informal learning vary widely, from a modest impact to a revolutionary rethinking of traditional, formal education. Nearly all work on informal learning, however, suggests that it is a productive and provocative place to extend *where* education happens.

Somewhat paradoxically, while research into informal learning and especially digital media emphasizes that *learning* is not bound to school but happens across many different places, both physical and digital, most of the work on *teaching* remains focused on school-like settings. Some literature and some training programs do examine corporate or workplace training (see, for instance, Quinn, 2014; Wick, Pollock, & Jefferson, 2010), while others look at informal settings such as museums (see Marcus, Stoddard, & Woodward, 2011, for example), though instruction there often strongly resembles school-like practices. It is perhaps surprising that while we have a large and growing body of research around where teaching and learning happens, so little of it actually focuses on the teaching itself, analytically or prescriptively.

A multipedagogies perspective instead directly acknowledges that teaching does indeed happen outside of formal educational institutions in a range of sites. Informed by the concept of informal learning, multipedagogies frame these nonschool sites as productive places where teaching happens and opens up these spaces for deeper interrogation, critique, and interventions into the kinds of teaching that go on in them. Furthermore, by highlighting these teaching acts outside of the institutional control of schools, it democratizes teaching for those people not formally certified by the state or other governing body yet engaged in deep and critical moments of teaching of all kinds.

TEACHERS AS A DIVERSE GROUP

Digital media and Internet technologies have rapidly accelerated the ways we look at and conceptualize *informal* learning environments. Claims about digital media often center on new forms of participation, and on the ways they reconfigure *how* learners connect and interact with other people and with learning "content"; this configuration is seen as different (and often better) than that of traditional school environments. As Jenkins and colleagues (2009) argue, the promise of digital media is in the creation of "participatory cultures" that "shift the focus of literacy from individual expression to community involvement" (p. 6). Literacy in this definition means situated knowledge and action, so Jenkins and colleagues argue that digital media are a means to engage with other social actors in a specific context that is generally interest-driven, voluntary, provisional, and made up of a range of different people with different sets of expertise and goals. Digital learning communities allow more people to be considered experts, and the community of participants can determine what "counts" as expertise and whom to validate (Gee, 2003; Gee & Hayes, 2010). In formal educational settings, by way of contrast, teachers are credentialed and afforded expert status through a rigorous, standardized process controlled by a governing agency or institution, and few students are free to judge the teacher's competency or to certify his or her expertise.

Various learners participate in learning communities at different levels or in different ways (Ito et al., 2009). Participants learn *how* to participate in these communities by observing and tinkering, as well as through feedback from other participants. And, because of the highly complex nature of the networks of participation in the digital arena, participants can be experts in one domain (say, how to create artwork in Photoshop) while being relatively unskilled in other domains (say, writing fan-fiction stories) (Gee & Hayes, 2010). Nevertheless, valuable peer-to-peer interactions form one of the core claims about digital media and learning, particularly how peers learn from each other (Ito et al., 2009, 2013). Despite the fact that it's easy to see participants learning by observing and listening to others as the result of *teaching* by others, little emphasis is placed on how these other participants actually engage in teaching. Instead, most of the focus is on what learners "pick up" through their participation and interactions in learning communities.

As in the move to validate sites of teaching outside of institutional control, a multipedagogies perspective similarly reflects that people of all sorts teach, and we can appropriately treat them as "teachers." While they are not credentialed teachers of the sort found in schools, they nevertheless perform many of the same functions and use many of the same techniques. More importantly, treating them as teachers does not necessarily de-professionalize certified teachers by implying that just anyone is an "expert" teacher (which is, after all, the point of credentialing teachers after often intense preparation). It does, however, mean that we can look at a range of activities done by many different people for insight into effective teaching—regardless of who does it—and look at ways to improve the teaching that people encounter in their everyday experiences.

A CASE STUDY:
DOTA 2 AS A DISTRIBUTED TEACHING AND LEARNING SYSTEM

The videogame *Dota 2* is an illuminating example of how a multipedagogies approach to teaching and learning manifests around a complex space like a videogame, and in particular through the ways that teaching and learning happen via multiple different channels in and around the game. *Dota 2* is designed by Valve, Inc., has more than 10 million active players each month, and has annual revenue of over $200 million (Grubb, 2015). At its core, the game is much like "capture the flag," with two teams of up to five players each trying to capture the other team's base while defending their own. To start the game, players choose from more than 100 different characters, each with its own unique skills, abilities, and weaknesses. Team composition is important, as the characters are designed to fill certain roles, from high-damage dealers to supporting characters who help and strengthen the other players, so communication and group cooperation is critical. There are hundreds of variables and thousands of possible combinations of teams and play styles. While the concept of the game might be simple (capture the other base, don't let yours get captured), how to go about achieving this goal can be quite complex.

Dota 2 can be seen as a *distributed teaching and learning system* (DTALS) in which different learners/players across different sites teach other players how to navigate the complex nature of the game. Some teaching (designed explicitly by Valve) occurs within the game, while other instruction occurs on third-party sites such as forums or YouTube videos. How these teaching resources are designed and configured is particularly interesting as far as who is doing the teaching and where the teaching is taking place in the game—demonstrating the power of multiliteracies as enacted through these distributed systems.

Valve, the makers of the game, designed a number of overt teaching resources. The central resource is an optional, multipart tutorial. Sequenced tutorial modules cover everything from basic game mechanics to higher-level concepts. The tutorial sequence is highly scaffolded. In the early tutorial levels, many textual cues and prompts and visual symbols such as arrows pointing to parts of the interface regularly appear for players; by the later levels very few of these interventions appear. Early levels are particularly "easy" and nearly impossible to fail, while later levels are nearly as difficult as the "real" game and may require multiple attempts before the player succeeds. Similarly, each module builds on the skills, concepts, and processes of the earlier modules. The proficiency a player gains in each tutorial level is the foundation for the subsequent modules.

In fact, the way these modules are designed to teach—through scaffolded instruction with overt showing and telling, reinforcement, and a ramping up of difficulty, while reducing direct instruction toward practical application—aligns closely with concepts like the Zone of Proximal Development (Vygotsky, 1986) as well as many contemporary methods of teaching found in traditional classrooms. In this sense, the tutorials look a lot like school—albeit a rather dynamic, interactive, and responsive version of school—so it is not that difficult to see these tutorials as a way of teaching. It is also possible to consider Valve as the designer of the teaching, and the game itself as the vehicle or "teacher." It is an interesting question (but outside the scope of this chapter) to delve deeply into the relationship between the gamemaker and the game itself and ask "who" or "what" is the actual teacher, so here let us simply think of the game's designers as teachers using the game to teach.

Many video games use tutorial levels or elements. It is a common enough trope in games that we can assume game designers understand and leverage these tutorials as a primary channel for teaching players to play the game. The same holds for many of the other overt elements Valve includes in *Dota 2*, such as a resources library within the game client that has textual and statistical information for each character, item, and ability, with video demonstrations of each ability in action. Valve also hosts guides for the game on its website; they include detailed information, analysis, and tips for players. These resources can be accessed on-demand and as needed.

Teaching players how to play the game, then, is distributed across different sites within these various elements found in the game structures and platforms. Elsewhere, I have called these *designed teaching elements* (Holmes, 2015). They are made by Valve to overtly teach; Valve is responsible for designing the game resources and for the methods for distributing them. Players can interact with them (or not, since they are all optional), can use them in different ways (they can play part or all of the tutorial more than once, they can read a guide or use the library and try out the tips), but all in the service of learning how to play the game, and all designed under the "control" of Valve as the teacher.

Valve also includes another kind of teaching resource that makes the present discussion of multipedagogies clearer and more nuanced. Valve designed a set of tools and features for other players to "populate," what I have called *designed-for-emergent-teaching elements*. For example, the game includes a "coach mode." In this special mode, a player can invite a friend or other peer to coach (teach) them as they play. This coach has special tools within the game client, such as the ability to draw on the other player's screen and control parts of the player's interface. The player and coach also have a special voice-chat channel and text-chat channel that only they can see. Teaching in the coach mode is done by another player using these features, not by Valve. In the tutorial, Valve is the controller of all the content (the terms, the topics, the pace and so on), but in coach mode, Valve is only the designer of a set of tools—it is up to players to actually do the teaching. Valve anticipated what people might need to teach (private chat channels, interface control) and designed around those assumptions. But *what* people actually teach is not up to Valve; players can just as easily teach how to cheat or exploit the game as teach how to play the "right" way. Players are also limited by the affordances of the tools Valve provides in the game, so they cannot do things like replay moments or change the mechanics of the game. Through the coach mode, teaching is also distributed—not just distributed as one of many resources in the client but also distributed between Valve, designer of the tools, and the players who actually populate those tools.

There is one other type of teaching and learning resource around *Dota 2* that can inform this analysis of where teaching happens and who teaches. Like many online pursuits, *Dota 2* inspires a great deal of "affinity spaces" (Gee, 2003; Gee & Hayes, 2010). They include learning spaces like forums and FAQs, YouTube walkthroughs and tutorials, theory-crafting websites where people exchange data-driven ideas about the game, wikispaces and guides, and many other activities. These affinity spaces are driven by players' interests in specific aspects of the game, and while the domain (*Dota 2*) is the same the focus and content can be radically different among these various sites. Hardcore players who care about maximizing their performance may populate theory-crafting sites and create and access highly specialized guides for characters and abilities. Casual fans may care more about connecting with other players, and look for ways to increase their social gameplay. People enamored of the story and lore may create and maintain detailed information on the backgrounds of the characters and other narrative elements.

Each of these groups teaches and learns about specific aspects of the domain, but together they make up the broader system around it; these are *emergent teaching resources* in that they are made and enacted not through the design of the game's maker but by people as they interact and engage with the game. The content they make and the tools they use are similarly outside of the control of Valve. People can teach others about specific aspects of the game just as readily as they can teach how to cheat. Learners can access these sites at their discretion and can create their own pathway through these various resources. However, significant social mediation often occurs within and between these sites, such as linking to other sites, and recommending some resources over others. So learners must have some savvy when navigating these emergent sites, often gaining a great deal of metaknowledge about the domain along the way.

These extra-game resources point back toward the game itself, but are controlled by people other than the game's designers. These people design their own teaching around the game but also influence the design of the game; things like streaming were popular before *Dota 2* and likely played a large role in Valve's including such features into the designed teaching elements. Further, Valve benefits greatly from the participation of outside teachers, since it does not have to develop all the materials but can leverage players' learning outside of the game at little cost to the company.

BRINGING VIDEO GAMES INTO LEARNING CONTEXTS

Dota 2 shows that it is possible to address both of the propositions raised at the beginning of this chapter: that *where* teaching happens is both important and often very fuzzy, and that *who* teaches is not necessarily bound to professional or credentialed teachers but can include many different kinds of people in many different configurations, from gamemakers to more knowledgeable peers. Teaching happens in many different sites around *Dota 2*, from the designed elements like the tutorial and the library to designed-for-emergent elements like the coach mode to emergent sites like forums and walkthroughs. None of these sites are necessarily tied to any formal educational institution. Some of these sites are formally designed or sanctioned by Valve, and as the game's maker Valve might see them as the "institution" since they have direct control over the game and its content. But the ways the designed-for-emergent and emergent teaching resources allow people to teach outside of Valve's control (even things like how to cheat or exploit the game) further show that teaching happens in places beyond any institution.

Dota 2 also shows how many different people and entities can teach. Valve certainly makes design decisions that, coincidently or not, align to many good teaching principles (like scaffolded instruction, managing the player's attention, providing just-in-time and on-demand resources and so on). The inclusion of the designed-for-emergent elements also functions to extend the role of teacher to the players themselves, and Valve's inclusion of these elements again reflects both its vested economic interests in the community (since players working together in the game are more likely to continue playing it) as well as the importance of players in shaping the kind of teaching and learning that happens around the game. And, while there is a great deal of variation in how overtly and directly emergent resources teach, in aggregate they are meant to introduce players to new ideas, new ways of playing, new understandings of the game and the community around it, and new ways of thinking about their own play. These sites are designed and populated by different people who act as teachers outside of the control of the game's makers. Together, all of these elements highlight the ways that both the game designer and players themselves actively and collaboratively create teaching resources. Teaching here is done by many different people.

But *Dota* 2 also shows how multipedagogies, when enacted through distributed teaching and learning systems, can address the complex ways we teach and learn deep problems. A player can learn to play the game by accessing any number of the designed and emergent sites and in many various configurations; they may begin in the "official" channels and play the entire tutorial before starting to play the game, or they may watch guides on YouTube before ever launching the game, or they might have a friend sitting in the room with them, "armchair" teaching them as they play. It is even possible for players to skip any explicit teaching resource and just learn to play through trial and error. The game is designed to give enough meaningful guidance and feedback to support these players too, although the learning may be slow and frustrating (hence why Valve creates the designed teaching elements in the first place). Learning any deep problem—whether it's *Dota 2* or calculus or auto repair—is likely never again going to be "contained" in any single teaching site or through any single teaching resource; it will almost certainly spread across many different times, places, and objects, and require practice, feedback, and iteration. *Dota 2* makes obvious how those various sites—both the "formal" ones designed by Valve and the emergent sites that players themselves create—form a system to teach the deep and interesting problems that make up the game.

Thinking about the design and organization of the systems that emerge around these deep problems provides an important area of inquiry into how these systems come about, what they look like, and how they are maintained. This thinking also indicates that tracing a specific learner's pathway through many different sites might provide insight into how they learn, what kinds of teaching they encounter, and how this pathway is constructed. Such insight might provide an interesting method of analyzing how people learn across many different teaching encounters, and how we might construct better pathways as designers and teachers. A multipedagogies perspective opens up the discussion of these spaces, people, and tools as sources of teachings and can extend where we research, create, and implement teaching.

Multipedagogies, especially in relation to DTALSs, do not necessarily preclude classroom or school-based teaching. Indeed, "institutional" teaching can often leverage many people and sites as teachers. Fieldtrips, YouTube clips in an English class, the sequencing of math courses through high school, inviting a local expert in to talk to a class— all these and many other instances show that school can certainly incorporate teachers beyond the professional *teacher* and can utilize teaching and learning spaces outside of any classroom walls. Multipedagogies within schools may help to stress the many opportunities that teachers have to incorporate and curate good teaching moments, whether they are ones they design themselves or those offered by others outside of the institution. School could be a "hub" that connects in- and out-of-school teaching and learning and centers teachers as expert designers, curators, and practitioners.

Nevertheless, school remains a central institutional force that certifies the learning a young person does. Learners often have little say in how the resources are organized, when they encounter them, or the ability to seek alternatives. The research in informal learning, as noted above, suggests that learning outside of a classroom, whether it's in a videogame, an afterschool program, or "messing around" in digital tools like Photoshop, can be important and even essential to a learner's success in a rapidly changing world. Multipedagogies, and especially those enacted in DTALSs, provide ways for learners to structure alternatives to the institutional control of teaching and learning and to organize meaningful learning pathways of their own.

In fact, such control on the part of a learner addresses one final important facet of the NLG's original manifesto. The NLG argued that the civic nature of schools and the state should act "not to impose standards [but] as neutral arbiters of difference" among a "civic pluralism" (p. 69). Furthermore, they argue, "the role of pedagogy is to develop an epistemology of pluralism that provides access without people having to erase or leave behind different subjectivities" (p. 72). Society, from the view of the NLG, should be made up of people with many different interests, points of views, and values, and teaching should be a way of bridging these differences rather than forcing them to change to adhere to a single sense of identity or discourse. The NLG's position essentially means that diverse sets of people together form and inform the civic discourse and that school's place is to enable people to participate in civic life but also maintain their own identity.

Dota 2 provides an interesting parallel here. Many different people want to play the game for different reasons and in different ways: some socially with their friends, others competitively, some as hard-core players looking to maximize their damage output or skill, still others for casual recreation. The game supports all of these different play styles and interests and offers channels for each (competitive play modes, spectator mode, casual mode, and so on), while still maintaining the cohesion of the game as a domain of participation. While these groups create their own emergent spaces (theorycrafting sites, forums, game streams, fan art sites) they still return to the central hub of the game in order to engage with it. In a sense then, Valve has designed a way to help these communities negotiate how and where they play while still contributing to the larger community of *Dota 2*. The game, like schools in the NLG's vision, arbitrates these differences while not forcing one particular play style or identity but allowing players to maintain their "subjectivities."

Furthermore, the game offers insight into how these kinds of spaces might be designed to promote such engagement. The NLG's concept of *design* suggests that designmakers create objects or actions that are meant for others to redesign in order to make them meaningful; that is, to invite "recipients" to take up the design and rework it for themselves. This is how, for the NLG, people create their own social futures. The way Valve includes the various designed-for-emergent elements is an invitation for players to participate in the design and redesign of the game for themselves, as well as to create the social and technical contours of the domain. Valve gives players tools to actively construct their own social futures in a sense, since they can actively engage in the design of their games in ways that are meaningful to them. Players can also navigate and connect emergent sites outside of the game, constructing pathways through particular ways of playing and specific interests that they have. They can connect to people and resources and actively design their experience with learning about the game and align it to their own motivations. In other words, *Dota 2* shows how it might be possible for teachers to provide the means for learners to act as engaged citizens actively participating in the design of their own learning and their own place in the social world around them. *Dota 2* also illustrates how lots of different people can act as teachers regardless of where the teaching happens.

REFERENCES

Bennett, E. (2012). *A four-part model of informal learning: Extending Schugurensky's conceptual model.* Retrieved from www.adulterc.org/proceedings/2012/papers/bennett.pdf

Bessen, J. (2014, August 25). Employers aren't just whining—the "skills gap" is real. *Harvard Business Review.* Retrieved from hbr.org/2014/08/employers-arent-just-whining-the-skills-gap-is-real

Cappelli, P. (2014, August). *Skills gaps, skills shortages and skills mismatches: Evidence for the US.* (Working Paper 20382.). Retrieved from National Bureau of Economic Research website: www.nber.org/papers/w20382

Davidson, C., & Goldberg, D. (2009). *The future of thinking: Learning institutions in a digital age.* The John D. and Catherine T. MacArthur Foundation Reports on Digital Media and Learning. Cambridge, MA: MIT Press.

Falk, J., & Dierking, L. (2010). The 95 percent solution. *American Scientist,* 98(6), 486–493.

Gee, J. P. (2003). *What video games have to teach us about learning and literacy.* New York, NY: Palgrave Macmillan.

Gee, J. P., & Hayes, E. (2010). *Women and gaming: The Sims and 21st century learning.* New York, NY: Palgrave Macmillan.

Grubb, J. (2015, March 24). Dota 2 makes $18 million per month for Valve—but League of Legends makes that much every 5 days [Web article]. Retrieved from http://venturebeat.com/2015/03/24/dota-2-makes-18m-per-month-for-valve-but-league-of-legends-makes-that-much-every-5-days/

Holmes, J. (2015). Distributed teaching and learning systems in Dota 2. *Well Played,* 4(2), 92–111.

Ito, M., Baumer, S., & Bittani, M. (2009). *Hanging out, messing around, and geeking out: Kids living and learning with new media.* The John D. and Catherine T. MacArthur Foundation Reports on Digital Media and Learning. Cambridge, MA: MIT Press.

Ito, M., Gutiérrez, K., Livingstone, S., Penuel B., Rhodes, J., Salen, K. . . . Watkins, C. (2013). *Connected Learning: An agenda for research and design.* Irvine, CA: Digital Media and Learning Research Hub.

Jenkins, H. (2006). *Convergence culture: Where old and new media collide.* New York, NY: New York University Press.

Jenkins, H., Purushotma, R., Weigel, M., Clinton, K., & Robison, A. J. (2009). *Confronting the challenges of participatory culture: Media education for the 21st century.* Cambridge, MA: MIT Press.

Marcus, A., Stoddard, J., & Woodward, W. (2011). *Teaching history with museums.* New York, NY: Routledge.

Marsick, V. (2009). Toward a unifying framework to support informal learning theory, research and practice. *Journal of Workplace Learning,* 21(4), 265–275.

New London Group. (1996). A pedagogy of multiliteracies: Designing social futures. *Harvard Educational Review, 66*(1), 60–92.

Quinn, M. (2014). *Revolutionize learning and development: Performance and innovation strategy for the information age*. New York, NY: Pfeiffer.

Schugurensky, D. (2000). *The forms of informal learning: Towards a conceptualization of the field* (WALL Working Paper No. 19). Retrieved from Ontario Institute for Studies in Education of the University of Toronto website: https://tspace.library.utoronto.ca/handle/1807/2733

Sefton-Green, J. (2004). *Literature review in informal learning with technology outside of school*. NESTA Futurelab Series, report 7, HAL 00190222

Vygotsky, L. S. (1986). *Thought and language*. (Newly revised and edited by Alex Kozulin). Cambridge, MA: MIT Press.

Wick, C., Pollock, R., & Jefferson, A. (2010). *The six disciplines of breakthrough learning: How to turn training and development into business results*. New York, NY: Pfeiffer.

CHAPTER 10

What Scholars of Multiliteracies Can Learn from Embodied Cognition

Mary B. McVee, James R. Gavelek, and Lynn E. Shanahan

Literacy publications, conferences, and books reveal burgeoning explorations of theories, methods, and pedagogical practices related to multimodality that grew out of the multiliteracies framework of the New London Group (NLG) and particularly the work of NLG members Gunther Kress and James Gee. Clearly, scholars have taken seriously the charge of exploring the multiple semiotic modes that create meaning and have done so through varied approaches (Jewitt, 2009). Literacy scholars have explored pedagogical practices, research methodologies, and theoretical nuances of semiotic modes and affordances for meaning-making (e.g., Jewitt & Kress, 2003; Miller & McVee, 2012; Mills, 2016; Serafini, 2013).

"Although communication has always exhibited multimodal qualities, it is since the 1990s that conceptualizing multimodality has enjoyed renewed critical interest. Initially associated with the scholarly work of the NLG, multimodality is rooted in semiotics" (Page, 2010, p. 4). Since the original publication of *A Pedagogy of Multiliteracies* (New London Group, 1996), one of the most influential and dynamic developments in literacy research has been the multimodal turn, or more accurately, the "semiotic turn" (Siegel & Panofsky, 2009, p. 99).

The study of multimodality in general, and semiotic signs in particular, is a complex domain as new media introduce new opportunities for multimodal design and analysis. Also, despite the work that has been carried out, some modes—for example gesture and audio signs—remain underexplored in literacy pedagogy, practice, and learning (cf. Shanahan, 2012; Shanahan & Roof, 2013). Clearly literacy scholars and practitioners can and should continue to explore multiliteracies of design. Scholars should continue to mine the substrata of modes, naming, exploring, analyzing, and articulating pedagogical practices and methods pertaining to multiliteracies, and continuing to examine and delineate learning and teaching through multimodality as grounded in theories of social semiotics (Hodge & Kress, 1988; Kress, 2010).

While we fully support this agenda, in this chapter we look beyond multimodality as grounded in the original NLG multiliteracies publication. To be clear, we are not positing that work on multimodality is complete; recent handbooks (e.g., Jewitt, 2009), newly founded journals (e.g., *Multimodal Communication*; *Visual Communication*), and conferences (e.g., International Conference on Multimodality) make clear that multimodality is still an emerging area of study. Rather, we argue that there are foundational theoretical perspectives related to multimodality and multiliteracies that researchers must attend to in order to fully excavate semiotic signs related to literacy learning, teaching, and meaning-making. By including the concept of embodiment or embodied cognition, we argue that researchers might avoid some of the pitfalls of previous iterations of literacy research (McVee, Dunsmore, & Gavelek, 2005).

This chapter explores the relationship between multimodality, as presented within the multiliteracies framework, and theories of embodiment drawn from second-generation cognitive science. Such perspectives attend to the embodied sense of meaning and to modes as material and ideational tools through which literacy events are mediated. Failure to attend explicitly to the relationship between multimodality and embodiment hampers efforts to further explore principles of multiliteracies set forth in the NLG manifesto and limits explorations of multimodality by reproducing, if even unintentionally, dualist and cognitivist representations of learning and teaching. Given the brevity of this chapter, we will merely scratch the surface of embodied cognition as we consider (1) embodiment and multimodality within the original NLG multiliteracies framework, (2) embodiment in second-generation cognitive science, and (3) embodiment as it matters to scholars and teachers of multimodality and multiliteracies.

EMBODIMENT AND A PEDAGOGY OF MULTILITERACIES

As a construct, embodiment is essential to a multiliteracies framework even though it does not figure prominently in the original NLG (1996) publication. For example, the now-well-known figure included in the original publication (see Figure 10.1) identified a metalanguage for describing modes and design elements and included an outer ring labeled "Multimodal." This figure could have included the context "Embodied Lifeworlds," since the modes (audio, spatial, gestural, visual, and linguistic) are manifestations of lifeworlds referred to in the original publication.

The word "embody" does appear during discussion of the importance of design: "Different conceptions of education and society lead to

Figure 10.1. New London Group Manifesto Chart

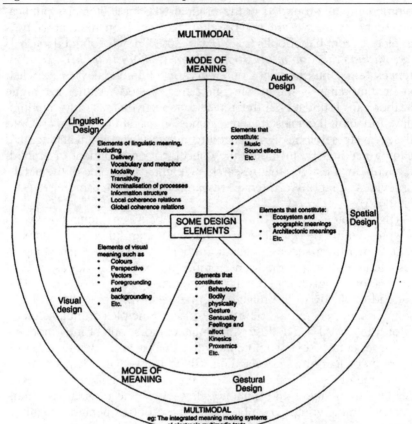

very specific forms of curriculum and pedagogy, which in turn *embody* [emphasis added] designs for social futures" (p. 73). The term "embody" is used generally to indicate the ways in which design is situated within curriculum and pedagogy that, in turn, affect how design, available design, and re-design are employed in the context of lifeworlds.

In the original multiliteracies publication, a second reference to embodiment is more substantial, because it connotes a particular theory of human mind and learning:

Our view of mind, society, and learning is based on the assumption that the human mind is *embodied* [emphasis added], situated, and social. That is, human knowledge is initially developed not as "general and abstract," but as embedded in social, cultural, and material contexts. Further, human knowledge is initially developed as part and parcel of collaborative interactions with others of diverse skills, backgrounds, and perspectives joined

together in a particular epistemic community, that is, a community of learners engaged in common practices centered around a specific (historically
and socially constituted) domain of knowledge. (NLG, 1996, p. 82)

Here, the NLG is explicit: "the human mind is embodied, situated, and social." These themes were articulated throughout the original
publication in relation to discourse, design, pedagogy, literacy, and
multiliteracies. Clearly there are connections between multimodality
(i.e., experiencing the world through our senses) and embodiment.
After all, the human organism can only experience the world through
sensory modes because it has a body capable of perceiving *and* enacting through the senses, a point made by John Dewey in 1896. While
the idea of embodiment was implied in the 1996 NLG publication, it
was not foregrounded or explicitly theorized in the original multiliteracies publication or in the edited volume (Cope & Kalantzis, 2000),
although, as discussed below, members of the NLG have explored perspectives related to embodiment in their work. The lack of explicit
theory and development of the construct in relation to multiliteracies
may be one reason why literacy researchers have been slow to take
up explicit discussion and exploration of embodiment. We take up this
discussion from the perspective of second-generation cognitive science
but acknowledge that critical social theorists (e.g., Bourdieu, Deleuze,
Foucault, Freire) also make valuable and important connections to embodiment. We do not, however, have sufficient space to address those
intersections in this chapter.

THE MEANING OF EMBODIMENT

Some original NLG members have directly discussed embodiment.
Gee (2004) argues, for example, that learning and reading—acts often
viewed primarily, or even exclusively, as cognitive—are not only social
but also embodied. Gee writes:

> Learning does not work well when learners are forced to check their bodies
> at the schoolroom door like guns in the old West. School learning is often
> about disembodied minds learning outside any context of decisions and
> actions. When people learn something as a cultural process their bodies are
> involved because cultural learning always involves having specific experi-
> ences that facilitate learning, not just memorizing words. (p. 39)

Gee (2000) also refers to this separation of mind/body indirectly
in the NLG multiliteracies book (Cope & Kalantzis, 2000). He links the
mind/body to culture, language, and socioeconomic class when noting

that discourses of school often force learners to "exit" their "lifeworlds" (Gee, 2000, p. 66). Rather than draw from embodied experiences of everyday life, students must draw upon experiences—often highly decontextualized and abstracted—in school settings.

The notion of embodiment lines up particularly well with the notion of lifeworlds referred to in the original NLG publication and later articulated in various publications by Gee (2000, 2007, 2008) and Kalantzis and Cope (2008, 2012). Around the time of the original NLG publication, interdisciplinary groups of scholars (e.g., Varela, Thompson, & Rosch, 1991; Lakoff & Johnson, 1999) were beginning to explore embodiment. Johnson (1987) writes of embodiment:

> Meaning includes patterns of embodied experience and preconceptual structures of our sensibility (i.e., our mode of perception, or orienting ourselves, and of interacting with other objects, events, or persons). These embodied patterns do not remain private or peculiar to the person who experiences them. Our community helps us interpret and codify many of our felt patterns. They become shared cultural modes of experience and help to determine the nature of our meaningful, coherent understanding of our "world." (p. 14)

Although Johnson's ideas may not seem radical in the present day, in the 1980s the concept of mind was largely thought of as a computer with inputs, scripts, and output—a metaphor that eschewed the social, transactional, and embodied (McVee, Dunsmore, & Gavelek, 2005). At the same time, scholars across disciplines such as linguistics, philosophy, and psychology were working to explore new metaphors of mind as pattern recognizer or connected network (Clark, 1993). Philosopher Mark Johnson refers to these multimodal actions and experiences using Dewey's term, the "body-mind" (Johnson, 2007, p. 139). Johnson notes that much of what we know comes through a "felt sense" (p. 26) even before we have conscious awareness of those ideas, an idea also expressed earlier by William James (1890) who famously said "as we think we feel our bodily selves as the seat of the thinking" (p. 242). Such learning is something rooted in experience, action, and the body rather than an abstracted cognition or mental process.

This notion of the body-mind is important as it relates to dualism. Dualism presupposes that humans have both physical and mental properties and that these properties are separate or discrete. In contrast, embodiment posits that thought is not just about mental process or the brain, and while the brain is an obviously necessary organ for learning, it is not all that is necessary. The body and the senses are essential for cognition, even in areas often thought of as most abstract, such as mathematics (cf. Edwards, Ferrara, & Moore-Russo, 2014; Núñez, 2008). That bodily senses are essential to learning is unlikely to be disputed by those involved in education, but despite this, many educational policies and pedagogies treat children as if they were disembodied brains fit for only cognitive mental processing. It is incredibly challenging to break out of the dualist epistemologies that undergird views of education and learning because our own learning and life experience is steeped in these epistemologies.

Imagine this scenario. Children work in an individualized reading program based on computer assessments of reading fluency. This is the majority of their reading program (i.e., little classroom time is spent on authentic engagement with texts).

Compare Figure 10.2 to an illustration titled "At School" by the artist Jean Marc Côté (circa 1900) (Figure 10.3). The illustration in Figure 10.3 is from a series first published in France to envision what the world would look like in the year 2000. Looking at the pictures in tandem is intriguing. First, the underlying metaphor for both educational practices is knowledge or learning as transmission. In Figure 10.2 no teacher is present, whereas in Figure 10.3, the teacher's role is to feed books into the hopper. The hopper breaks down texts/knowledge to be transmitted directly by wires to student learners. How different is this scenario from much of what goes on in 21st century classrooms governed by high-stakes test preparation?

We cannot know what other activities the children in Figure 10.2 have engaged in, although presently there is growing concern about the lack of physical movement and recess in U.S. schools (Barros, Silver, &

Figure 10.2. Children Working on a Reading-Based Computer Program

Figure 10.3. *At School* by Jean Marc Côté

Stein, 2009). But, both images represent a long-held belief in Western societies, that learning, and particularly reading, is something abstract that happens in the head, something separate from the world. Consider the wires in Figure 10.3, which connect only to the heads/brains of the students, while all the bodies sit still in the same forward-facing position. It is a dualist representation of knower as separate from known, learner separate from the act and actions of learning. This notion of "in-the-head" learning is continually recycled in western educational movements.

Consider the current emphasis on brain-based learning. One of the problems with brain-based learning as a term (not necessarily the science behind it although some of that is questionable as well [e.g., Hruby & Goswami, 2013]), is that the term "brain-based learning" repeats the cognitivist idea that learning or information processing happens only in the brain—that our brains are what really matters. The question here is not *do* brains matter—they most surely do—but the question is *how* do brains matter.

Shapiro (2011a, 2011b) talks about embodied cognition using this comparison. Consider the engine of a car. One could argue that the engine is the most important part of a car. After all, if the engine is removed, all the other systems go offline. However, if we tend only to the engine, ignoring all other parts, we are not attending to the whole system. A car needs fuel to go, tires to move forward as well as many other working parts. By extension, if we consider reductive, schoolish practices, a narrow focus on basic skills, and even current talk about brain-based learning, our attention is on the engine—the brain, mental processes of cognition—while ignoring the other relevant aspects of the body that function as a system to support embodied learning.

Studies in neuroscience across a number of interdisciplinary fields, including longstanding work by Lakoff and Johnson (1980, 1999), support the notion that human learning and development are profoundly embodied. Embodied cognition brings a highly complementary perspective to existing work on multiliteracies, design, and multimodality. In particular, embodied knowledge foregrounds engagement and action through experience in the ways that Dewey, Rosenblatt, James, and others wrote about in the early 20th century and that the NLG highlighted in writing about multiliteracies.

EMBODIMENT AND MULTIMODALITY

Building on the work of the NLG, multiliteracies, and multimodality, Miller (2013) has made one of the most explicit linkages between multimodality and embodiment in the context of literacy research and second-generation cognitive science. In a metasynthesis of research related to digital multimodal composing, Miller writes: "Multimodal text creation in diverse sociocultural contexts draws on and develops embodied experience, thus developing embodied cognition through multimodal tools. In the digital world, youth have first-hand experiences with these ways of understanding in newly available texts, literacies, and representational modes" (p. 389). Miller observes that key concepts in multimodality such as transmediation are related to embodiment and, in particular, to embodied learning and lifeworlds (2013, pp. 418–420; Miller & McVee, 2012).

It is important to note here that *transmediation* indicates "translation of content from one sign system into another" (Suhor, 1984, p. 250) or what Kress refers to as "transduction" (e.g., Bezemer & Kress, 2008, p. 175). This translation process is more than cognitive but may foster development of a wide range of cognitive, aesthetic, and psychomotor skills which remain untapped in most traditional classrooms. Transmediation can be highly generative and engaging for students, enabling design and meaning-making beyond typical school-like practices and allowing learners to make connections to their own lived experiences (i.e., lifeworlds) (cf. Bailey, 2006; Mills, 2011; Bruce & Chiu, 2015).

The idea of transmediation is one point where embodied perspectives become critically important to understanding and conceptualizing multimodality within a multiliteracies framework. It is not that the perception of modes leads to construction of new schemata or conceptual knowledge becoming "cognitivized" and therefore important.

While there clearly is a perceptual aspect to mode, the holistic process includes *perceptual* and *enactive* dimensions of knowledge even for language-based practices such as narrative (Caracciolo, 2012). In contrast, many educational settings value internalized cognitive skills (e.g., getting a correct answer, explaining a sound rationale, decoding a word, interpreting a poem correctly). Contrast this hyper-cognitive view of learning with Kress's (2010) descriptions of modes:

> In the reception of a sign the *materiality* of modes interacts with the physiology of bodies. When I see a gesture I understand it in large part in an action of "silent" or actual *mimesis* (Wulf, 2005): I come to understand its meaning—say the extent of the sweep of a hand-movement or its pace—mimetically both by an inner, invisible, "parallel" performance for myself or through an outer, visible performance, in which I experience in my body what the meaning of that gesture might be. I have caught myself attempting to imitate gestures which I had noticed in order to "feel" their meaning. There are, as well, the meanings suggested by signs in the accompanying environment. Signs made in gesture are culturally shaped as are all the signs in any mode. (Kress, 2010, p. 76)

Kress's description here is similar to what Johnson, Dewey, and James have described and what we referred to earlier as "felt sense"—the idea that we feel meaning in our bodies as much as we think meaning in our heads.

Kress's writing also provides an interesting example of the ties between multimodality and embodiment since it echoes the description of mirror neurons as described by Vittorio Gallese. Gallese (2009) writes: "The discovery of mirror neurons and of other mirroring mechanisms in the human brain shows that the very same neural substrates are activated when these expressive acts are both executed and perceived" (p. 520). This means that neurons in the brain of the person watching a gesture are activated similarly to those of the individual making the gesture. Mirror neurons are but one example of discoveries that support the idea that the body plays a primary role in the construction of knowledge through perception, enaction, and transaction.

Research in literacy education and pedagogy pertaining to the linguistic, social, and now social semiotic turn make clear that culture, social interaction, and language are critical elements of child development. But even linguistic signs are mediated in embodied ways through pitch and prosody. Consider, for example, how a child in utero will respond and move toward a mother's voice. Children acquire language as they move through the world and engage with others in embodied actions and spaces. Deb Roy's *Birth of a Word* (2011) provides a brilliant demonstration of this. Roy video-recorded nearly every moment of his young son's life—all embodied actions and interactions and language interactions—until his son clearly produced his first word, "water." Roy demonstrates that "water" is not grounded in mental structures but in the spaces, social interactions, and embodied experiences around the thing called "water."

THE IMPORTANCE OF EMBODIMENT IN THE CONCEPTS OF MULTIMODALITY AND MULTILITERACIES

Modes are clearly enacted and perceived only through the body. For example, we use sight to read images in terms of color, shape, spatial representation and so on. In much multiliteracies research to date, the body figures implicitly rather than explicitly (Leander & Boldt, 2013). It is not merely the taking in of semiotic signs and the creating of semiotic signs that hold the most dynamic power for multimodality. Rather it is the fact that these signs are grounded in the body-mind. A focus on design, redesign, available design without explicit attention to the body-mind runs the risk of foregrounding aspects of design such as visual grammars and metalanguages rather than the ways in which designs are grounded in the body-mind and embodied lifeworlds of children, youth, and teachers.

There is often a misunderstanding among those unfamiliar with multiliteracies and multimodality, in particular, that multimodal teaching and learning is merely "hands-on" practice. Many teachers will even comment, "I already do hands-on learning." But what we are positing here is much more than hands-on learning. It is a paradigm shift that involves radically transforming our perspective so that we are considering "minds-on–bodies-on" as students engage the body-mind and researchers consider what it means to learn from a body-mind perspective.

Ben, an emerging bilingual who had been in the U.S. for only 6 months, worked across several days with Dimitri to build a rubber band–powered car. At several points Ben actually indicated aloud that he could not express his ideas in English, but he was able to communicate by drawing, gesturing, demonstrating with artifacts, and even by making engine noises. Observing these embodied interactions makes clear why scholars have asserted that "Children enter language hands first" (Goldin-Meadow, 2007, p. 741).

As Ben worked to communicate, his partner Dimitri played an active role in listening, asking questions, and also engaging with artifacts. While we could break this interaction down into different modalities or discuss transmediation across modes, we contend that the meaning-making was not in the mode but in the transaction of body-mind-action-artifact. Focusing on multimodality is necessary but not sufficient to explain the dynamic learning that took place in this context.

CONCLUSION

In sum, there are several principles that we encourage researchers and educators to consider more directly with regard to multimodality and multiliteracies:

1. Our biological structures determine our sensory interactions with the world.
2. The representations of these interactions exist in the body-mind, that is, at the point of perception and enaction.
3. This knowledge of the body-mind is situated in the transactions between the individual and the world.
4. Such transactions are mediated by socially and culturally enacted practices.
5. These practices are carried out through material artifacts, felt sense, and actions.

There are also numerous questions that researchers can explore related to the body-mind. For example, what is the relationship between transmediation/transduction, embodiment, and multiliteracies? What affordances emerge when multimodality is studied as transaction and not only as design? How do ideas surrounding activity, action, and space change when teachers foreground embodied learning alongside design? How might perspectives of embodiment and multimodal design be used synergistically to encourage individuals to explore race, gender, class, and language within a multiliteracies framework? These are but a few of the many questions that have yet to be explored.

REFERENCES

Bailey, N. M. (2006). *Designing social futures: Adolescent literacy in and for new times.* (Unpublished doctoral dissertation). State University of New York, Buffalo, NY.

Barros, R. M., Silver, E., & Stein, E. K. (2009). School recess and group classroom behavior. *Pediatrics, 123*(2), 431–436.

Bezemer, J., & Kress, G. (2008). Writing in multimodal texts: A social semiotic account of designs for learning. *Written Communication, 25*(2), 166–195.

Bruce, D., & Chiu, M. M. (2015). Composing with new technology: Teacher reflections on learning digital video. *Journal of Teacher Education, 66*(3), 272–287.

Caracciolo, M. (2012). Narrative, meaning, interpretation: An enactivist approach. *Phenomenology and the Cognitive Sciences, 11*(3), 367–384.

Clark, A. (1993). *Associative engines: Connectionism, concepts, and representational change*. Cambridge, MA: The MIT Press.

Cope, B., & Kalantzis, M. (Eds.). (2000). *Multiliteracies: Literacy learning and the design of social futures*. New York, NY: Routledge.

Dewey, J. (1896). The reflex arc concept in psychology. *The Psychological Review, III*(4), 357–370. Retrieved from http://www.comp.dit.ie/dgordon/Courses/ILT/ILT0003/TheReflexArcConceptIinPsychology.pdf

Edwards, L. D., Ferrara, F., & Moore-Russo, D. (Eds.). (2014). *Emerging perspectives on gesture and embodiment in mathematics*. Charlotte, NC: Information Age Publishing.

Gallese, V. (2009). Mirror neurons, embodied simulation, and the neural basis of social identification. *Psychoanalytic Dialogues, 19*, 519–536.

Gee, J. P. (2000). New people in new worlds: Networks, the new capitalism. In B. Cope & M. Kalantzis (Eds.), *Multiliteracies: Literacy learning and the design of social futures* (pp. 43–68). New York, NY: Routledge.

Gee, J. P. (2004). *Situated language and learning*. New York, NY: Routledge.

Gee, J. P. (2007). *What video games have to teach us about learning and literacy* (2nd ed.). New York, NY: Palgrave Macmillan.

Gee, J. P. (2008). Video games and embodiment. *Games and Culture, 3*(3–4), 253–263.

Goldin-Meadow, S. (2007). Pointing sets the stage for learning language— and creating language. *Child Development, 78*(3), 741–745.

Hodge, R., & Kress, G. (1988). *Social semiotics*. Ithaca, NY: Cornell University.

Hruby, G., & Goswami, U. (2013). Educational neuroscience for reading education researchers. In D. Alvermann, N. Unrau, & R. Ruddell (Eds.), *Theoretical models and processes of reading* (6th ed., pp. 558–588). Newark, DE: International Reading Association.

James, W. (1890). *The principles of psychology* (Vol. 1). New York, NY: Henry Holt & Co.

Jewitt, C. (Ed.). (2009). *The Routledge handbook of multimodal analysis*. London, UK: Routledge.

Jewitt, C., & Kress, G. (Eds.). (2003). *Multimodal literacy*. New York, NY: Peter Lang.

Johnson, M. (1987). *The body and the mind: The bodily basis of meaning, imagination, and reason*. Chicago, IL: The University of Chicago Press.

Johnson, M. (2007). *The meaning of the body: Aesthetics of human understanding*. Chicago, IL: University of Chicago Press.

Kalantzis, M., & Cope, B. (2008). *New learning: Elements of a science of education*. New York, NY: Cambridge University Press.

Kalantzis, M., & Cope, B. (2012). *Literacies*. New York, NY: Cambridge University Press.

Kress, G. (2010). *Multimodality: A social semiotic approach to contemporary communication*. New York, NY: Routledge.

Lakoff, G. J., & Johnson, M. (1980). *Metaphors we live by*. Chicago, IL: University of Chicago Press.

Lakoff, G., & Johnson, M. (1999). *Philosophy in the flesh: The embodied mind and its challenge to Western thought*. New York, NY: Basic Books.

Leander, K., & Boldt, G. (2013). Rereading "A pedagogy of multiliteracies": Bodies, texts, and emergence. *Journal of Literacy Research, 45*(1), 22–46.

McVee, M. B., Dunsmore, K. L., & Gavelek, J. R. (2005). Schema theory revisited. *Review of Educational Research, 75*(4), 531–566.

Miller, S. M. (2013). A research metasynthesis on digital video composing in classrooms: An evidence-based framework toward a pedagogy for embodied learning. *Journal of Literacy Research, 45*(4), 386–430.

Miller, S. M., & McVee, M. B. (2012). *Multimodal composing: Learning and teaching for the digital world*. New York, NY: Routledge.

Mills, K. A. (2011). "I'm making it different to the book": Transmediation in young children's multimodal and digital texts. *Australasian Journal of Early Childhood, 36*(3), 56–65.

Mills, K. A. (2016). *Literacy theories for the digital age*. Bristol, UK: Multilingual Matters.

New London Group (1996). A pedagogy of multiliteracies: Designing social futures. In B. Cope & M. Kalantzis (Eds.), *Multiliteracies: Literacy learning and the design of social futures* (pp. 9–37). New York, NY: Routledge.

Núñez, R. E. (2008). Mathematics, the ultimate challenge to embodiment: Truth and the grounding of axiomatic systems. In P. Calvo & T. Gomila (Eds.), *Handbook of cognitive science: An embodied approach* (pp. 333–353). San Diego, CA: Elsevier.

Page, R. (2010). Re-examining narrativity: Small stories in status updates. *Text & Talk, 30*(4), 423–444.

Roy, D. (2011, March). The birth of a word [TED Talk audio file] Retrieved from http://www.ted.com/talks/deb_roy_the_birth_of_a_word?language=en.

Serafini, F. (2013). *Reading the visual: An introduction to teaching multimodal literacy*. New York, NY: Teachers College Press.

Shanahan, L. (2012). Use of sound with digital text: Moving beyond sound as an add-on or decoration. *Contemporary Issues in Technology and Teacher Education, 12*(3), 264–285.

Shanahan, L. E., & Roof, L. M. (2013). Developing strategic readers: A multimodal analysis of a primary school teacher's use of speech, gesture, and artefacts. *Literacy, 47*(3), 157–164.

Shapiro, L. (2011a). *Embodied cognition*. New York, NY: Routledge.

Shapiro, L. (2011b, March 25). Embodied cognition with Lawrence Shapiro [Audio podcast]. Retrieved from http://brainsciencepodcast.com/bsp/embodied-cognition-with-lawrence-shapiro-bsp-73.html

Siegel, M., & Panofsky, C. P. (2009). Designs for multimodality in literacy studies: Explorations in analysis. *Literacy Research Association Yearbook, 58*, 99–111.

Suhor, C. (1984). Towards a semiotic-based curriculum. *Journal of Curriculum Studies, 16*(3), 247–257.

Varela, F. J., Thompson, E., & Rosch, E. (1991). *The embodied mind: Cognitive science and human experience.* Cambridge, MA: The MIT Press.

CHAPTER 11

The Expression of Multiliteracies and Multimodalities in Play

Karen Wohlwend

Two decades have passed since the New London Group (NLG, 1996) radically expanded the definition of literacy in the landmark manifesto *A Pedagogy of Multiliteracies,* which introduced the notion that literacies are multiple, both modally and culturally. This reconceptualization extended the concept of *text* to include animation, video, music, websites, drama, and live-action play, among other multimodal forms for making meaning. Since that time, digital technologies and global networks have stretched multiliteracies even further. When information is conveyed not through print but primarily through image, video, and apps, more expansive methodologies and pedagogies are needed to identify and respond to the complexity and movement of multibodied and multispatial interactions. This is particularly true in *play*, where players collaborate, compete, or otherwise coordinate activity to create and maintain a shared pretend scenario or game. This chapter examines the NLG's foundational concepts of multimodal design and multiliteracies, as well as recent critiques of the concepts, to understand where these concepts fit well with play, where play slips past definition, and how these slippages might inform contemporary pedagogies.

MULTILITERACIES AND PLAY

The NLG's recognition that literacies are multiple and diverse, situated in everyday practices, created a major strand of multiliteracies research that critically engages culture as more than a universalized monolith. Literacies involve both embodied ways of using materials to make meanings and sets of physical tools and the artifacts they produce. Literacies, like all cultural tools, can provoke power relationships, which means reading, writing, playing, and designing are ideological practices to wield rather than autonomous skill sets to master (Street, 1995). Over time, particular ways with literacies and their meaning-products come to be expected and tacitly valued within cultural groups. The situated nature of literacy in *A Pedagogy of Multiliteracies* drew upon NLG author James Paul Gee's (1996) theorization of Discourse, in which certain combinations of reading, writing, playing, or making are accompanied by ways of talking, sitting, walking, eating, and so on, and their co-occurrence comes to be expected as the normal way of being and doing among a group of people. Although not an NLG participant, linguistic anthropologist Ron Scollon shared many of the same commitments to the study of language and literacy in cultural contexts: Literacy practices are imbricated and entangled with language practices and other social practices. For example, Scollon's *nexus of practice* explains how webs of social practices make up naturalized ways of participating and mediating cultures. Particular combinations of practices act as markers of membership and identity (e.g., insider/outsider; novice/expert) that uphold unspoken patterns of inclusion and exclusion, justified by widely circulating discourses (Scollon, 2001; Gee, 1996, 1999). Literacies are powerful ways of making meaning and belonging, situated in a culture's mesh of engrained social practices and dispositions, materialized in automatic routines that members expect of one another.

Mediated discourse theory provides a thread to connect multiliteracies to cultural production in play. In mediated discourse theory (Vygotsky, 1978; Wertsch, 1991), meanings are mediated, or co-constructed and made accessible, through social practices with cultural tools. When children come together in play, they mediate conventional meanings of physical actions and material props through negotiation, until they agree upon who is playing whom and what their characters will do and say. These agreed-upon meanings are improvised in the moment with materials that are available in the immediate environment and permitted for children's use according to family, school, or other institutional rules. An example illustrates this: A group of kindergarten boys rolling and taping paper tubes instantly recognized the tubes as props—*Star Wars* light sabers—in response to one child's fencing move that initiated a silent multiplayer duel sequence. Just as quickly, when the teacher approached, they improvised, flipping their paper tubes sideways to turn prohibited pretend weapons into electric eels and an undersea pretense that would be tolerated at school.

> It is through play that children foreground particular potential meanings of artifacts while backgrounding others by adding physical play actions, talk, and sound effects that make one meaning more relevant. We tend to look for some print on a page when we consider children's literacy products and to discount and overlook the action texts that children play. When

the boys enacted eels, they quietly held the tubes horizontally and maneu-
vered individually, walking side-by-side, sometimes tumbling the tubes in
slow circling motions or undulating waves. When they enacted light sabers,
they turned toward each other, tilted the tubes diagonally or vertically, and
voiced the shoom, shoom, shoom, of humming light sabers as they engaged each other in momentary fencing moves. (Wohlwend, 2013, p. 112)

In this way, a toy (e.g., neon-glowing plastic light saber or child-
made rolled paper tube substitute) is an aggregate of meanings and materials situated in a cultural context, entangled with the power relations
and prevailing discourses in global flows that circulate in the classroom
(e.g., teacher/student power relations in educational discourses such as
developmentally appropriate practice) and outside school (e.g., popular
media fan identities and discourses). Discourses justify particular ways
of "using language, other symbolic expressions, and 'artifacts,' of thinking, feeling, believing, valuing, and acting that can be used to identify
oneself as a member" (Gee, 1996, p. 131). Educational discourses make
some materials, modes, and meanings unavailable in classrooms (e.g.,
children should be reading and writing and not playing, pretend weapons are not allowed in school). A still-prevalent singular print-intensive
autonomous model (Street, 1995) keeps school literacy securely insulat-
ed, boxed in on all sides by a grade level and by a discipline matrix of
tightly-framed standards.

Multimodality and Play

Another NLG legacy redefined Design, recognizing critical agency in
designers' active appropriation that strategically makes or redesigns
texts to fit their social purposes using available resources. This concept
drew on NLG author Gunther Kress's (1997) research on early writing
that theorized young children as designers who craft drawings, block
constructions, or writings intentionally. Kress closely followed the drawing and writing of young children, demonstrating how young children
developed a sense of agency in the complex wielding of color, line,
and shape in paper car constructions. Careful observation revealed children's inventive and thoughtful decisions about, say, where to cross a
T, or how to color a paper car to make it appear shiny, and when to
cut it out from its paper frame to turn a representation into an object for
play. Kress's analysis (1997) of a child's action cutting out a car brings
a drawing or representation into the world of action and is fundamental to understanding children's action texts. Children are not limited to
representing their thinking on paper; they craft with actions, making
worlds, and things with enough substance to support interactions in

three dimensions. "The relation between form and meaning is a motivated one, and this motivation arises out of the young maker's interest" (Kress, 1997, p. 142). Meanings are motivated by the physical properties of materials, which influence their sensory affordances and their sociocultural uses. The interplay of semiotics, materiality, and culture constitutes a mode—a sensory aspect of the environment in a system of culturally-produced meanings developed over histories of use (Kress, 1997, 2003; Pahl & Rowsell, 2010). Figure 11.1 displays a non-exhaustive range of modes that can provide resources for meaning-making with bodies, places, and things.

Kress (1997) showed that children at play demonstrate signs that they craft with bodies and modes in their environments, not to compensate for their emergent language but because they intend to convey the richest meanings possible in their designs. In *A Pedagogy of Multiliteracies,* the relationships among Design, Redesign, and Available Designs have implications for early literacy research and teaching, shifting the focus from young children's emerging competencies with literacy skills to their purposeful, playful engagements in multimodal composition and cultural production. This repositions children as knowledgeable cultural participants. Even very young children are experienced media consumers who interact daily with video, apps, games, and other multimedia. Through these media histories, children develop expectations for multimodal interactions (e.g., visual effects, music, speech, scene layout, sound effects, etc.) according to film, television, and videogame conventions. In other words, young literacy

Figure 11.1. A Sampling of Action Modes

	Embodied	Environmental	Designed
Visual	Gaze	Color	Image, Print
Audio	Speech	Sound	Sound Effect, Music
Spatial	Movement	Layout	Animation, Landscape
Gestural	Posture, Gesture	Proxemics	Affect
Tactile	Haptic	Texture, Temperature	Shape, Depth

learners *think in film*, knowing that action-based performances on screens mean differently than page-based formats. In videos or animations, meanings are created in an enacted narrative but also through fleeting multimodal interactions in the composition of scenes, unfolding action sequences of shots within scenes, and juxtaposed relationships among subjects and objects within a shot.

However, play is an unruly literacy, flexible and ambiguous (Sutton-Smith, 1997), whimsical and capricious, enabling both doings and undoings. Its fluidity of meaning creates a productive tension with pedagogical aims such as the need for cohesion in storytelling. This was a challenge that early childhood teachers in Literacy Playshop studies faced when trying to hold on to children's free-flowing and meandering play narratives, "like nailing Jell-O to a wall" (Wohlwend, Buchholz, Wessel-Powell, Coggin, & Husbye, 2013, p. 45). Tensions among play and storytelling are further complicated when collaborative production with digital technologies intersects with children's participation that unfolds according to their purposes, social relationships, play histories, and friendships in classroom and popular cultures (Wohlwend, 2011b).

Modal Bubbling

The study of play has prompted researchers and theorists to search for new theoretical and inquiry approaches that can account for its emergent, contentious, joyful, and multiply messy character, and this search leads to new understandings of literacies in general. In children's pretend play, player actions and interactions with other players and materials *are* the meanings; thus the foregrounded modes convey meanings that move across space and time. Play scenarios are crafted with bodies, modes, and objects in moments of experience that are emergent, spontaneous, and often temporary. Play exists in the moment, challenging the future-focused concept of design articulated in *A Pedagogy of Multiliteracies*. This is a main premise of a landmark critique of NLG's privileging of linguistic text and representation. Through a Deleuzian analysis of a boy's joyful and intense manga play, Leander and Boldt (2013) examined his activity as an emergent, emotion-packed, and embodied literacy performance in a mobile, meaningful, lived, and felt experience—one that should not be analytically pinned down and flattened into a strategic, orderly, and intentional text.

In play, collaborative meanings are imagined with immediate materials in the moment, improvisations that are transitory and always provisional. An imagined scenario is a collective representation of an agreed-upon context that suspends (one) reality and replaces its conventional meanings of things in an immediate place with pretend ones.

In the next section, I explore a more mobile and less *planned model* of multimodality that accounts for the quicksilver shifts in moments of experience as modes bubble up, grow, shrink, and burst to be replaced by another.

ANALYZING PLAY ACTIONS, MODES, AND MEANINGS

Jewitt (2009) makes a distinction among approaches to multimodal analysis, including two that were represented in *A Pedagogy of Multiliteracies*: a social semiotic approach focused on textual analysis of meanings and multimodality (e.g., NLG's Fairclough and Kress) and a linguistic anthropology approach focused on interactional analysis of discourse and cultural contexts (e.g., NLG's Gee and Cazden; also Scollon). In the anthropological strand, Norris (2004) developed a multimodal interactional analytic tool—*modal density*—that provides a way to examine literacy interactions for *modal complexity*, or the number of modes that are in active use, and *modal intensity*, or the relative attention each mode attracts or requires. In this way, the relative modal density of a particular event can be represented in a modal map where a large number of circles indicate high modal complexity and larger circles to indicate higher intensity of more frequently used or foregrounded modes. Interestingly, in social semiotic framing, modes also can be compared for their functional load, that is, to see which mode is doing more work in carrying a design's meaning (Kress & Jewitt, 2003). Both approaches are relevant in analyzing play activity.

The construct of modal density captures the juxtaposition of modes in a moment of experience and allows an unhinging or mapping of young children's play and media production as emergent collaborative flows of embodied actions, modes, and meanings, rather than individual and fixed processes, products, or effects of discourse. Specifically, how does action-oriented analysis of young children's digital storytelling reveal their negotiation of the complexity of an emergent and fluid text? In this view, play is a literacy, a set of social and semiotic practices that produces action texts, animated or live-action pretense collaboratively enacted with other players in an imaginary context, whether a dollhouse, a puppet show, an animation app, or a video game. I have described this kind of interactive spatial production as an action text, focusing on its co-enacted pretense. This perspective recognizes play not only as a literacy but also as a tactic, a way of remaking power relations by making alternative spaces through pretend as-if worlds (Wohlwend, 2011b). To examine literacy practices and material artifacts as sites of engagement and to understand play cultures in early childhood settings, I draw on nexus of practice to analyze how children wield literacies when they play together, tracking nexus in their collaborative production and negotiation of shared meanings to see how play affects patterns of belonging in school and peer cultures.

The following vignette is excerpted from a study of multimodality and meaning-making action texts in children's play, films, and media production in ongoing ethnographic Literacy Playshop research (Wohlwend et al., 2013) in early childhood classrooms (10 teachers, more than 120 3- to 8-year-old children). This episode of classroom play and filmmaking was recorded in a K–1 classroom where two teachers co-taught 50 5- to 7-year-old children during a 1-month thematic unit on storytelling, imagination, and making. Video analysis programs synchronized video data of children's play and filmmaking activities with video of children's handling of video cameras, puppets, and props while creating films. Mediated discourse analysis identified video clips for close multimodal mapping (Wohlwend, 2011a) of modal complexity (Norris, 2004) to locate changes in film meanings and classroom participation.

An Action Text: Coloring Arms and Quacking Hands

Three children are seated on the carpet of the K–1 classroom, liberally coloring their forearms and hands with patches of green, yellow, orange, and blue, using watercolor markers. One child picks up the digital camera, and with it the roles of camera operator and director. Aiming the camera at one of two girls, he signals "Go!" She immediately arches her mallard-colored arm and makes quacking gestures by holding her hand horizontally and touching her thumb to her fingers. Animating her hand as a duck's bill, she quacks to the tune "Twinkle, Twinkle, Little Star": "Mwack, mwack, mwack, mwack," and so on. As she sings, the second girl joins in, reaching two quacking hands toward the camera, which creates a blur effect. Cautioning "too close!" the camera operator quickly pulls the camera back to zoom out. At the end of the song, he turns the camera on the other player but she is again decorating her arms. Instead, he turns the camera on his own forearm, playing with movements as he brings his green fingers close to the lens and moves then away again. He accompanies his hand movements with the quacking song, dragging out each syllable slowly, then improvises a burst of sounds and wordplay, "Beesha bosha basha pa pa pa way . . .," punctuated with a few Donald Duck vocalizations.

When a passing child asks, "Why are you coloring on your arms?" the director replies, "It's okay, it's part of our story" and, dropping the pitch of his voice, he switches into his duck character, "Now don't ever ask us again." After reassuring the bystander that they have teacher permission to draw on their bodies, the three players resume filming, alternating turns in front of the camera to continue quacking their varia-tions on the tune. As the film moves from duck to duck, the action and quacking slows to a crawl at times, distorting the syllables and morphing a few notes to a minor key.

Multimodal analysis of this instance of young children's filmmak-ing reveals emergent and improvised meanings in the manipulations of modes (e.g., proximity, music, color, tempo) in the child-made video. The children moved their hands in and out of the camera frame, filling the screen with blurry images of colorful fingers, slowing down the song and their actions in places, playing with speech sounds to create rhythmic wordplay. Each action, mode, or meaning is further thickened by modal intra-actions within the multiple actions among cameraperson and actors in a collaborating film crew, within the multiple semiotic systems in costume production and performance in a live-action music video, and within the multiple improvised characterizations by multiple actors:

1. Multiple actions overlap in film crew collaboration as children coordinated filmmaking roles in a single film. For example, the cameraperson needed to move the camera away from the actor's hands when she moved too close to the lens while he tried to hold the camera steady. Players also coordinated the timing of their performances, taking individual turns and singing together.
2. Multiple modes combined in multimodal interaction through music, sound effects, color, and movement that enlivened the children's storytelling. The multimodal interaction repeated the meaning "duck" through an exaggerated nasal voice quality, Disney's Donald Duck sound effects, quacking hand gestures, and patches of coloring that match the solid green of a drake's head and dots of brown on forearms that simulated the brown speckling of a feathered body.
3. Multiple meanings pooled in multiplayer improvisations and emerging story ideas in shared pretense. Such storylines vary according to genre. In this music video, rather than proceeding in a beginning-to-end flow of narrative, the children looped the melody over and over, adding variations to create new stanzas.

Semiotic and social effects were created as well by interactions among actions, modes, and meanings. Semiotic effects are visible in the ways modes combine with meaning and mediated actions with cultur-al tools and materials. For example, children designed with the mode *gaze* by attending to subjects in the camera framing or changing the camera angle, panning to capture more action, or zooming in to create a cut-in closeup of quacking hands. These actions held social effects in peer culture when children were included or excluded in shots or activities that conveyed insider status. Children wielded the creative space opened by costume-making to safely transgress school culture. They justified deliberately coloring on their bodies with markers, clearly enjoying the ability to engage in a practice that was against the rules (i.e., "Color on paper, not people"), as it would be in many early childhood classrooms. They also forestalled a peer's threat to tattle by referencing their teacher's approval: "Mrs. B said we could, if it's for our story. And it is."

BUBBLING UP, BUBBLING OVER, AND BURSTING

This moment of coloring arms while another child quacks with hand motions to an improvisation on a nursery rhyme tune, while a third child films the action shows the difficulty of applying simple analytical frames for examining a foregrounded practice to parse out how social actors' attention is divided among modes. In this early childhood example, modes seemed to *bubble up* as a story element emerged, *bubble over* as actions/modes/meanings clumped into assemblages, and then *burst* before disappearing into the background.

> **Bubbling Up:** Children's play texts are emergent and fluid
> (Leander & Boldt, 2013). The action texts are co-constructed in
> a collaboratively imagined context, a fragile and fluid pretense
> sustained by players' shared agreements to pretend this means
> that, which at the same time opens up the played context and its
> underlying pretexts for negotiation, remaking, and improvisation,
> allowing new directions to pop up.
> **Bubbling Over:** The data show productive assemblages of actions,
> modes, and meanings built through repetitions and modes in
> motion. The children's film featured cyclical repetitions of the
> "Twinkle, Twinkle" melody, repetitions that were also remakings
> as different children improvised on the melody. The humor of
> quacking gestures and comical facial expressions was amplified
> by gaze and proximity in camera work, as zooming in and out
> was achieved by physically changing the camera's proximity and
> moving closer to actors' bodies, while actors also changed their
> own proximity by leaning toward and leaning away from the
> camera.
> **Bursting:** Play can be temporary, partial, and fast-paced. The
> transitory meanings and quick transformations in children's
> play are emblematic of its inventiveness and its fragility, where
> meanings change on a whim.

Rather than a modal density measure of user attention or a modal load to measure the relative semiotic strength of a text, I suggest this metaphor of modal bubbling to capture the emergent, productive, and temporary nature of children's play texts (see Figure 11.2).

This analysis of a moment of play reveals the complexity of children's designs created moment-to-moment in collaboration with peers. In the case of classroom filmmaking, additional factors add to the tensions among emergence, production, and transience in their storying. The framing camera lens of a digital camera requires shared onscreen/offscreen awareness by both players and camera operators, as ducks move in and out of frame. These collaborations show children's abilities to imagine what the camera "sees" as they move bodies and cameras to manage multiplayer actions with multiple modes of proximity and image in zoom in/zoom out relationships.

Literacy practices are not static. Instead they are composed of a confluence of actions, modes, and meanings in the trajectories that flow into and emanate from a moment or site of engagement. Mediated discourse analysis takes an action orientation to literacy, materiality, and culture and shines an analytic focus on mediated action, the ways we wield things and rework their meanings to belong. Mediated actions

Figure 11.2. Modal Bubbling: Coloring Arms in Duck Song Film

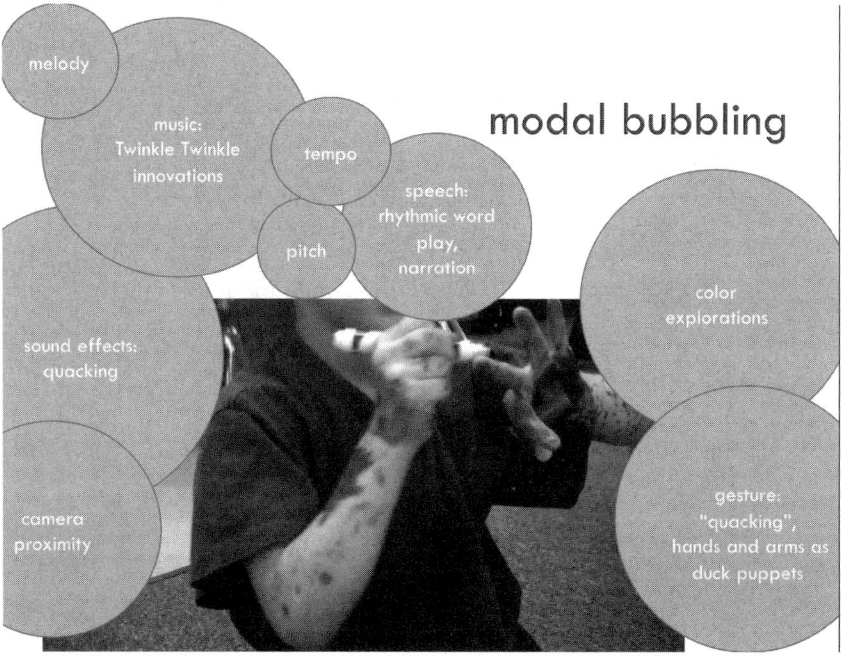

are engrained into bodies through histories of use (Bourdieu, 1977) or ways with things. And at a fundamental level, literacy is how we make meaning with stuff, how we use bodies with tools and materials to fashion artifacts and resemiotize the meanings of the things around us. The products of this meaning-making leave traces that may or may not be tangible and durable objects. I argue that children's pretend play, transitory in the moment, produces a vibrant text full of meanings for its participants. The action texts of play can be transformative whether or not they leave a permanent record through a photo, film, or a saved game.

CONCLUSION

The fluid transformations that occur in children's action texts suggest the potential of play and media production as key sites for understanding new practices of meaning-making and cultural participation for children and youth. Recognizing the semiotic potential of play is key to re-establishing play spaces in early childhood classrooms, spaces that are disappearing as play is squeezed out to prepare children for high-stakes testing. It is just as important to recognize the educational significance of play for older youth and to integrate play into all classrooms. Through play, children can collaboratively engage converging imaginaries that matter to them (Medina & Wohlwend, 2014). In this way, play aligns with NLG's Design and Redesign with potential for transformative effects on texts and equitable participation in school and peer cultures. Play is a literacy for making and remaking taken-for-granted identities and texts that circulate widely through imaginaries, but it is also a literacy for *unmaking,* its bubbling and bursting uniquely suited to respond to fast-paced flows of imaginaries and technologies. Literacy research on play-based pedagogy is urgently needed to understand how play functions as a key meaning-making practice in the context of imaginaries and powerful digital tools that easily record and amplify action texts. Children who already "think in film" need teachers who understand and teach video production. But filmmaking is just a comfortable first step—with familiar elements: a linear text, story arc, and so on. Meanwhile children's lived literacies move on. More responsive and nimble pedagogies are needed now to quickly catch up and follow children across shifting landscapes along the path opened by *A Pedagogy of Multiliteracies.*

REFERENCES

Bourdieu, P. (1977). *Outline of a theory of practice.* Cambridge, UK: Cambridge University Press.

Gee, J. P. (1996). *Social linguistics and literacies: Ideology in Discourses* (2nd ed.). London, UK: Routledge Falmer.

Gee, J. P. (1999). *An introduction to discourse analysis: Theory and method.* London, UK: Routledge.

Jewitt, C. (2009). Different approaches to multimodality. In C. Jewitt (Ed.), *The Routledge handbook of multimodal analysis* (pp. 28–39). London, UK: Routledge.

Kress, G. (1997). *Before writing: Rethinking the paths to literacy.* London, UK: Routledge.

Kress, G. (2003). *Literacy in the new media age.* London, UK: Routledge.

Kress, G., & Jewitt, C. (2003). Introduction. In C. Jewitt & G. Kress (Eds.), *Multimodal literacy* (pp. 1–18). New York, NY: Peter Lang.

Leander, K., & Boldt, G. (2013). Rereading "A pedagogy of multiliteracies": Bodies, texts, and emergence. *Journal of Literacy Research, 45*(1), 22–46.

Medina, C. L., & Wohlwend, K. E. (2014). *Literacy, play, and globalization: Converging imaginaries in children's critical and cultural performances.* New York, NY: Routledge.

New London Group. (1996). A pedagogy of multiliteracies: Designing social futures. *Harvard Educational Review, 66*(1), 60–92.

Norris, S. (2004). *Analyzing multimodal interaction: A methodological framework.* London, UK: Routledge.

Pahl, K., & Rowsell, J. (2010). *Artifactual literacies: Every object tells a story.* New York, NY: Teachers College Press.

Scollon, R. (2001). *Mediated discourse: The nexus of practice.* London, UK: Routledge.

Street, B. V. (1995). *Social literacies: Critical approaches to literary development.* Singapore: Pearson Education Asia.

Sutton-Smith, B. (1997). *The ambiguity of play.* Cambridge, MA: Harvard University Press.

Vygotsky, L. (1978). *Mind in society* (A. Luria, M. Lopez-Morillas, & M. Cole, Trans.). Cambridge, MA: Harvard University Press. (Original work published 1935)

Wertsch, J. V. (1991). *Voices of the mind: A sociocultural approach to mediated action.* Cambridge, MA: Harvard University Press.

Wohlwend, K. E. (2011a). Mapping modes in children's play and design: An action-oriented approach to critical multimodal analysis. In R. Rogers (Ed.), *An introduction to critical discourse analysis in education* (pp. 242–266). Mahwah, NJ: Erlbaum.

Wohlwend, K. E. (2011b). *Playing their way into literacies: Reading, writing, and belonging in the early childhood classroom.* New York, NY: Teachers College Press.

Wohlwend, K. E. (2013). Playing Star Wars under the (teacher's) radar: Detecting kindergartners' action texts and embodied literacies. In V. M. Vasquez & J. W. Wood (Eds.), *Perspectives and provocations in early childhood education* (National Council of Teachers of English Early Childhood Assembly Yearbook) (pp. 105–115). Charlotte, NC: Information Age.

Wohlwend, K. E., Buchholz, B. A., Wessel-Powell, C., Coggin, L. S., & Husbye, N. E. (2013). *Literacy playshop: New literacies, popular media, and play in the early childhood classroom.* New York, NY: Teachers College Press.

CHAPTER 12

Imagination, Creativity, and Design

Dawnene D. Hassett and Christiane L. Wood

Building on the New London Group's (NLG, 1996) depiction of curriculum as a design for social futures, this chapter examines the importance of imagination in the semiotic process of designing and constructing meaning potentials. We provide examples from a study of play, literacy, and innovation (Wood, 2016) that illustrated how children's imaginations work in and through the semiotic processes of meaning-making. These examples served as guides for our thinking about the range of support we can offer children as they draw on their imaginative resources to socialize, create, and innovate with their peers. In the end, we argue that imagination is both serious and playful, guided and spontaneous, and overall, an integral part of the design process within a pedagogy of multiliteracies.

IMAGINATION AND DESIGNS OF MULTIMODAL MEANINGS

Twenty years ago, in their seminal work *A Pedagogy of Multiliteracies*, the NLG advanced the concept of "pedagogy as design," proposing that "*curriculum is a design for social futures*" (1996, p. 73, emphasis in original). Twenty years later, at least in the United States, we see two different visions of curriculum and pedagogy that are at odds with each other, and often are present in classrooms or schools at the same time. The first vision is about preparing children to be uniformly fast and furious reciters of texts and facts supported by rote instruction, similar to that of the 19th century industrial model of top-down, outcomes-driven education. This vision for the future is captured in standardized, uniform, and often scripted curriculum. It is built on the rhetoric of equal access, because theoretically everybody is learning the same thing in an efficient manner. Yet much has been written about literacy education as big business, where market-driven forces not only created the inequalities and fading opportunities that we see today, but also continue to maintain a façade of equal access and education for democracy (e.g.,

Biesta, 2007; Friedrich, Jaastad, & Popkewitz, 2010; Shannon, 2007).

The second vision for education and society focuses on being thoughtful and deliberate about one's pedagogical framework in order to create opportunities to support students' becoming more collaborative, innovative problem-solvers. This vision is evident in the surge of pedagogical trends practiced widely by educators around the globe, such as focused integration of science, technology, engineering, the arts, and math (STEAM), or the implementation of project-based learning (PBL) and makerspaces. These approaches have a larger worldview that sees teachers and students on an equal footing in terms of what they each can bring to a particular project or problem. In terms of literacy education, even schools and classrooms that use mass-marketed standardized curricula tend to have times and spaces where students problem-solve and collaborate with their peers. These times and spaces often involve play and creativity, in reading and writing lessons, but also in literacy activities across the curriculum.

As the NLG (1996) originally noted, "Different conceptions of education and society lead to very specific forms of curriculum and pedagogy, which in turn embody designs for social futures" (p. 73). In this chapter, we address the second vision for education and society, one that is designed for innovation, collaboration, and creativity: the one that focuses on *design* itself. The NLG based its framework for a multiliteracies curriculum around the concept of design, where the already-known conventions and grammars of a semiotic system (*available designs*) are taken up and iteratively transformed through the semiotic process of meaning-making (*designing*) that results in "a new meaning, something through which meaning-makers remake themselves" (p. 76) (*the redesigned*). We use this model of the design process to consider the ways in which imagination is a part of the semiotic process of meaning-making. For our analysis, we also use the elements of design depicted by the NLG as metalanguages to describe and interpret the ways in which different resources offer different ways of designating meaning, knowing full well that designs of meaning operate across modes and are therefore multimodal.

DEFINING IMAGINATION

To define imagination, we turn to Lev Vygotsky (2004), who sees imagination as a creative activity. He makes an important distinction between creative activity and reproductive activity, associating reproductive activity with memory, such as "repeating previously developed and mastered behavioral patterns or resurrecting traces of earlier impressions" (p. 7). Creative activity, on the other hand, is "based on the ability of our brain to combine elements, [and] is called imagination or fantasy in psychology" (p. 9). Unlike reproductive activity, such as recalling where you grew up or repeating a known equation, creative activity requires the creation of new images or actions. According to Vygotsky, "All human activity of this type, activity that results not in the reproduction of previously experienced impressions or actions but in the creation of new images or actions is an example of this second type of creative or combinatorial behavior" (2004, p. 9). For Vygotsky, all human activity of this second type is imaginative.

Imagination in children is something that we think of as quite common, and often directly related to their play. In play, children act from what they know, as they imitate careers and stories from their real lives, including their real lives of watching TV, playing video games, or hearing music. But in imaginative play, children do something more than duplicate what they have seen or heard. To distinguish imaginative play from imitation based on memory, Vygotsky (2004) points out:

> A child's play is not simply a reproduction of what he has experienced, but a creative reworking of the impressions he has acquired. He combines them and uses them to construct a new reality, one that conforms to his own needs and desires. (pp. 11–12)

In play, children are able to create both reality-based imaginations and imagination-based realities, which allow them to design new realities, ways of being, or rules for life.

In relation to the NLG's (1996) framework of the design process, this view of imagination, especially young children's imaginations, helps us to discuss the role of imagination within the semiotic process that takes us from *available designs* through *designing* toward *the redesigned*. While it is very clear that "everything the imagination creates is always based on elements taken from reality" (Vygotsky, 2004, p. 13), which includes the conventions and grammars of *available designs*, imagination also has a complex relationship with reality, such as when the elements we take from reality to feed our imaginations come from other places, such as a ghost story we heard around the campfire or a television show we saw about a moment in history. In these cases, the *available designs* that occur in our realities are the end product of someone else's imaginative creation, combined with our contextual experiences of campfires or our knowledge of history. The imagination's role in the process of *designing*, then, includes the recombination of *available designs* that can correspond to both real and unreal occurrences, experienced vicariously or first hand. As Vygotsky (2004) notes, "there is a double, mutable dependence between imagination and experience. If, in the first case, imagination is based on experience, in the second case experience is based on imagination" (p. 17). Here, the creative work we do to recombine *available designs* informs our own imaginations, which inform our experience of reality too.

Vygotsky (2004) notes that the imagination's complex relationship with reality is also an emotional one. He explains that in a psychological sense, "we see everything with completely different eyes depending on whether we are experiencing at the same time grief or joy" (p. 18), and this "internal logic of feeling will represent the most subjective, most internal form of imagination" (p. 19). Emotional states can influence our perspectives, how we think in the moment, and thus how we imagine ourselves within the world around us. While emotions can have a direct influence on how we are able to imagine, our imaginations can have a direct influence on our emotions, too. Vygotsky writes, "This means that every construct of the imagination has an effect on our feelings, and if this construct does not in itself correspond to reality, nonetheless the feelings it evokes are real feelings, feelings a person truly experiences" (pp. 19–20). In the process of *designing* meaning with the imagination, then, it is the imagination's association with the full range of emotions, from empathy to disgust, that helps us to comprehend literature, art, and music because "the emotions that take hold of us from the artistic images on the pages of books or from the stage are completely real and we experience them truly, seriously, and deeply" (p. 20).

Finally, imagination is integral to *the redesigned* aspect of the NLG's (1996) framework because, according to Vygotsky (2004), "absolutely everything around us that was created by the hand of man, the entire world of human culture, as distinct from the world of nature, all this is the product of human imagination and of creation based on this imagination" (pp. 9–10). It is *the redesigned* that can bring the imagined to fruition, but imagination, in many ways, has to come first. While the NLG offers an analytic framework for understanding the semiotic work of meaning-making, in our examples from a primary school we see the imagination running in and through the entire creative process.

IMAGINATIONS IN THE MAKING

In this section, we describe situations where children's imaginations combine and recombine multimodal design elements in four overlapping ways: (1) children use designs available in everyday classroom life to spark imaginations; (2) children's imaginary worlds *become* the available designs for further use; (3) the imagination is used in the semiotic work of designing personal meaning; and (4) the imagination is used for critical framing, redesign, and the transformation of oneself.

Our examples come from Wood's (2016) study about the intersections among literacy, play, and innovation. While the data for this chapter come from her research, we chose never-before-analyzed data specifically for this chapter on imagination and multiliteracies. Wood's study took place over the course of two years in New Orleans, at a K–3 public charter school called Bricolage Academy, which was designed specifically to be a school for play and innovation. For example, the school houses an Innovation Room, where children spend extended time together for the sole purpose of inventing, talking, and playing with a variety of different material objects at their disposal. The classroom contexts in Wood's study shed light on the workings of social educational environments that were fully conceptualized and intentionally built with play and innovation in mind. In short, the children became thinkers, doers, and innovators in spaces that the teachers filled with the materials, organizational structures, and spaces for imaginative play.

IMAGINATION'S USE OF AVAILABLE DESIGNS IN THE EVERYDAY CLASSROOM

Our first example of how children's imaginations function within the NLG's (1996) *Designs of Meaning* framework depicts a child using an everyday mode, the teacher's oral language, as an *available design* to fuel her imagination. It comes from a kindergarten classroom where the teacher is conducting her daily reading workshop. Teachers often start reading workshops with focused minilessons carefully designed to guide children to use a particular strategy or reading technique (e.g., Atwell, 1998; Keene & Zimmerman, 1997). However, teachers may not always plan or design exactly *how* they will talk to their students during focused minilessons in terms of linguistic design elements, such as intonation or word choice (New London Group, 2000). Yet linguistic design is probably one of the most basic tools teachers have at the ready to create meaning in a minilesson, through the types of verbal delivery, vocabulary, or metaphor that they use.

On this day, a kindergarten teacher in one of the classrooms intentionally locked into children's imaginations through her choices of words and her commitment to the reality of a "superpowers" metaphor:

Readers have superpowers. Today your superpower gives you the tools to read smoothly—sometimes we need to read word by word but other times we try our best to read like we are talking. So today your superpower can help you try and sound just like the character or just like somebody is talking.

This teacher was not alone: all the kindergarten teachers in Brico-lage used the idea of "superpowers" to help their students try on different strategies for reading and thinking about reading. The superpowers that individual teachers chose to highlight on any given day could be anything that they wanted to emphasize in their focused minilessons, including superpowers that would help children read and talk about books, superpowers that could help them focus on beginnings and ends of words, or superpowers that would help them imagine a character's feeling. In these cases, the teachers overtly gave their students the idea of superpowers as a way for children to experience familiar and unfamiliar literacy concepts during minilessons. This was in the teachers' lesson plans and on charts around the room to guide children in their own use of imagined superpowers as they engaged with text.

Days after the superpowers minilesson mentioned above, a kindergarten girl made a shield out of cardboard in the Innovation Room of the school. She called it her "superpowers shield scooper." She told the class, with serious dedication to her play and imagination, that her shield is filled with superpowers, and if a friend ever needed a superpower, she could give it to them to help them out with their reading. There is a reality in what she says, and one that is backed by her teacher: Her superpowers shield scooper is a socially acceptable tool for scooping up things to help with reading.

In this example, the available design that the kindergartener used was presented linguistically by her teacher, but certainly was gestural, visual, and spatial as well. The linguistic terms were enough, though: The teacher put forth the vocabulary of superheroes with superpowers, a metaphor that is easy to imagine, and she delivered it as a truth—*readers have superpowers*. That available design, then, found the spark of a little girl's imagination, and voilà, the design of a superpowers shield scooper. In this case, her imagination, which linked "superpowers" to a "superpowers shield scooper" became a part of the semiotic process for meaning-making that was spontaneous and playful. The actual physical superpowers shield scooper that you can hold is important enough, but her imagination in the making extends beyond the end product and into her real life, where she has superpowers that most likely *feel* real, because she can use them herself or share them with a friend during reading time, sometimes with the teacher's guidance and sometimes not.

This vignette provides an example of how a teacher can guide imaginations toward serious business, like learning to read. It also provides an example of how available designs can get taken up by children in spontaneous and playful ways, and then taken through the entire design process to the physical creation of a something new. While the kindergarten teacher was intentional in her choice of words and delivery, she did not assign children to make a shield for reading strategies, nor did she ask that this shield remain in the classroom to be used as a future available design for further imaginative play, both about and not about reading.

IMAGINATION AS AVAILABLE DESIGN

In this next vignette, the teacher in the Innovation Room recounts a story where a child's imagination, once going, just takes over, illustrating how imagination becomes the *available design* itself in a spontaneous and playful way:

> There was a little boy who built a truck. It started out as something else, but he added boxes and it ended up looking like a truck—all he needed to do was add wheels. He brought it up to me so I could see. He had a cab, doors that open, antennas, grill—it was all there except the wheels. He and I found some things that could be used to make wheels. We put the wheels on with a skewer. They were cardboard wheels with masking tape. It looked just beautiful—he made this incredible thing. The next day the kids came in and wanted to play with it—and the kids were running it back and forth and the wheels came off. . . . We put it back together, and he put the wheels back on six or seven more times.

The resources for making the truck—the cardboard, the masking tape, the skewer, and so forth—didn't spark "truck" in the little boy's imagination. He wasn't out for "truck" when he first saw these things. Instead, the available design for "truck" came in the process of building something else. He was tentative, not knowing quite what was in the making. Somewhere in the process of playing with boxes and tinkering with the many possible futures for these boxes, his creative process produced the semiotic possibility of "truck." Working through the imagination itself provided available designs for the little boy to consider.

Now once "truck" gave meaning to the boxes, there was no turning back. A full day later, with wheels falling off, tape peeling, skewers broken, it never became "not-truck." The imagination took over for everybody playing with it. At this point, it was a full-blown socially accepted (no longer imagined) truck. But it was the boy's search for something—in his imagination and in the process of designing—that greased the wheels in the first place.

This brings up the point that if we are to think of imagination functioning within the semiotic process of making meaning, we have to remember that *available designs* might come about through the process of imaginative work in the first place. As Vygotsky (2004) said earlier, "in the first case, imagination is based on experience, in the second case experience is based on imagination" (p. 17). While "truck" is certainly something that exists in reality and is always an *available design*, the creative work in this case *started out as something else*, and required some tinkering and building before the boy saw "truck" as an *available design* for him. Once it became "truck," of course the other semiotic pieces fell into (or out of) place, like its "wheels." The point is that the imagination may need some time to play around with various resources before an *available design* like "truck" can be thinkable in the first place. Maxine Greene (1995) notes:

> As the young move into the life of language, . . . as they begin thematizing and symbolizing their experiences, horizons are breached; the landscape is transformed; experiences are clarified. The prereflective, that is, what we perceive before we reflect upon it, becomes the launching place of rationality. (p. 53)

In the case of "truck," the little boy began his playing and thinking spontaneously, trying things out pre-reflectively, clarifying whether different pieces fit within his creative process. Then, when his imagination stuck on "truck," and when it made its public debut with his peers, the truck became the launching space for a rational situation, where all of play, construction, and reconstruction that ensued was based on the grammar and social conventions of truck-play and truck-rebuilds.

Imagination in the Social Semiotic Work of Designing

Our third example focuses on imagination as a social process of *designing*. In this case, a group of four girls engaged in the implicit design of a play episode that combined semiotic resources to capture emotions, feelings, and lived experiences. The girls created multimodal repertoires that, unbeknownst to them, would last throughout the day in both serious and playful ways. This example takes place in a kindergarten classroom, where free play is a part of the morning routine.

On this particular morning, a small girl named Layla started humming an intriguing melody while seated at a rectangular table with three other girls. While she hummed, one of the other girls, Chloe, stated that she would be traveling over a really big bridge to meet her grandmother in Key West. As she spoke, she illustrated a palm tree with a brown trunk, coconuts, and green branches. Parallel to Chloe, Layla continued singing while listening and coloring at the same time. Layla explained:

> This is my tree I am writing about it because my parents had the tree cut down. I am so sad about it and I just can't get it out of my mind.

The tree's name was Calliope—it was my Calliope tree [a southern magnolia tree]. It had pink blossoms. I would look at it everyday from my bedroom window and now it's gone. My parents had no idea how much that tree meant to me.

Chloe, who continued to work on her drawing of Key West, began to mimic Layla's tune and hum along with her. Together they shared melody and rhythm in a collaborative composition of Layla's sad story.

Later that afternoon, the girls' imaginative play continued in the Innovation Room. Layla, still sad about her tree, joined in play with the three other girls. In this play episode, Chloe was the princess who was leaving the castle to go on vacation—drawing upon her excitement about her upcoming travels to Key West. Layla was the sad princess, and Mila and Avery helped take care of both Layla and Chloe. Mila and Avery collected materials found in the Innovation Room and carefully constructed a paper book representative of a passport and a suitcase made from cardboard for Chloe's travels. Layla continued to hum, sing, and talk about her Calliope tree while Avery and Mila tended to her needs and provided reassurance that she would be okay. Using cardboard, construction paper, crayons and tape, Avery and Mila made a new tree for Layla.

This whimsical play took on an array of social and emotional dimensions whereby the girls, individually and collectively, resided in a community process of *designing* enactive and symbolic representations of their lived experiences. Both Layla and Chloe, each in their own way, provided *available designs* (i.e., the Calliope tree, the trip to Key West) for the social semiotic imaginative work of making meaning for and with each other. Their play became a textual representation through language and image (drawing, writing, creating with paper),"borrowing from, and responding to, the articulated world around them" (Dyson, 2013, p. 159). In the process of designing, the girls were performing a multiliteracies curriculum that escapes most publishers: a curriculum for "communities of learners that are diverse and respectful of the autonomy of lifeworlds" (New London Group, 1996, p. 73). The emotional and affective elements of imagination make this respect for diversity possible. As Greene (1995) states: "Imagination is what, above all, makes empathy possible" (p. 3).

IMAGINATION AND THE REDESIGNED SELF

Our final example focuses on Tyrone, who used a cardboard box to construct a boat. In both the Innovation Room and the 1st-grade classroom, Tyrone and his 1st-grade colleagues had been learning about motors and how things move as a part of a transportation unit designed to integrate literacy, science, and innovation. At one point, the children were guided, by a teacher's suggestion, to design something from a spool, a rubber band, and a pencil. Tyrone constructed a boat out of a cardboard box with a rubber band and spool motor. The pencil was the propeller in the back. Tyrone stated:

> This is a battle ship that pushes things for hurricanes to make a wall to protect the land. I was in one hurricane. It was so much water . . . . it was coming in the house. I was 5 now I am 7. We were safe.

While the *available designs* for this project were presented in class and through various media, Tyrone's battleship reflected a lived experience as the basis for *designing*. Tyrone's imagination in the making of this boat then became an innovation, with the *redesign* of a boat into something could better protect the land from a hurricane's floods. The outcome was a battleship that wasn't about battling people, but instead about battling hurricanes.

In Tyrone's description, he not only explains his battleship in terms of what it does, he also makes sure his listeners know he has experience with these sorts of things, and that his family was safe. This reminds us that children are aware, as they are making things, that the functions, structures, and design elements of their creations communicate meaning to real people who have authentic concerns and genuine interests (Kalantzis & Cope, 2005). In general, *critical framing*, as discussed by the NLG (1996, p. 86), as well as by Kalantzis and Cope (2002, p. 247), is the consideration and interpretation by students of how the meanings of their designs and textual practices work to explain, problem-solve, or talk back to issues within larger cultural and social contexts. In this specific example, Tyrone had a chance to imagine and create a new kind of battleship innovated to "talk back" to hurricanes. Two whole years after Tyrone and his family personally experienced the devastation of a hurricane, he learned about motors, and with that new knowledge he wanted to solve a problem that continually persists in New Orleans. As an older boy now, at seven, Tyrone could remake himself as an inventor who solves problems and designs for the future, by using a spool, a rubber band, and a thread of imagination.

Conclusion

In this chapter we described how imagination works within the New London Group's (1996) *Designs of Meaning* curricular framework, and we have provided examples of how imagination functions within semiotic processes of meaning-making through creativity and design. We have also seen the ways in which imagination is both serious and playful, guided and spontaneous, but nonetheless an integral component that transformed children's wonderings into creations and designs, extending their individual thinking into the collaborative culture found in the classroom spaces of this school. As we go about designing curriculum for social futures based on collaboration and innovation, a few principles for thinking about imagination as an integral part of the semiotic design process include the following:

1. Imagination is present in all aspects of a design process, from *available designs* through *designing* and the *redesigned*, which leads to a new creation, an innovation, or a transformed practice.
2. Children's imaginations can make use of any *available designs*, but when teachers are aware of design elements at their disposal, they may be in a better position to create *available designs* for both curricular and imaginary purposes.
3. At the same time, something a child imagines can *become* an available design for the child to use further, or for other children to use when it becomes socially available.
4. Imagination can be used in a meaning-making sense as an individual alone with words and thoughts, smells and feelings, or imagination can be socially performed in the process of social semiotic meaning-making. But as a part of a semiotic activity, the imagination relies on known entities even as it creatively combines or discombobulates them.
5. The imagination can critically frame children's engagement with the world in self-transformational ways.

Broader implications from this research suggest that cultivating the imaginations of young children can guide them to further understand innovative thinking and the processes of designing something new. This, at its essence, is what it means to create a curriculum designed for social futures, the kind of curriculum where children are given the semiotic toolkits and the freedom to design for social futures themselves.

REFERENCES

Atwell, N. (1998). *In the middle: New understandings about writing, reading, and learning.* Portsmouth, NH: Boynton/Cook.

Biesta, G. (2007). Why "what works" won't work: Evidence-based practice and the democratic deficit in educational research. *Educational Theory, 57*(1), 1–22. doi:10.1111/j.1741-5446.2006.00241.x

Dyson, A. H. (2013). *Rewriting the basics: Literacy learning in children's cultures.* New York, NY: Teachers College Press.

Friedrich, D., Jaastad, B., & Popkewitz, T. S. (2010). Democratic Education: An (im)possibility that yet remains to come. *Educational Philosophy and Theory, 42*(5–6), 571–587.

Greene, M. (1995). *Releasing the imagination: Essays on education, the arts, and social change.* San Francisco, CA: Jossey-Bass.

Kalantzis, M., & Cope, B. (2002). A multiliteracies pedagogy: A pedagogical supplement. In *Multiliteracies: Literacy learning and the design of social futures* (pp. 239–248). New York, NY: Routledge.

Kalantzis, M., & Cope, B. (2005). *Learning by design.* Melbourne, Australia: Victorian Schools Innovation Commission.

Keene, E. O., & Zimmerman, S. (1997). *Mosaic of thought: Teaching comprehension in a reader's workshop.* Portsmouth, NH: Heinemann.

New London Group. (1996). A pedagogy of multiliteracies: Designing social futures. *Harvard Educational Review, 66*(1), 60–92.

New London Group. (2000). A pedagogy of multiliteracies: Designing social futures. In B. Cope & M. Kalantzis (Eds.), *Multiliteracies: Literacy learning and the design of social futures* (pp. 9–42). London, UK: Routledge.

Shannon, P. (2007). *Reading against democracy: The broken promises of reading instruction.* Portsmouth, NH: Heinemann.

Vygotsky, L. S. (2004). Imagination and creativity in childhood. *Journal of Russian and East European Psychology, 42*(1), 7–97.

Wood, C. L. (2016). *The literacy of play and innovation: A case study of Bricolage* (Unpublished doctoral dissertation). Madison: Department of Curriculum & Instruction, University of Wisconsin–Madison.

Exciting Times for New Scholars

Doctoral Students Consider the Past and the Future of Multiliteracies Research and Pedagogy

Dani Kachorsky, Maria Goff, Lori Talarico, Olivia G. Stewart,
Megan Hoelting, Kelly Tran, Kewman Lee, and Kristin Elwood

In spring 2015, a group of Arizona State University doctoral students in the Learning, Literacies, and Technologies (LLT) program participated in a biweekly seminar wherein we studied the works of, and met with, some of the original members of the New London Group (NLG), as well as other literacy scholars. Our transdisciplinary doctoral program brings together students from varied backgrounds and wide ranges of research interests, such as adolescent literacies, educational technologies, gaming studies, the learning sciences, new literacy studies, social justice, social media studies, teacher education, and visual and multimodal literacy.

This seminar afforded us the opportunity to dialogue with key scholars who established and worked within the field of multiliteracies. For each biweekly session, we were assigned seminal and contemporary works by one of the scholars we were to meet. Using video-chat technology, we spent time discussing their published works and their current ideas concerning the future of multiliteracies research. Coordinated by our professor, Frank Serafini, visiting scholars included members of the NLG as well as other scholars influenced by their work, including James Paul Gee, Allan Luke, Len Unsworth, Donald Leu, Gunther Kress, and Colin Lankshear. During our discussions, each of them reflected on the manifesto's influence on the field of literacy research and pedagogy, its influence on their own work, and their hopes for educational research in the future. These discussions form the primary source material for this chapter. What we share here is a composite of those discussions and our reflections as new scholars on a field that has influenced us all.

THE FOUNDATIONS OF MULTILITERACIES

To explore the ways in which the NLG has shaped our experience as students, we first examined the original manifesto *A Pedagogy of Multiliteracies* and the circumstances that led to its writing. In 1994, the group that gathered in New London, NH, came together from diverse backgrounds and theoretical perspectives. They agreed that the term *literacy* in the traditional sense was insufficient to describe the diverse practices that group members had observed. Up to that point, literacy had often been narrowly defined as a set of mental processing skills acquired by an individual, rather than as socially and culturally situated practices (New London Group, 1996). Scholars generally believed that there was a single, universal, and autonomous model of reading and writing (Street, 1995). However, NLG members thought this traditional model of literacy did not apply to diversified societies and their practices in an increasingly networked and digitalized world; rather there were multiple—indeed numerous—literacies (Cope & Kalantzis, 2015; New London Group, 1996).

DEFINING MULTILITERACIES

The NLG defined the prefix *multi* in *multiliteracies* in a variety of ways. Firstly, group members recognized the "enormous and significant differences in contexts and patterns of communication in the realities of increasing local diversity and global connectedness" (Cope & Kalantzis, 2015, p. 3; New London Group, 1996, p. 64). They viewed traditional, print-based literacy as multiple due to the diverse practices associated with it. These practices can differ by culture, as described in the work of Brian Street (1995), or by smaller social groups within a culture, as described in the work of James Paul Gee (personal communication, June 2016). Different cultures have different conceptions of literacies, and in a world of increasing diversity, it is important for researchers, teachers, educators, and policymakers to recognize these conceptions (New London Group, 1996).

The NLG also applied the concept of *multi* to modalities (Cope & Kalantzis, 2015, p. 3), in which various modes (e.g., text, images, and sound) are all important for meaning-making. These characterizations of literacy differ significantly from the traditional view of it, in which language-based, printed text is often privileged. At the time, work in multimodality was still in the early stages. Consequently, the group's inclusion in the document became profoundly influential on further work in multiliteracies and new literacies (Lankshear & Knobel, 2003, 2013). This notion of literacy referring to more than printed text led to the conception of diverse literacy practices; for example, media, art, and science all have forms of literacy within this framework.

The broadness of the term *multiliteracies* as defined by the NLG allowed group members to come together with a common goal despite being from diverse fields. Indeed, with the exception of Bill Cope and Mary Kalantzis, many NLG members now prefer to use alternative terminology, depending upon their specific interests and fields of study (e.g., critical discourse analysis: Fairclough, 2013; the New Literacy Studies/big D Discourse: Gee, 2015; multimodality: Kress, 2009; critical literacy: Luke, 2000). Although each member was prompted to redefine literacy at the meeting in New London by different pressures in their respective fields (e.g., the questions about genre addressed by Kress, and the interest in new capitalism, which motivated Gee), multiliteracies provided common ground on which the group could convene. In a sense, it is this broad definition that allowed research in multiliteracies to be taken up in diverse ways.

RESEARCH IN MULTILITERACIES

Since the original publication of *A Pedagogy of Multiliteracies*, the term *multiliteracies* has been adopted in diverse ways across research, pedagogy, and practice. According to Cope and Kalantzis (2015), a recent Google search for *multiliteracies* yielded more than 196,000 webpages, a Google Scholar search resulted in more than 12,700 mentions in academic articles and books, and an Amazon search revealed 193 books for sale that included the term as part of their titles. Moreover, the term has been taken up in various fields including literacy education, second language education, science education, multilingualism, learning technology, and applied linguistics. These results show that the concept of multiliteracies is used extensively, and that researchers have made an effort to reconcile and expand the notion of multiliteracies. A discussion of how our invited scholars have taken up research in multiliteracies is addressed in the following sections.

THE CONCEPT OF MULTIMODALITY IN LITERACY

Multimodality has been developed both theoretically and practically by many prominent scholars around the world (e.g., Jewitt, 2008, 2009; Rowsell, 2013; Serafini, 2013; Unsworth, 2011). Most of our visiting scholars, in fact, discussed the role of multimodality in multiliteracies research either explicitly or implicitly. One of the most notable was Gunther Kress, who focused on how his thinking has evolved since his initial work in social semiotics (Kress, 1993). Emphasizing that the signs people use to convey meaning are always embedded in social contexts and with specific purposes, Kress urged us to question how we reconcile multimodal research within the Western ideology, which he argued professes wrongly that language is capable of fully representing all types of knowledge. Our class was also privy to the evolution of his thinking, from understanding that each mode is capable of providing information in ways that other modes cannot, toward accepting new methods of research that value and incorporate these affordances and limitations. By better understanding the ways in which people represent ideas, researchers can more fully understand how to conduct research on multimodal phenomena. For us, this exposure to the ways in which these notions developed for such a prominent scholar in the field of literacy was invaluable.

THE ROLE OF DIGITAL TECHNOLOGIES IN LITERACY

Several scholars highlighted the expanding, complex relationship between multimodality, multiliteracies, and technology. Luke noted that the NLG could never have truly predicted how interrelated this relationship would become, despite NLG's original acknowledgment that research under a multiliteracies lens must inherently address technology as new technologies continuously shape literacies. Throughout the semester, the ways in which technology changed the nature of literacy research became a frequently discussed topic. Leu and Lankshear both shared the sentiment that as technology constantly changes so does literacy itself.

While many researchers may agree on this changing landscape, this belief is not always reflected in practice in schools. Leu argued that while technology use has been increasing in schools, particularly within the realm of assessment, it is still frequently logocentric; assessment remains the same, with technology used only to aid in faster data collection. Therefore, he posed the question "How do we assess students' ability to assess things on the Internet?" His current research utilizes online research and comprehension assessments (ORCAs), which aid researchers in understanding how students comprehend multimodal texts on the web (Leu et al., 2014).

Leu's current research echoes arguments made in Leu, Kinzer, Coiro, Castek, and Henry (2013) that the Internet is a tool that not only defines learning and literacies but also requires new kinds of literacies to unlock its full potential. Gee similarly discussed the need to recognize that digital technologies are more than just the tools and their use. Instead, digital technologies involve ways of acting, interacting, valuing, believing, and knowing, as well as often using other sorts of tools and technologies, including very often oral and written language, all of which work together to form a culture of meaning-making and communication that surrounds the use of digital tools.

Gee (2015) warned against analyzing the digital world as something radically different, noting that we often forget the lessons we have already learned about communication, culture, and meaning-making in the physical world. However, the physical world is reciprocally changing through digital technologies. For example, as a result of flexible, multimodal platforms that allow for personalized design, Lankshear asserted, there is now a more central focus on creativity for students as they utilize these platforms. Though these are only brief examples, they illustrate the profound and far-reaching effects that digital technologies have on current multiliteracies research.

MULTILITERACIES AND TEACHER EDUCATION

The NLG suggested the limitations concerning what schools can do in terms of changing the world, and 20 years later, we continue to have this same discussion. Luke discussed how "the Googling of the world" and its impact on a multiliteracies approach in education can be an opportunity for empowerment for disenfranchised students. Furthermore, he believes that we, as new researchers, need to take up where the NLG left off and repoliticize multiliteracies by teaching students to critically analyze new content for authorship, purpose, and context. But what does this mean for teacher education? Citing Freire's (Freire & Macedo, 1987) call for critical pedagogy by "reading the world," Luke described how researchers need to teach both teachers and students how to be critical of technology—critical of who owns and controls the technologies we use, as well as critical of how we engage and conduct ourselves when interacting with those technologies. These are all areas Luke believes teachers should address with their students; however, there is an absence of this instruction within teacher education programs. During the seminar, we noted that while the scholars we studied promoted a shift in literacy approaches, legislative mandates such as the No Child Left Behind Act (2002) pushed education toward a particular evidence-based curriculum resulting in high-stakes testing and a teach-to-the-test mentality (Darling-Hammond, 2007).

As a possible direction for teacher education, the NLG (1996) suggested that literacy be couched in terms of design and redesign, even purporting that "teachers and managers are seen as designers of learning processes and environments, not as bosses dictating what those in their charge should think and do" (p. 73). While best practices in teaching have moved toward a more student-centered classroom, recent educational reforms have branded teachers the villains instead of "professional classroom learning designers" (Smagorinsky, 2014). If teacher preparation and professional development continue to focus on standards-based assessment and pay-for-performance initiatives, how will teachers begin to prepare students for the innovative, inquiry-based practices they will need in today's global society?

In the seminar, Leu predicted that in 10 years, global connections between classrooms to conduct collaborative problem-solving will be common practice. However, while pedagogical integration of technology has increased in the past decade, it has not increased at the expected rate (Project Tomorrow, 2013), and many novice teachers still feel underprepared for the realities of teaching with and about new technologies (Ertmer & Ottenbreit-Leftwich, 2010). This suggests that teacher preparation and professional development are not keeping pace with advances in technology and its influence on our society. They further recommended a focus on "how students and teachers learn how to learn" and predict that problem-based learning may be a possible answer (p. 276). McLean and Rowsell (2013) added to this argument that teacher education approaches to language and literacy should expand to include the practices teachers and students need for today and the future. Coincidentally, this hearkens back to the NLG's suggestion that multiliteracies be framed through a design process. Leu, Kinzer, Coiro, Castek, and Henry (2013) echo Snow's (2014) call for action that classroom research with teachers should focus on the skills, tools, and instructional models teachers need. Universities will need to form partnerships with schools for the development to be ongoing and effective while meeting teachers' and students' needs.

The Future of Multiliteracies Research

Overall, our visiting scholars were positive about the potential that research stemming from multiliteracies has for enacting change in today's schools and in other learning environments. Looking toward the future, they responded to our request for advice on the direction of our own research with what they believed to be rich opportunities for new scholars and the research community as a whole. Their advice covered the following areas: (1) the role of the researcher, (2) research methodologies, (3) areas for potential research, and (4) the dissemination of research.

Role of the Researcher

Many visiting scholars encouraged an expanded vision of the role the researcher plays in literacy research to include the roles of *innovator*, *collaborator*, and *advocate*. Gee suggested that it is important for new scholars and current researchers to become theoretical innovators because progress in educational research has come to a halt. He explained that without new theories, educational research will not survive. Leu and Unsworth seconded the importance of innovating through theory building. Unsworth pointed out the need to theorize about how to investigate new technologies and their corresponding literacies. To that end, Leu et al. (2013) assert that literacy is deictic and, as such, requires a dual-level theoretical framework to better understand its patterns of change. They suggest that we must look across all of the lower-case "new literacies" to detect patterns of use and then apply those patterns to an upper-case "New Literacies" theoretical framework.

Through our discussions about the role of researcher as innovator, we came to the conclusion that in order for people to be innovative, they cannot be isolated within their research fields. Rather, as the seminar organizer Frank Serafini explained, scholars need to work with those with whom they have disparate views. Other visiting researchers claimed that collaboration is a crucial characteristic of the researcher role. Luke stressed the importance of working with the educational community as a whole, while Lankshear felt that the only way to innovate or move forward within educational research was through connecting and working with other stakeholders or communities. Lankshear also pointed to collaboration as a form of advocacy in which communities and individuals gain a stronger, or less subterranean, position in the sociohistorical landscape. Similarly, Luke recommended researchers become advocates for students. He felt it was important for researchers to work *with* minority communities not to *give* them a voice, but to *make space* for their voices.

In addition, visiting scholars addressed the need for future researchers to be aware of increasing global interactions and researchers' changing roles as a result. For example, Leu discussed how globalization allows researchers to examine communication around the world and where problems emerge; Lankshear emphasized this affordance by asserting that "transnationality is the new local." Because of increased access to, and socialization through, technologies, interactions and meaning-making happen on a more global level. Researchers are capable of observing worldwide interactions, crossing contexts and cultural values, and this access suggests a responsibility. Indeed, Lankshear encouraged us to identify points of inspiration and to become "accidental researchers"— those open to following leads and responding to new ideas rather than simply asking questions to which a stance has already been developed.

Effective Research Methodologies

As we look to the future, another important consideration is research methodology. For our research to have the greatest impact on the field,

Leu felt that methodologies need to evolve and focus on mixed-method research, as funding agencies, policymakers, and schools want to see numbers and replicable data that is characteristic of experimental studies. This can be seen in practice in Leu's research on online research and comprehension assessments (ORCAs); his work uses traditional quantitative methods to analyze data, but is firmly based in New Literacies theories that view literacy as a social practice (Leu et al., 2014).

Conversely, Lankshear stressed the importance of doing "a lot of ethnography" as we seek to understand how meanings are made multimodally. Lankshear and Knobel (2007) present a case for the value of ethnographic methods suggesting that if researchers move toward "full-blown real-time ethnography, [they] could capture insider perspectives and understandings about what was going on at different 'levels' of engagement within the discourse" (p. 233), allowing them to gain a fuller picture of how separate discourses interface with each other.

From another perspective, Luke suggested that scholars use critical theory as a lens of analysis to examine issues of power, including ownership of content, and to help understand what needs to be taught regarding new technologies. Luke urged us as emerging scholars to consider "issues of access" and to design studies that question how access to technologies affects literacy. While the advice visiting scholars gave us regarding methodologies may seem diverse and contradictory, we can see, upon closer inspection, that they are urging us to examine our research questions and select tools that focus on the details that are important to our perspectives on multiliteracies, such as access, communications practices, and multimodal composition.

Areas for New Research

As mentioned by Leu et al. (2013), there remains a dearth of research in the area of multiliteracies, suggesting that research in this area should begin by determining what is essential to multiliteracies acquisition and its support. The visiting scholars responded to this dearth and to our request for guidance by providing us with generous suggestions on the areas of need in multiliteracies research. Both Leu and Luke stressed that communications practices (e.g., instant messaging, blogging, and tweeting) are changing rapidly with the advent of digital technologies, and schools are struggling to adapt. Lankshear, Knobel, and Curran (2012) found that studies in this area often address the "(dis)continuity" between out-of-school literacy practices and the traditional literacy practices of formal education. To this end, Leu felt that universities needed to partner with schools to develop research-based solutions that provide students access to communicative technologies (e.g., "providing email access to second graders"). Along those same lines, in order to resolve parental and administrative concerns regarding student access to communicative technologies, Luke suggested research should focus on helping to provide schools and students with "ethical tools" to teach students communicative ethics and how to conduct themselves with technology. He further emphasized the need for studies that consider minority voice in the use of digital tools to compose multimodally, echoing his previous sentiment that urges us to consider issues of power and access.

Finally, both Kress and Unsworth feel that multimodal composition is an area that still needs more focus, perhaps using tools from film studies to focus on the interface between image and language and how meaning-making works as other modes are added into the mix.

Improvements in Dissemination of Research

Finally, visiting scholars saw an opportunity for future improvement in the dissemination of our research. Kress and Unsworth both advocated for the use of more flexible platforms for the dissemination of research. They suggested the scholarly community has long encountered repeated challenges in sharing research due in part to space limits, copyright concerns, and the logocentricity of prominent journal formats. Kress advocated for using multiple modes for research dissemination, explaining that different modes both achieve different ends and require different epistemological commitments. Furthermore, Kress posited that image alone can be a much more precise mode for disseminating and analyzing research.

Unsworth pointed to the increasing use of multiple platforms by writers of children's literature as a model for researchers. He explained that different platforms (e.g., paper media, film, digital text, etc.) have different affordances, and as such, publishing in multiple outlets could be useful. Kress echoed this suggestion by stating that not only do different platforms offer different affordances; they also offer different structures, limitations, and audiences. In discussions, we interpreted this to mean that, as researchers, we will need to consider whom we intend to reach and how we intend to reach them. This is not simply an issue of framing and presenting our research in a manner that is accessible to a particular audience. This involves considering the limitations of any one mode for presenting, representing, and communicating knowledge. We must ask ourselves what are the best modes for communicating our work.

Luke and Leu were also concerned with the audiences for multiliteracies research. In their respective lectures, these scholars stressed the importance of disseminating multiliteracies research not just to other researchers but to teachers and administrators, as well. To this end, Kress and Unsworth's concerns about which platforms are ideal for reaching which audiences take on new meaning. Since teachers are the ones engaging with students in the classrooms and making daily decisions about pedagogy, they are the ones who most need access to the research we will conduct.

CONCLUSION

To echo the words Donald Leu gave us: We live in an exciting time to be new scholars. The notion of multiple literacies that the NLG put forth in 1996 through *A Pedagogy of Multiliteracies* inspired scholars across educational disciplines to push the question, "What is literacy?" As evidenced by our discussions with several scholars from the NLG and with other contemporary scholars of literacy, there are still many areas for theoretical and empirical research to take up. It is up to current and emerging scholars to continue developing the multiliteracies framework through innovative and responsible research that advocates and makes room for a multiplicity of voices, cultures, and practices.

As we look to the future of multiliteracies research, we must continue to be conscious of the past, careful to keep the lessons we have learned in mind as we develop and test new theories. However, we must remain flexible and not force the technologies and literacies of the future into preexisting theories and frameworks that reflect a less globalized community. Furthermore, as researchers in an increasingly interdisciplinary field, we must make a concerted effort to work not only with other researchers whose views do not necessarily reflect our own, but also with teachers, administrators, and policymakers if we are to have true impact in the world. This means being community partners as well as managing and disseminating knowledge in new ways.

REFERENCES

Cope, B., & Kalantzis, M. (2015). The things you do to know: An introduction to the pedagogy of multiliteracies. In B. Cope & M. Kalantzis (Eds.), *A pedagogy of multiliteracies: Learning by design* (pp. 1–36). Basingstoke, UK: Palgrave Macmillan.

Darling-Hammond, L. (2007). Race, inequality and educational accountability: The irony of "No Child Left Behind." *Race Ethnicity and Education, 10*(3), 245–260.

Ertmer, P. A., & Ottenbreit-Leftwich, A. T. (2010). Teacher technology change: How knowledge, confidence, beliefs, and culture intersect. *Journal of Research on Technology in Education, 42*(3), 255–284.

Fairclough, N. (2013). *Critical discourse analysis: The critical study of language*. New York, NY: Routledge.

Freire, P., & Macedo, D. (1987). *Reading the word and the world*. Westport, CT: Bergin & Garvey.

Gee, J. P. (2015). *Social linguistics and literacies: Ideology in Discourses* (5th ed.). New York, NY: Routledge.

Jewitt, C. (2008). Multimodality and literacy in school classrooms. *Review of Research in Education, 32*(1), 241–267.

Jewitt, C. (Ed.). (2009). *The Routledge handbook of multimodal analysis*. London, UK: Routledge.

Kress, G. (1993). Against arbitrariness: The social production of the sign as a foundational issue in critical discourse analysis. *Discourse & Society, 4*(2), 169–191.

Kress, G. (2009). *Multimodality: A social semiotic approach to contemporary communication*. New York, NY: Routledge.

Lankshear, C., & Knobel, M. (2003). *New literacies: Changing knowledge and classroom learning*. Buckingham, UK: Open University Press.

Lankshear, C., & Knobel, M. (2007). Researching new literacies: Web 2.0 practices and insider perspectives. *E-Learning, 4*(3), 224–240.

Lankshear, C., & Knobel, M. (2013). *A new literacies reader: Educational perspectives*. New York, NY: Peter Lang.

Lankshear, C., Knobel, M., & Curran, C. (2012). Conceptualizing and researching "new literacies." *The Encyclopedia of Applied Linguistics*, (1998). doi:10.1002/9781405198431.wbeal0182/full

Leu, D. J., Forzani, E., Rhoads, C., Maykel, C., Kennedy, C., & Timbrell, N. (2014). The new literacies of online research and comprehension: Rethinking the reading achievement gap. *Reading Research Quarterly, 50*(1), 37–59.

Leu, D. J., Kinzer, C. K., Coiro, J., Castek, J., & Henry, L. A. (2013). New literacies: A dual-level theory of the changing nature of literacy, instruction, and assessment. In D. E. Alvermann, N. J. Unrau, & R. B. Ruddell (Eds.), *Theoretical models and processes of reading* (6th ed., pp. 1150–1181). Newark, DE: International Reading Association.

Luke, A. (2000). Critical literacy in Australia: A matter of context and standpoint. *Journal of Adolescent & Adult Literacy, 43*(5), 448–461.

McLean, C. A., & Rowsell, J. (2013). (Re)designing literacy teacher education: a call for change. *Teaching Education, 24*(1), 1–26.

New London Group. (1996). A pedagogy of multiliteracies: Designing social futures. *Harvard Educational Review, 66*(1), 60–92.

No Child Left Behind Act of 2001, Pub. L. No. 107-110, U.S.C 20 §1425 (2002).

Project Tomorrow. (2013). Learning in the 21st century: Digital experiences and expectations of tomorrow's teachers. Speak Up 2013. Retrieved from http://www.tomorrow.org/speakup/tomorrowsteachers_report2013.html

Rowsell, J. (2013). *Working with multimodality: Rethinking literacy in a digital age*. New York, NY: Routledge.

Serafini, F. (2013). *Reading the visual: An introduction to teaching multimodal literacy.* New York, NY: Teachers College Press.

Smagorinsky, P. (2014). Authentic teacher evaluation: A two-tiered proposal for formative and summative assessment. *English Education, 46*(2), 165–185.

Snow, C. (2014). Rigor and realism. Doing educational science in the real world [Wallace foundation distinguished lecture]. *Educational Researcher, 44*(9), 460–466.

Street, B. V. (1995). *Social literacies: Critical approaches to literacy in development, ethnography and education.* London, UK: Taylor & Francis.

Unsworth, L. (Ed.) (2011). *Multimodal semiotics: Functional analysis in contexts of education.* New York, NY: A&C Black.

Glossary

Critical Discourse Analysis: An interdisciplinary approach to the study of discourse that views language as a form of social practice. Scholars working in the tradition of critical discourse analysis focus on investigating how societal power relations are established and reinforced through language use.

Design: The process of representing meanings to oneself, such as reading, listening, or viewing, or to the world in communicative processes such as writing, speaking, or making pictures. The multiliteracies view of design has three aspects: Available Designs (culturally available representational forms); the Designing one does (the work you do when you make meaning, how you appropriately transform available designs); and the Redesigned (how, through the act of Designing, the world and the person are transformed).

Discourse: Language above the sentence level. Gee (1999) distinguished between Discourse with a "big *D*" and discourse with a "little *d*," defining discourse with a little *d* as language used to enact identities and activities, and Discourse with a big *D* as a way of being in the world or in a specific context.

Embodied Cognition: The theory that many features of human or other types of cognition are shaped by aspects of the body beyond the brain. The features of cognition include high-level mental constructs and human performance on various cognitive tasks, such as reasoning or judgment.

Ideology: A set of socially constructed ways of thinking and acting that become embedded and naturalized in a particular culture to the extent they become invisible or taken as common sense. A set of conscious and unconscious ideas that constitutes one's worldview or way of looking at things and that affects the meanings people construct.

Lifeworlds: Virtual or material spaces for community life characterized by distinctive subcultures, discourses, and languages.

Media: The technologies used for the rendering and dissemination of texts; in particular, multimodal ensembles. Television, radio, the Internet, electronic books, and DVDs are all examples of types of media.

Metafunction: Aspects of language and visual images that make it possible to communicate across time and space. Metafunctions serve as a device for organizing how language and visual images

199

work. The three primary metafunctions are ideational, interpersonal, and textual.

Metalanguage: A language used to describe the structures and uses of languages or visual images. Metalanguages are often used to describe the meaning-making resources of language and visual images.

Modality: The degree to which we are to consider the realistic or fictional qualities of an image or multimodal ensemble. A high degree of modality suggests the image is very realistic, while a low degree of modality suggests the image is very fictional or abstract.

Mode: A system of visual and verbal entities created within or across various cultures to represent and express meanings. Photography, sculpture, written language, paintings, music, and poetry are types of modes.

Multiliteracies: The reconceptualization of literacy as a multidimensional set of competences and social practices in response to the increasing complexity and multimodal nature of texts. This concept suggests literacy is not a single, cognitive set of skills, rather an array of social practices that extend beyond reading and writing printed text.

Multimodality: An interdisciplinary approach that understands representation and communication extend beyond written language and that includes a multiplicity of modes. It refers to the theory that meanings are represented and communicated across and within cultures by a wide variety of semiotic resources.

Semiotic Resource: An umbrella term used here to refer to the various means for representing and communicating meanings. It is a material and social resource used for communicative purposes. Semiotic resources have a meaning potential, based on their past uses, and a set of affordances based on their possible uses, and these will be actualized in concrete social contexts.

Social semiotics: A branch of the field of semiotics that investigates human signifying practices in specific social and cultural circumstances, and that tries to explain meaning-making as a social practice.

Systemic Functional Linguistics: An approach to understanding language as a social system. The focus is on language in use and how it shapes social practices.

Textual Metafunction: Also referred to as the compositional metafunction, it refers to the way language or a visual image is organized. Based on the work of Halliday, it is one of the three metafunctions of language, ideational and interpersonal being the other two.

About the Contributors

Sandra Schamroth Abrams is an associate professor in the Department of Curriculum & Instruction at St. John's University in New York, NY. Her examinations of digital literacies and video-gaming focus on layered meaning-making and agentive learning.

Elvis Arancibia attended Claremont Academy in Worcester, MA. He is originally from Peru. He was a member of the Poetry Inside Out research group at Clark University in Worcester.

Julianne Burgess teaches English to newcomer youth at Mohawk College in Hamilton, Canada.

Jill Castek is associate professor, Department of Teaching, Learning, and Sociocultural Studies at the University of Arizona in Tucson.

Julie Coiro is associate professor, College of Education and Professional Studies, University of Rhode Island, Kingston.

Bill Cope is a professor in the Department of Education Policy, Organization & Leadership, University of Illinois, Urbana-Champaign. His recent research has focused on the development of digital writing and assessment technologies.

Katharine Cowan is a senior teaching fellow at the University College London Institute of Education, United Kingdom. Her research interests include exploring the connections between the Reggio Emilia approach and multimodal perspectives on learning, including the ways different forms of learning are recognized and documented.

Saint Cyr Dimanche is studying at Brandeis University, Waltham, MA, with a major in International Relations. He is originally from the Central African Republic. He was a member of the Poetry Inside Out research group at Clark University.

Kristin Elwood is a doctoral student in the Learning, Literacies, and Technologies PhD program in the Mary Lou Fulton Teachers College at Arizona State University, and she has an ME in Educational Technology with a BA in English. She taught high school English and graphic design for 12 years and researches Design Thinking as it intersects with teacher preparation and digital literacy.

James R. Gavelek is associate professor and coordinator of the Literacy, Language and Culture PhD program at the University of Illinois at Chicago. His research interests are focused on semiotics and the embodied nature of meaning-making.

James Paul Gee is the Mary Lou Fulton Presidential Professor of Literacy Studies and a Regents' Professor at Arizona State University. He is a member of the National Academy of Education and an AERA Fellow.

Maria Goff is a doctoral candidate in Arizona State University's Learning, Literacies, and Technologies PhD program. Her research looks at the intersections of adolescent literacies, multiliteracies, and teacher education and development.

Dawnene D. Hassett studies curriculum theory and literacy education in the Department of Curriculum & Instruction at the University of Wisconsin–Madison. She is interested in social semiotics and the role that imagination plays when young children make meaning with visual and interactive texts.

Megan Hoelting is a PhD student whose research interests include participatory cultures, young adult literature, and cultural identities in the classroom.

Jeffrey B. Holmes is the assistant director of the Center for the Art and Science of Teaching in the Mary Lou Fulton Teachers College at Arizona State University. His research focuses on teaching in informal settings, especially in digital media such as video games.

Carey Jewitt is a professor of Learning and Technology at the Institute of Education, University College London, United Kingdom. She is a leading researcher in multimodality and multimodal analysis, and is the founding editor of the journal *Visual Communication*.

Dani Kachorsky is a doctoral student in the Learning, Literacies, & Technologies program in the Mary Lou Fulton Teachers College at Arizona State University. Her research interests include multimodal and visual literacy with an emphasis in how teachers and students take up these literacies in classrooms.

Mary Kalantzis was dean of the College of Education at the University of Illinois, Urbana-Champaign, from 2006 to 2016. With Bill Cope, she has co-authored numerous books, including *New Learning: Elements of a Science of Education* (Cambridge University Press, 2012).

Carita Kiili, is a postdoctoral fellow in the Department of Education, University of Oslo & University of Jyväskylä.

Gunther Kress is professor of Semiotics and Education and co-director, Centre for Multimodal Research, at the University College London Institute of Education, United Kingdom. His research covers communication and meaning-making in contemporary environments.

Kewman Lee is pursuing his PhD degree in the Learning, Literacies, & Technologies program at Arizona State University. His current research focuses are digital literacy practices in transnational online affinity spaces, translingual practices, multimodality, and unified discourse analysis.

Deborah Diaz Lembert is an undergraduate at Clark University, Worcester, MA, studying Spanish literature and education. She was a member of the Poetry Inside Out research group at Clark.

Mary B. McVee is professor of literacy education and director of the Center for Literacy and Reading Instruction at the University at Buffalo, SUNY. Her research traverses positioning theory, social and embodied learning; digital literacies and multimodality; narrative, disciplinary literacies, and diversities of language, literacy, and culture.

Sarah Michaels is a professor of education at Clark University, Worcester, MA, and the Senior Research Scholar at the Hiatt Center for Urban Education. A sociolinguist by training, she works on issues of language, culture, and multiliteracies, with teachers as researchers and with youth researchers, emphasizing the central role of productive talk in building classroom cultures of public reasoning.

Abby Moon is an undergraduate at Clark University, Worcester, MA, where she is a double major in Cultural Studies and Art History. She was a member of the Poetry Inside Out research group at Clark.

Jie Y. Park is an assistant professor of Education at Clark University, Worcester, MA. Her research interests include adolescent literacy and language practices in in-school and out-of-school settings. For the past 2 years, she has been studying how 1st-generation immigrant students acquire academic discourses, and what cultural and linguistic resources they bring to their schooling.

Rebecca Rogers is a Professor of Education in the College of Education, University of Missouri–St. Louis. She specializes in literacy studies, teacher learning, and critical discourse studies. She is a former Fulbright Scholar in Critical Discourse Studies at the Universidad de San Martin, Buenos Aires, Argentina.

Jennifer Rowsell is professor and Canada Research Chair in Multiliteracies at Brock University, St. Catharines, Canada.

Kevin Sanchez was born and raised in San Juan, Puerto Rico. Currently he attends a local community college in Worcester, Massachusetts. He was a member of the Poetry Inside Out research group at Clark University.

Lynn E. Shanahan is an associate professor of Literacy Education in the Department of Learning and Instruction at the University at Buffalo, SUNY. Her research on video reflection, the development of strategic readers and writers and disciplinary literacies, is based in social semiotics, multimodality and embodied theoretical perspectives.

Olivia G. Stewart is a PhD candidate in the interdisciplinary Learning, Literacies, and Technologies Program at the Mary Lou Fulton Teachers College at Arizona State University. Her research interests are in how digital media can be used to enhance classroom learning and the literacy practices surrounding their uses.

Lori A. Talarico is a PhD candidate in Education–Learning, Literacies and Technologies at Arizona State University with interest in how online literacies can expand our understanding of literacy learning. Before beginning her doctoral studies, Lori taught both middle-school and community-college writing.

Kelly M. Tran is a PhD candidate and researcher of video games and online communities. Her research focuses on the sociocultural aspects of learning through games and digital media.

Lina Trigos-Carrillo is a postdoctoral fellow at the Campus Writing Program of the University of Missouri. Her research focuses on critical perspectives to academic writing, and community and family literacy of minorities and emergent bilinguals across the Americas.

Karen E. Wohlwend is associate professor of Literacy, Culture, and Language Education at Indiana University. She studies young children's play as an embodied literacy, produced with popular media and digital technologies in online spaces and in childhood cultures.

Christiane L. Wood is assistant professor of Literacy Education in the School of Education at California State University, San Marcos. Her work focuses on children's meaning-making at the intersection of literacy, play/tinkering, and design in classroom contexts.

Index

Note: *Italicized* page numbers indicate glossary terms.